Treatment
Collaboration

A Norton Professional Book

Treatment Collaboration

Improving the Therapist, Prescriber, Client Relationship

Ronald J. Diamond, MD
Patricia L. Scheifler, MSW

W.W. Norton & Company
New York • London

For information about permission to
reproduce selections from this book, write to
Permissions, W. W. Norton & Company, Inc.,
500 Fifth Avenue, New York, NY 10110

Production Manager: Leeann Graham
Manufacturing by Haddon Craftsmen

Library of Congress Cataloging-in-Publication Data

Diamond, Ronald J., 1946–
    Treatment collaboration : improving the therapist, prescriber,
client relationship / Ronald J. Diamond and Patricia L. Scheifler.–
1st ed.
        p. ; cm.
    "A Norton professional book."
    Includes bibliographical references and index.
    ISBN-13: 978-0-393-70473-0
    ISBN-10: 0-393-70473-4
    1. Therapeutic alliance. 2. Psychotropic drugs.
3. Psychotherapist and patient. 4. Psychopharmacology
consultation. 5. Drugs–Prescribing. I. Scheifler, Patricia L.
II. Title. [DNLM: 1. Mental Disorders–drug therapy.
2. Communication. 3. Interprofessional Relations.
4. Professional-Patient Relations. WM 402 D537t 2007] GML
RC489.T66D53 2007
616.89'17–dc22   2006030937

W. W. Norton & Company, Inc., 500 Fifth Avenue, New York,
N.Y. 10110
www.wwnorton.com

W. W. Norton & Company, Ltd., Castle House, 75/76 Wells St.,
London W1T3Qt

1 3 5 7 9 0 8 6 4 2

One of the most enjoyable parts of writing a book is being able to write a dedication. This is a book about collaboration, and the kids in my life have been the people who have taught me the most about this. This book is dedicated to my daughter Sara, who has been in my life from the beginning, and to Natan, Saul, and Aaron, who came into my life a bit later.

—Ronald J. Diamond

I dedicate this book to Emil and Frances Scheifler, my parents, who made my social work career possible by supporting my college education.

—Patricia L. Scheifler

Contents

Acknowledgments

The best ideas of this book have been developed through my collaboration with the consumers and staff at the Mental Health Center of Dane County, where I have worked over the past 30 years. The center is a unique place that for three decades has tried to put values into action. Dr. Len Stein, the original architect of mental health services in Dane County, explored and taught many of the ideas in this book before we had much of a vocabulary to even talk about them. The academic acknowledgments are too numerous to list, but the ideas of Leston Havens, Stephen Rolnick, William Miller and Pat Deegan are readily apparent throughout the book. I want to acknowledge the Center for Community Change, a think tank organized more than 25 years ago by Paul Carling, that seriously explored consumer empowerment and consumer participation. The Center has long since disbanded, but I have continued to be influenced by many of the people in this group, and my participation started me on my own journey of recovery and collaboration that has led to this book. And finally, I want to acknowledge the work of my wife, Cherie. Although her name is not listed as an author, much of the best parts of the book are due to her.

—Ronald J. Diamond M.D.

I am greatly indebted to many individuals for shaping my professional career, practice, beliefs, and ultimately the content of this book. Dr. William H. Bradshaw taught me skill building strategies and stimulated my interest in using rational emotive therapy for managing persistent symptoms. Dr. Cynthia Bisbee taught me about psychoeducation and launched my dedication to educating clients and their families about mental illness. Dr. Humphry Osmond engaged me in collaborative medication decision making and taught me to participate in a dynamic partnership with a prescriber and client. Special credit is due Tom R. Hobbs, Ph.D., the Partial Hospitalization staff, and clients at Western Mental Health Center, Inc., the practice base where I have been encouraged to develop and implement new treatment concepts and strategies. I am especially indebted to my husband, James T. Kemp DSW, who supports my career in innumerable ways and who spent endless hours listening, rereading, and consulting with me throughout the writing of this book.

—Patricia L. Scheifler MSW, PIP

Treatment
Collaboration

Introduction: Collaborative Medication Management

This is a book about how clients, therapists, and prescribers can work together to make medication decisions, to ensure that medication is as effective as possible, and to work collaboratively to manage mental illness so that clients can achieve personal goals. Throughout this book, the point is repeatedly made that medication is a tool that can help clients manage their illness and achieve their preferred roles and life goals. Other illness management tools are also included because they can significantly impact and influence medication management decisions and outcomes. A major premise of the book is that *recovery* is the goal, not medication adherence. A guiding principle is that collaboration, rather than authoritarianism, is most likely to promote, achieve, and sustain recovery.

Some Words about Words

Language is both complicated and important. Throughout this book, specific words have been chosen with conscious, deliberate thought. In some instances, the choice was made for the sake of simplicity. In other instances, the choice was made for therapeutic, conceptual, or ideological reasons.

1

Client instead of *consumer, patient, member,* or *person with mental illness.* There is significant and heated disagreement about what term should be used to refer to people who have mental illness. We chose *client* for the sake of simplicity and consistency.

Therapist instead of *counselor, social worker, case manager, nurse, psychologist,* or *rehabilitation specialist.* We use the term *therapist* to refer to a variety of different mental health staff who function in the role of treatment provider or coordinator of services. The word *clinician* is sometimes used to refer to the therapist and prescriber collectively.

Prescriber instead of *doctor, physician, psychiatrist, prescribing nurse,* or *prescribing psychologist.* We chose the term *prescriber* to acknowledge the growing role of nurses and other professionals with prescribing authority. However, in instances where the role of a physician seemed uniquely important, we used terms such as *psychiatrist* or *doctor* instead of *prescriber.*

Collaboration instead of *client driven.* The concept of collaboration conveys partnership, teamwork, cooperation, alliance, and working together toward common goals. It is a dynamic, flowing, energy-invested relationship. No one person is "in charge." The amount of control, input, or responsibility that each person has fluctuates. That fluctuation is what makes collaboration a dynamic relationship. There may be times when one person's input is 10%, whereas at another time that same person's input may be 70% or more. This degree of input changes based on the circumstances and the other participants.

Medication instead of *drugs.* The term *drugs* is used to refer to street drugs such as marijuana, cocaine, and speed. The term *medication* is used to refer to the psychotropics that are prescribed for the treatment of mental illness.

Treatment instead of *treatment and rehabilitation.* Some services for people who have severe persistent mental illness are considered treatment oriented, whereas other services are generally consider more geared toward rehabilitation. We use *treatment team*, *treatment plan*, and *treatment* to encompass both treatment and rehabilitation, realizing that we have blurred the distinction for the sake of simplicity.

Think or **believe** instead of *feel*. The words we use to identify thoughts and feelings have been given careful consideration. The word *feel* is commonly used incorrectly in everyday communication. Again and again, the word *feel* is substituted for what is actually a thought. This error can typically be identified by use of the phrases "I feel that..." or "I felt like..." but in either case what follows is almost always a thought, not a feeling. Feelings are generally held to be valid and indisputable. However, feelings arise from thoughts. Thoughts may be conscious or unconscious, accurate or mistaken, based in facts or drawn from assumptions. It is often possible to influence a person's thoughts and beliefs through education and discussion. These are important distinctions in treatment. Education can play a decisive role in helping people better understand mental illness, participate in collaborative medication decision making, and effectively manage their illness so that they can achieve their personal life goals. For example, we may not be able to directly change how anyone feels about medication. However, through education, people may gain an understanding that medication can be a useful tool and begin to think differently about how it can help them achieve their goals.

Practice instead of *try*. The distinction between *practice* and *try* is important in sections of the book that discuss choosing and making changes in lifestyle habits. Often when a person says "I will try..." the contract and unspoken intent may be to avoid change. If I agree to try, and fail, I can always say, "Well, I tried." That was the only contract: that I "try." *Try* is often the "out" a person uses when faced with coercion to change. Too often a client agrees "to try" to do what a therapist or prescriber wants. In fact, the client may have little real intention to do what is recommended or requested. The "agreement" is really just going along with what the therapist or prescriber wants. To *practice* suggests a commitment to repeat the behavior, to get better at it, to hone it to the point that it becomes a skilled habit.

Chapter Summaries

Chapter 1. The Role of Medication in Mental Health Treatment. Medication often plays a central role in mental health treatment. Although medication alone is never enough, it can be a powerful tool that clients use to control some of the problems caused by their mental illness, and to help them achieve their own personal life goals while supporting the process of recovery. For medication to be most effective, it is important for the client, the prescriber, and the therapist to agree on the goals. Identifying "target symptoms" can help client, therapist, and prescriber monitor how well a medication is actually working and what problems it may be causing. If the goal of medication is to help the client "do better," then all involved must agree on what "doing better" means. Collaboration among the three parties is at the center of the effective use of medication.

Chapter 2. The Prescriber–Therapist–Client Relationship. Mental health treatment typically involves a relationship between therapist and client, between prescriber and client, and between prescriber and therapist. Other members of the client's treatment team and informal support team are also present in this web of relationships. It is often confusing who is responsible for what. At times it seems as though the prescriber is responsible for treatment decisions, especially if the prescriber is a physician. At other times, the therapist, who knows the client best, may have a sense of responsibility. And of course it is the client's life, and the client is ultimately responsible. Further confusing this multiplicity of relationships are the realities of differences in power between the various members of the team, which influence how they work and communicate with each

other. The role of different kinds of expertise, different values regarding what is important, and different views of the problem provide additional complications that must be understood for the team to work effectively.

Chapter 3. Collaboration in Medication Decision Making. Effective collaboration requires that the therapist, the prescriber, and the client all put time and effort into making the collaboration work. There are issues of vocabulary and communication style that can get in the way of collaboration. Therapists and prescribers need to learn how to invite the client to be part of the collaboration. Prescribers need to actively invite therapists and clients to be part of the collaboration. Although collaboration is partly a matter of attitude, it is also facilitated by specific skills. Specific skills for the client, the therapist, and the prescriber can help facilitate a collaborative relationship. Some of these skills focus on how to invite information to be shared; others focus on how to arrive at common targets and goals. Much of the expertise required for collaboration focuses on how to communicate with other members of the treatment team, who may have very different styles and assumptions.

Chapter 4. Medication Management Strategies. A number of strategies can be utilized to develop respectful, collaborative relationships. Empathy, listening, and finding areas of agreement are all very important. Another kind of strategy is to structure the conversation around logical "chunks" that can be considered one at a time. Thinking about the various possible changes that can be made with a medication is one way to do this. This chapter explains eight key strategies that are used in medication decision making. These strategies can be used as a framework for sharing information, decreasing personal confrontation, and initiating a give-and-take process in the conversation that may help all participants consider what options are possible.

Chapter 5. The Pros and Cons of Medication. Therapists and prescribers often have difficulty in understanding why a client discontinues a medication, especially a medication that seems to be working well. If a medication is really effective in helping a client control symptoms and live a better life, then why would the client stop taking it. The reality is that most people with a mental illness or medical illness are ambivalent about medication. There are many problems that can be caused by medication, even a medication that is working well. These include side effects, risks, cost, embarrassment, a sense of dependency, and the constant reminder of the illness. The therapist and prescriber can help the client cope with the ambivalence surrounding medication taking and enhance the client's motivation to change.

Chapter 6. Psychiatric Presentation of Medical Illness. Medical illness is extremely common in people with major mental illness, much more common than in the general population. People with major mental illness tend to have worse medical care than the general population. Medical illness can cause psychiatric symptoms or worsen psychiatric symptoms in a person who is known to have a mental illness. It is important for therapists and other nonmedical members of the treatment team to know something about medical illnesses that can present as a psychiatric problem. The goal is not for the therapist to become a doctor, but rather for the therapist who knows the client best to be sensitive to some of the medical problems that are most common and be able to better communicate with the client's physician. The therapist is often in the best position to alert the physician to symptoms or problems, the knowledge of which can help direct a more focused and purposeful medical evaluation.

Chapter 7. Working with Primary Care Physicians. Despite the obvious importance of a therapist and a client's primary care physician talking with each other, such collaboration is very rare. Both therapists and physicians agree on the importance of such communication, but neither is likely to initiate it. Therapists and physicians rarely know each other, have very different communication styles, and each tends to find talking to the other difficult and frustrating. This chapter reviews some of the reasons underlying this communication difficulty and suggests practical strategies for the therapist to use to overcome the barriers that are commonly present.

Chapter 8. Beyond Medication. This chapter sets the stage for Chapters 9–11, emphasizing that although medication is often essential, medication alone is almost always insufficient. Medication is a central component of helping people manage mental illness, but medication management is interdependent with other symptom and illness management tools and strategies.

Chapters 9–11. These three chapters are written in workbook format. Rather than just being read, these chapters are intended to be used as psychoeducational resources. The materials can be used in individual sessions, as part of a group, in psychoeducation classes, or for self-study. The format and layout of the materials differs from the other chapters in the book: the vocabulary is intentionally less technical, and the worksheets include check boxes, spaces to write personal responses, opportunities to select preferred choices, and the option to decline the listed choices. Options and lists of options and check boxes are either numbered or lettered to make them easier to use and discuss as specific psychoeducational tools. In these three chapters, acquisition of knowledge, learning new skills, making personal choices, taking action, and practicing to create new habits are central themes. Specifically:

Chapter 9. Beyond Illness to Recovery. This chapter is intended to help clients understand recovery, identify personal life goals, put together a recovery team, and create an initial plan to attain life goals. This chapter can also help clients make the connection between managing mental illness and achieving personal life goals by encouraging them to identify role recovery goals, functional recovery goals, and symptomatic recovery goals.

Chapter 10. Recovery Lifestyle Habits: Recovery is a Way of Life. This chapter encourages clients to learn about, choose, and practice habits that can increase their chances of better controlling their symptoms and reducing the risk of relapse. It suggests ways to manage mental illness so that the illness itself becomes less of an obstacle to reaching personal life goals.

Chapter 11. Relapse Management. This chapter is divided into five sets of worksheets to help clients learn about, and choose ways to successfully recognize and respond to, relapse:

Worksheet 1: What Problems Have Past Relapses Caused for You?
Worksheet 2: What Are Your Early Signs of Relapse?
Worksheet 3: What Caused Your Relapse in the Past?
Worksheet 4: Making a Relapse Action Plan
Worksheet 5: How You Can Use Medication to Help When You Are Beginning to Relapse

Who Might Read and Use This Book, How, and Why?

This is a practical, how-to-do-it book that is designed for front-line therapists and prescribers who work with people who have mental illness. Although the experience of the authors and the examples in the book focus on people with serious mental illness, many people with a range of illness severity take psychiatric medication, and much of the book will be relevant to this broader audience. This book is written for social workers, case managers, psychologists, psychiatric nurses, psychiatrists, and all mental health clinicians. This is also a book for people with mental illness and their families. All of these members of the client's treatment team need to work together, collaboratively addressing medication and other important treatment issues. Although collaboration about medication decisions is the primary focus of the book, other areas of treatment also require collaboration between different clinicians and between the client and clinicians. Unfortunately, collaboration is more often talked about than actually practiced, and there are few books or papers on how to do it. This is a book about how to make collaborative treatment work better.

PART I

Collaborative Medication Decision Making

CHAPTER ONE

The Role of Medication in Mental Health Treatment

Medication has become widely accepted as a cornerstone of mental health treatment. Twenty years ago, various kinds of talk therapy were considered the mainstay of treatment, and both client and clinician needed to justify why a medication might be considered as well. Now the central role of medication in mental health treatment has become so accepted that it is assumed that medication will be strongly considered, if not actually prescribed, for virtually all mental health problems. There are many reasons for this change, including (1) the increased effectiveness and safety of psychiatric medications, (2) a push from both clients and insurance companies to experience improvement rapidly, and (3) a growing acceptance of the role of medication by both clients and society at large. There is increasing understanding of how the brain works and the role of brain chemistry in influencing mood, thought and behavior. There is also the influence of pharmaceutical companies in supporting research that demonstrates the effectiveness of medication and education that focuses on how therapists and prescribers can use medication to help clients get better.

This increased use of psychiatric medications has both its champions and its critics. Medications are clearly effective and can help many people with mental illness achieve a much better quality of life than would be possible without them. On the other hand, medications are too often used without enough consideration of what it is hoped the medication will accomplish, and without careful assessment of whether the medication has, in fact, helped. There is concern that not enough attention is paid to the risks and side effects of medication, and to how medications can make things worse as well as better. The debate over whether medication is "good" or "bad," "overused" or "not used enough," can obscure clear thought about how a particular medication might help this client at this time. It is important to have an explicit goal for each medication and then to assess to see if the medication really helps the client achieve this goal.

Medication is never a goal of treatment. Rather, medication is a tool that the client can use to accomplish his or her life goals. This means that treatment must start with clear goals about what it is hoped treatment will accomplish. The goals of treatment might be to get a job, move to an apartment, improve a relationship with family, get a girlfriend, or return to school. The overall goal of treatment is to improve the person's quality of life.

Medication is a tool, not a goal.

This is a more complicated task than it might initially seem. Who gets to decide on the appropriate goal or "target" for a medication? Traditionally prescribers focused on the goal of decreasing symptoms that could be observed during an office visit, or on a client stay out of the hospital. Prescribers often focus on stability or decrease in symptoms as goals for medication. Clients tend to focus on whether the medication helps their life improve. Therapists, who usually spend much more time with the client than does the prescriber, often have their own view of the appropriate goals for a medication, and make their own assessment about what the medication is doing or not doing. Often, clients take medication as directed, then discover that they still do not have a job or friends, do not feel any better, and thus decide that the medication is not worth taking. Too often, clients decide that their quality of life is not better, even if the prescriber believes that symptoms have decreased. If there is no clear agreement on the goal for a medication, there can be no clear agreement on whether the medication is actually helpful.

To increase the likelihood that a medication will actually be taken by a client, it is critical for client, therapist, and prescriber to agree on the importance and the goals of the medication. Prescribers make the decision about what to prescribe, but clients make the decision about what to take. The therapist also has an important role in developing the goals for medication, encouraging the client to take the medication, and assessing whether the medications are really helping. The client, prescriber, and therapist all need to collaborate. All participants have views, goals, ideas, and beliefs that will influence what medication is prescribed, what medication is actually taken, and how the effect of medication will be assessed. This is a book about how clients, therapists, and prescribers can work together to make medication decisions and to ensure that medication is as effective as possible.

Importance of Collaborative Medication Management

> Collaborative medication management is the process of actively involving prescriber, therapist, and client in a discussion about how medication can be used most effectively.

Medication is much more likely to be effective, and is certainly more likely to be taken regularly, if the prescriber, client, and therapist all agree about the need for it and the type and dose that will be used. As much as possible, decisions about medication are based upon collaborative input from the prescriber, client, therapist, and anyone who may have information about how well the medication is working, such as family members, caregivers, or other members of the treatment team. Medication management works best when the entire team is in agreement. It is much easier to get agreement if medication decisions are made as part of a discussion, if target symptoms are clarified, and different views are discussed. More often than not, if given a chance, team members can arrive at a consensus. At times, however, there is disagreement about what goals are important or what side effects are unacceptable. For example, the therapist might believe that paranoia may be an important target, but the client may disagree, believing that people are following him around and stealing things and that no medication will help stop someone else from stealing his money. The client is only going to be willing to take the medication if he believes it will do something that *he* thinks is important. Therefore, it is important for the client, prescriber, and therapist to find some target or goal for the medication that all agree on.

Unfortunately, there is little written about how to make this collaboration between prescribers, therapists, and clients actually work. Traditionally the roles of the therapist and the prescriber were very clear and very separate. Clients arrived at both doors with problems. Therapists used some combination of psychotherapy, skill training, psychoeducation, and case management. Prescribers prescribed. The prescriber might have attempted to involve the client in the process, but with limited time and a limited relationship, facilitating this involvement was often difficult. There was rarely enough time to help clients organize their own thoughts and feelings about their medication, develop a clear set of goals or target symptoms, and track the results over time. A prescriber might try to get some input from a therapist, but this input was generally considered neither necessary nor easy to obtain. Unfortunately this led to a commonplace situation in which the therapist, who usually knew the client best, had little input into an important part of treatment. It meant that the prescriber was forced to make medication decisions with much less information than he or she might want, and with little to no involvement from the client due to the limited time and structure of a typical "med check."

The prescriber, client, and therapist might all agree it would be better if all would share information and collaborate in decisions, but it is often difficult to convert this wish into reality. Prescribers often believe that they do not have the time to call a therapist and involve him or her in decisions. It may also be unclear as to how to involve the therapist. The prescriber, after all, has the responsibility for medication decisions. Does collaboration mean sharing this responsibility with the therapist? Does it mean listening to the therapist's views and information but not involving the therapist in the decision?

Equally unclear is the role of the client. If the ultimate responsibility for the prescribing decision is the prescriber's, what role does the client have? What does collaboration mean if the prescriber is still legally and professionally responsible for prescribing decisions? What happens if client and prescriber disagree? When is disagreement caused by a legitimate difference of opinion, and when is it caused by an impaired ability to make a decision? How can one even ask this kind of question within the context of a collaborative relationship? Collaboration requires flexibility, but it also requires clarity of roles.

The therapist may also have problems converting the idea of collaboration into a working reality. Nonmedical mental health therapists may know their client very well, but may have little expertise with medication and have no clear understanding of what a particular medication is supposed to do. They may also have trouble converting their knowledge of the client into clear target goals for the medication. There is often little informal or easily arranged opportunity for discussion between prescriber and therapist. The therapist and prescriber may work at different offices and have little informal occasion for contact. For the therapist to initiate contact often involves making a call to a busy prescriber, being put on hold, not having calls returned, and when finally making contact, feeling rushed, as though he or she were intruding into the prescriber's more important work. Even within the same building, to see the prescriber the therapist may have to sit for long periods of time and wait to be "worked in" between clients. The entire experience can discourage the therapist from attempting to bridge this gulf too often. In general, therapists may justifiably feel awkward about intruding into medication decisions. They are often unclear how much of a role they *should* have around medication decisions, and they are often ambivalent about how much of a role they *want* to have.

Other members of the treatment team and the client's support team can also be an important part of collaborative medication management. The *treatment team* refers to the mental health professionals and paraprofessionals who participate in different aspects of the client's treatment and rehabilitation. Different members of this team may have more or less input into medication management, but all members of the team will have their own views, their own information about the client, and their own influence on the client's willingness to take medication. The client's *support team* are the people in the client's life: friends and family, employer and neighbors. These people provide an important, even if informal, contribution to how well the client will cope, how he or she will think and feel about the use of medication, and what part medication will play in his or her life.

Agreeing on Target Symptoms

Collaboration requires that client and clinician find areas of agreement. For some clients, this is easy. For other clients, it is much more difficult to develop treatment goals with which both client and clinicians can agree. It can take significant skill for a therapist or prescriber to find target symptoms that the client will agree are important and could be helped by medication. This requires focusing on areas of agreement, rather than trying to convince a client out of an area of disagreement.

Paranoia

John is angry that people have broken into his apartment and stolen hundreds of thousands of dollars—cash that was given him in plain paper bags for past help that he had given to some very well known and wealthy people. When he called the police, not only did they not attempt to find the money, but they clearly did not believe that the money was really stolen. John was not willing to take medication if the target was to change his belief about the stolen money. He did agree, however, that when the police came in response to his various complaints, he would become so upset that he sounded "crazy" to them, which made his complaints even more difficult for them to believe. He also agreed that he got so upset about the money being stolen, and other bad things that had happened to him, that he sometimes was not sure what had really happened and what was just in his mind. The stolen money was real, but some other things might not have been. He was grudgingly willing to take medication if it would help him explain things better when he got upset, and if it helped him figure out what was real and what was not.

Depression

George says he is incompetent both in his job and with his family. Nothing is enjoyable. He cannot sleep or relax. He used to read all the time but now he cannot concentrate enough to pick up a book. Even following a TV show is a chore that takes more effort than it is worth. He is not suicidal, but he does think about death all of the time, and if he came down with a fatal disease he would find it a relief. He cannot believe that a medication could possibly help him think that he was doing his job well when he knows that he is not. He can, however, imagine a medication helping with his sleep and concentration and is willing to try a medication with these target symptoms in mind. With some prompting he acknowledges that he used to enjoy reading, and although he thinks it unlikely, he can imagine the possibility of enjoying this pleasure again. He is willing to add enjoyment of reading to the list of targets for a medication trial. In the process of discussing these target symptoms, George went from believing that nothing could possibly help, to being willing to try medication for long enough to see if it could possibly do any good.

Mania

Ralph enjoys the sense that he is faster, smarter, and more creative than most people around him. He has gone through periods of serious depression that he hates and fears, but he very much enjoys his period of feeling "high." He has tried a variety of mood stabilizers, but he sees no reason why he should take a medication that makes him feel slow and stupid. His irritability and impulsivity has lost him a number of jobs, including two that he really liked. He has been arrested twice, once after a fight and once after passing a bad check. He is in the unhappy process of having his car repossessed because of financial problems after the loss of his most recent job. He does not see himself as the source of these problems, but rather talks about getting frustrated at how slow and stupid everyone around him seems. He does agree that he would like to be able to get and keep a job that he enjoys, and he agrees that he would like some financial stability in his life. He acknowledges that there is a problem of "fit" between how fast he moves and thinks and how fast the rest of the world moves. He also agrees that as long as he moves so much faster than the rest of the world, there would be "crashes" between him and other people. He finally acknowledged that keeping a job and keeping his car would require that he either find other people who move as fast as he moves or that he take medication to slow himself down. He was not willing to take enough of a mood stabilizer to completely slow his mania to normal, but he was willing to take enough to slow down to the point of being less irritable with his new boss, being more consistent about getting to work on time, and keeping to a budget so that he could make car payments.

Agreeing on Tolerability Side Effects

There may be disagreements about what side effects are tolerable. A clinician's view of what would count as a "significant" medication-related weight gain for a client is often much more than that same clinician would be willing to tolerate if he or she were the one gaining weight. Clients are often much more concerned than staff with feeling "drugged out." There may be disagreements about "how much risk is too much," with prescriber, therapist, and client weighing risks and benefits differently. Client, therapist, and prescriber may also disagree about the importance of "doing it [managing symptoms] yourself" versus "relying on medication," with clients and staff often taking different sides of the disagreement. At times, the client may want a pharmacological solution to a problem that the staff think should be treated in a different way, while in other situations the staff may push for a pharmacological solution over the objections of the client.

It is not always clear whose view should prevail during such disagreements. Even when there is no legal coercion to take medications, significant pressure can be brought to bear by a therapist through control of money, access to resources such as rides or housing, or psychological pressure from people on whom clients may be dependent. On the other hand, clients can assert themselves by "forgetting" to take the medication, "cheeking" it, cutting the dose, or just not taking it. At times there may be no easy solution to the dilemma of differing perceptions and values. It is always preferable to support the values of the client. On the other hand, some clients with serious mental illness make decisions that lead to a life of disarray, preventing them from achieving those goals that they say are important to them.

What therapists and prescribers *can* do is listen to clients describe their goals, their values, and their perception of the cost–benefit ratio of medication. Often, a reasonable compromise is possible. Is the client more concerned about weight gain, hand tremors, sedation, restlessness, or sexual side effects? What options are available for managing the side effects about which the client is concerned? Is the client willing to take medication for a month or two, even if he or she is not willing to commit to a lifetime of medication use? Often, clients concerned about feeling "drugged out" are willing to take some medication, but less than the full dose recommended by the prescriber. At times, this smaller initial dose may have enough beneficial effect to encourage the person to take more. Or, if the client does not feel "drugged," he or she may be willing to take more. Still other times, this small initial dose leads to enough improvement that a higher dose is not needed. More is not always better, and coming to some agreement that all can live with may lead to a better long-term outcome than a solution that follows normal prescribing guidelines but is intolerable to the client.

What Does "Getting Better" Mean?

Medication is used to help the client "get better." What does *getting better* mean? What is the medication supposed to help with, and from whose perspective? Collaboration requires that the points of view of everyone involved be considered. Collaboration also requires acknowledgment of the legitimate role of both therapist and client in the prescriber's medication decision. The therapist can (1) help the client connect medication to his or her own life goals, (2) understand the beliefs and values of the client about medication, (3) have a major influence on how the client experiences medication, and (4) play a decisive role in whether the client will continue to take it. This collaboration with client and therapist does not challenge the authority of the prescriber; rather, it can increase the effectiveness of the prescriber.

As noted, prescribers are typically forced to make medication decisions after spending a short period of time with the client, and therefore with limited information about his or her life. The prescriber can rapidly assess if the client is currently depressed, continues to have panic attacks, or is bothered by hearing voices. However, it takes much more time and much more of a relationship with a client to know what he or she is hoping the medication might accomplish, what personal goals the client has for his or her own life, if the client is frightened of medication or has unrealistic expectations of what it might do. Collaboration allows more information and more points of view to be considered in the medication decision, and more comprehensive assessment of how well the medication may be working.

Why do any of us take a medication? It depends, in part, on the nature of the illness that we are trying to treat. We may take a medication because we are in pain and want the pain to go away. We may have an illness that we are afraid will get worse or even kill us if we do not take medication. We may have uncomfortable or painful symptoms from an illness and hope that by taking medication the symptoms will get better. We may take a medication because we hope that it will keep us from feeling bad or getting worse in the future, even though right now we have no symptoms from whatever illness we are trying to treat. In all of these examples we take a medication, whether for a medical illness* or a mental illness, because it will help us stay well or "get better." At times, we take medication because someone else wants us to take it. In this case it is this other person—a spouse or friend or family member—who believes that the medication will help us stay well or get better. Unfortunately, the idea of "doing better" or "getting better" is surprisingly complicated.

Every treatment that we offer to people with major mental illness is designed to help them get better. We judge whether a particular medication or other treatment works by whether it helps the person to get better. Unfortunately, it is not always clear what *getting better* means. Does it mean a cure of the illness, decrease in symptoms, staying outside of the hospital, functioning better, being able to get a job and get off disability? This confusion over what is meant by *getting better* is not just a problem for mental health but for all areas of medical care. When we think about medical illness, in general, we typically think of an acute infection such as pneumonia, for which getting better means a cure of the underlying illness. Most doctor visits for medical illness are not in response to acute illnesses that can be cured, however, but for chronic illnesses that don't have straightforward cures. Most distress and disability are caused by chronic illness rather than an acute illness that starts, is cured, and then goes away. Diabetes, high blood pressure, arthritis, and many other medical illnesses can be managed, but they are rarely cured. Although it does not happen often, it is possible for a serious, chronic illness to go into complete remission and

---

*We use the terms *medical illness* and *mental illness* to fit common thinking, although we believe that there is more overlap than difference between them. There is increasing data that "mental illness" is a biological brain disorder similar to medical illness, and there is increasing data that common "medical illness"—from diabetes to tuberculosis to heart disease to cancer—is strongly influenced by psychological and social factors.

appear to be completely "cured." This unexpected remission can happen even with serious, usually chronic medical illnesses such as rheumatoid arthritis. It can also happen with schizophrenia, depression, and bipolar disorder. Medical treatments seem to have little to do with these cures. Although we can always hope for this kind of wonderful outcome, it is not the typical way that we measure whether a treatment is helping or not.

With chronic medical illness, we often consider an improvement in symptoms as an indication that the person is getting better. An improvement in symptoms is thought to be connected with better function, less pain, and how the person will do in the future. If the pain of arthritis lessens, this decrease both improves current quality of life and is also assumed to indicate that there is less damage being done to the joint, with the hope there will be less pain in the future. A normalization of blood glucose levels in someone with diabetes is associated with lower risk of stroke and kidney failure in the future.

The traditional assumption in psychiatry is that a decrease in symptoms has the same ability to predict the future course of mental illness that it does in medical illness. This is probably an accurate assumption for some disorder such as depression OCD or phobias. A person who experiences an improvement in the symptoms of depression will have less distress, is likely to function better, and has a better chance of staying free of depression for longer in the future. However, there is a much lower correlation between some types of symptoms in other mental illnesses, such as schizophrenia, and either current or future function.

Positive symptoms, such as hallucinations and delusions, are the most obvious and dramatic symptoms of schizophrenia. These are the kinds of symptoms that clinicians typically monitor when they decide that the illness is "getting better" or "getting worse." Actually, these symptoms are only weakly correlated with ability to function, stay out of the hospital, work, live independently, or maintain a preferred quality of life. There is little data that current positive symptoms have any ability to predict how that person will do in the future. (However, some people who experience positive symptoms may consider them to be very distressing, distracting, or difficult to manage.) Negative symptoms such as lack of spontaneity, perseverance, and initiative are more strongly correlated with disability than are positive symptoms, but less likely to be considered as an indicator of improvement by clinicians. Cognitive symptoms, including memory deficits, short attention span, and problems making decisions, may be more strongly correlated with functional deficits for many people with schizophrenia and bipolar disorder. However, cognitive symptoms are also less likely to be considered by most clinicians in assessing whether a person is getting better.

If symptoms, at least positive symptoms, are not correlated with either function or future outcome, then what else counts as *getting better*? Often staying out of the hospital is seen as a sign of improvement. Unfortunately, the decision to hospitalize a person is more often influenced by the availability of a hospital bed, alternative services, or funding than by anything about the person's underlying illness. For people going through a difficult period with their illness, rehospitalization is more closely correlated with the availability of community supports than with the severity of their illness. One person may stay out of the hospital by staying on a huge dose of medication and doing nothing more stressful than watching TV at the group home. Another person may undergo a series of brief hospitalizations connected with the stress of learning to live independently, getting a job, or going back to school. Neither outcome necessarily reflects ability to function.

Ability to function is more closely connected with the concept of "getting better." Function is a relative matter whose backdrop is the environment in which the person is expected to function. There is an old quip that you "cannot vacuum in a vacuum"; that is, you cannot learn to handle money if you have no money to handle. It is hard to learn the skills to live independently if you have no chance to really live on your own. It may be more difficult to force yourself to attend to your own personal hygiene if you have no job to look good for and no friends who care what you look like or smell like. How well a person can function is connected to what is expected of that person by others, his or her social context, skills, and supports, as well as to illness.

Ability to work—to be self-supporting, pay taxes, and even get off Supplemental Security Income (SSI)—has sometimes been used as an indicator of getting better. As with function, this outcome is as determined by the availability of work-support programs, jobs, and skill training as it is by the state of the illness. There are very real barriers that make work impossible for many people with major mental illness, no matter how well they are doing in other areas. Many people simply cannot afford to work. A person with a major mental illness who receives SSI disability payments is likely to lose their health insurance, have their SSI payment decreased significantly, and have the rent for their subsidized apartment increased, all at the same time, if they earn too much money working. Others are afraid to work because of fear that their benefits may be reduced or even eliminated.

This is not to say that positive symptoms, negative symptoms, cognitive symptoms, mood symptoms, ability to function,

---

What do we mean by "getting better"?

- *Feel better*
- *Decrease symptoms*
- *Increase functioning*
- *Increase stability/stay out of hospital*
- *Improve subjective sense of well-being*
- *Improve quality of life*
- *Have meaningful roles in life*

community stability or getting a job are not connected with getting better, just that these are not the sum total of improvement from major mental illness. Two core concepts connected to improvement are *quality of life* and *recovery*.

The Goal of Any Treatment Is to Improve Quality of Life

The goal of every medical and mental health intervention is to improve *quality of life*, a term that has both subjective and objective components. We can consider the objective quality of a person's housing, physical health, or social supports. It is also important to assess the person's own subjective thoughts and feeling about his or her housing, social supports, or physical health. One person may dislike an apartment that appears objectively to be very nice, while someone else may very much enjoy living in an apartment that objectively appears less desirable. Different people will have very different views about the importance of such variables as location and friendliness of neighbors. Satisfaction with housing is also influenced by past experience and expectation. If the current housing is a step up from what they had before, then clients will more likely think it is better than if their current housing is a big step down. Similarly, if everyone else they know has much nicer housing, then they will likely rate their housing as less satisfactory than if, in comparison, their place seems pretty nice. Clinicians and family members may disagree with a client about the quality of housing, support system, or physical health. These different points of view must also be considered in assessing quality of life.

Quality of life is a multidimensional construct, a composite of a number of different, fairly independent dimensions. One person may feel great about his housing but very upset about his health. Another person may feel good about her friends but have major problems getting a job that she wants. Furthermore, not all of these dimensions are of equal importance. One person may believe that quality of housing is relatively unimportant, while work is very salient to his overall quality of life. Another person may think just the opposite and find the quality of her work much more important than the quality of her housing. There is research that suggests that, in general, women rate friendships as a more important part of their overall quality of life, while men tend to rate job-related issues as more important in their overall quality of life. Despite these complexities and the problems of measurement, quality of life is a core aspect of getting better.

Unfortunately, the connection between improvement in "quality of life" and treatment is far from clear. A person who has lived a very restricted life and avoided thinking about any personal goals may go through a period of feeling more dissatisfied as he or she develops a desire to add more to life. Quality of life is influenced by the gap (or lack thereof) between expectations and current reality. As a client begins to believe that more is possible for his or her life, expectations rise and, for a period of time, the gap widens between what is desired and what is achieved. Wanting more out of life may be the first step in a person's process of recovery, but may temporarily lead to a decrease in perceived quality of life. A medication that helps a person come out of a stupor and engage more with the world may similarly increase frustration initially and decrease perceived quality of life. Many research studies that purport to measure improved quality of life over a brief period of a few weeks really seem to be measuring changes in subjective feelings or changes in side effect burden, rather than other dimensions of quality of life. Changes in quality of life may take a long time. For example, a more effective medication may help the individual think more clearly and have more energy, but it may take months or more for this improvement to lead to a new job or more meaningful activities during the day.

Recovery Is a Central Goal in Modern Mental Health Treatment

For someone with a serious mental illness, *recovery* is very different from *cure*. Recovery is the process of experiencing more in life than just the illness. When a person is first diagnosed with a major illness, be it a heart attack, cancer, or schizophrenia, the illness tends to take over his or her life. The idea that the person is also a father, a bike rider, a piano player, or an artist gets pushed out of consciousness by everyone's overriding attention to the illness. That person becomes a "heart patient" or a "cancer patient" or a "schizophrenic patient." Over time, however, during the process of recovery, the person gets more in touch with all of these parts of him- or herself. The person is still someone with a damaged heart or is a cancer survivor or is even someone who continues to have significant symptoms from schizophrenia, but over time the illness becomes only one part of who the person is, rather than seeming as though it is all of who he or she is. Recovery is a process that can occur over time in both major physical illness and major mental illness.

Recovery is a profoundly personal journey. Some people become ill so early in their life that they have little to go back to upon recovery. The term *pro-covery*, conveying forward movement, has been used instead. The beginning steps that lead to this kind of recovery or pro-covery vary enormously from person to person. For one person it may start with getting a job, for another it may be getting his or her own apartment or having a friend, for another it may be getting a car. Often, the early parts of the journey are comprised of small steps; going to a nearby store or taking a bus, or merely leaving the fog of cigarette smoke and TV watching to begin taking a daily walk. It is impossible to know from the first few steps how far someone may be able to go or what direction his or her journey will eventually take.

Recovery is nonlinear. There is sometimes an assumption that we get "a little better every day in every way." This is not how we change. We all have good periods and bad periods, and people with major mental illness are no different. Journeys often include paths that are easier and paths that are more difficult, paths going in the right direction, and paths that lead to wrong turns. A person can get a job, then lose it, then get another job. A person can make a friend, then drift away from that friend. The journey of recovery is often a journey of ups and downs, areas where life is going better and areas that are not going as well. This journey can include long periods of inaction and periods of activity, similar to intervals of dormancy that alternate with growth periods in nature. A person may appear to make no progress for long periods of time, then make a substantial change all of a sudden. It is very important for clinicians, families, and clients themselves not get too frustrated by what appear to be periods of stagnation. It is important to hope and expect more, but not get frustrated during fluctuating periods of what appear to be lack of progress.

Recovery is an ongoing journey, a process that is never complete. As with recovering from alcoholism, high blood pressure, or diabetes, once the illness is under control, continued illness management typically remains necessary to keep it from exacerbating and interfering with personal life goals. Most of us are in the process of striving to make our lives better, and working to make life more of what we would like it to be. The process of recovery from a major mental illness is the process of taking

---

What is recovery?

- Recovery is not the same as cure.
- Recovery is the process of experiencing more to life than just illness.
- Recovery is a profoundly personal journey.
- Recovery is nonlinear with inevitable ups and downs.
- Recovery is an ongoing process that is never finished.

back one's life from illness and living a life that includes more of one's own goals. At the beginning of the journey of recovery, no one can know how far that journey might eventually take the traveler.

Importance of Personal Goals

Treatment must start with the person's own goals about how he or she wants his or her life to change. This goal identification is more complicated than it initially seems. People with major mental illness may be confused about their goals; they may have been told that their goals are unrealistic or are part of their illness. They may express goals in idiosyncratic ways that are difficult to understand. If their stated goals were criticized in the past, to avoid more criticism they may have learned to be careful about which goals they are willing to reveal. They may share their goals only with people whom they trust—and in some cases mental health professionals are not automatically on that list. People who have tried and failed, and tried and failed again, may be too afraid to try again. Naming a goal can mean taking another chance to fail.

Despite the problems, it is important to understand the goals of the individual. A person is much more likely to participate in therapy or take a medication if he or she believes that doing so will help him or her meet personal goals. The client is much less likely to take a medication if it is supposed to help with something that he or she does not want to change, or if he or she believes that the problem cannot possibly be changed by taking a medication.

Would you take a medication whose purpose was to turn your hair bright purple? Only if you wanted your hair to be purple. If you did not want purple hair, you would avoid that medication because it would not help you attain anything that you thought was important or desirable.

If you believed that someone had stolen a large amount of money, would you take a medication whose purpose was to remove your conviction that the money was really stolen? If you really believed that the money had been stolen, you would most likely get very angry if someone suggested taking a medication that would alter what you believe to be reality.

Initial Approach to the Use of Medication: Balancing risks and benefits

Medication is often seen as the cornerstone of treatment for people with schizophrenia, depression, and bipolar disorder. Too often, it is perceived as a panacea: If only the client would take medication, everything would be better. Any increase in symptoms must be caused by medication noncompliance. In reality, medication is often very important, but it is rarely a panacea and it is rarely enough by itself. More important, taking medication should never be considered a "treatment goal." Medication is a tool that can be used to help the person achieve *real* treatment goals. The question is: How can we use medication so that it will be most helpful in assisting the client to achieve recovery?

All medication, even aspirin, has risks and side effects. What risks are worth taking? If you are treating an illness that is always fatal, a very risky medication may be worth taking. If you are taking a medication for a headache, even a relatively small risk may be too much. Similarly with side effects: You might be

---

All medication has risks: Balance potential benefits versus risks:

- *What risks or benefits are most important to the client?*
- *What risks or benefits are most important to the clinician?*
- *What values and beliefs are involved?*
- *Who gets to decide?*
- *When is a risk "worth it"?*

willing to tolerate more bothersome side effects if the illness is very bad and the medication is very effective. Since *all* medications have risks and side effects, the prescriber, therapist, and client are always balancing the risk against the potential benefit. There is no way to achieve this balance without having a clear understanding of both sides of this ratio, including the risks of *not* taking medication.

Identifying Target Symptoms to Monitor the Effect of Medication

What are the potential risks and the potential benefits of this medication for this person at this time? Before starting any medication, the prescriber, client, and therapist come up with a list of "target symptoms"—what do we hope the medication will change? The client may take a medication hoping that it will make it easier to ignore voices, or make it less frightening to leave her apartment, or improve her concentration so that she can work more efficiently. The list of target symptoms is specific and unique for every individual. The target list clarifies what would count as improvement, and what would count as getting worse. If a client is constantly suicidal, then a few hours in which suicide is not even considered might be viewed as a major improvement. If a person hears voices that are so loud and intrusive that he cannot concentrate on anything else, having the

---

Develop "target lists" for each medication:

- *Targets must be detailed, specific, and concrete.*
- *Targets must include observable behavior.*
  - *What is the "target" of the medication?*
  - *What is the client hoping medication will do?*
  - *What behavior/feeling or experience does the clinician hope will change?*
  - *What are others hoping medication will do?*

voices recede enough to hold a reasonable conversation with someone might be a sign of significant improvement. It is also important to be clear about how long it will take to find out if a medication is going to work. If it is expected that it will take up to 4 weeks for a medication to work, then a 4-day trial would provide little reliable information about the potential benefit of the medication.

Medication Education

Ensuring that clients have adequate information about medication is an important part of a collaborative medication management process. In addition to the content information about the different classes of medication, an important part of this education is sharing information about what medication can do, and what it cannot. Medication will not change real-world problems: It will not give someone a job or friends. What a medication may do is help someone cope more effectively with these real-world problems. A medication may help someone tolerate the stress of a job, attend classes alongside other people without being so overwhelmed, or follow directions in a way that allows the person to keep a job. Sometimes it is difficult for clients to understand how a medication can change how people think or feel. To clarify this point, we use a common analogy: Most of us have had the experience of alcohol, coffee, or cigarettes changing how much energy we have, how alert we are, how clearly we can think, and how we feel. In short, our thoughts, feelings, and perceptions are heavily influenced by biology, which is heavily influenced by any substance we ingest.

Medication alone is not enough. Medication cannot control what we think, but it can influence how clearly we can think, how well we can deal with stress, how good we are at figuring out what to believe, what is real, and what is not. Medications can help, but medications are rarely able to correct all of the problems associated with mental illness. To have a better life and overcome, as much as possible, the difficulties caused by a serious mental illness, clients need to use all of the tools available. These tools often include medication, but they also include learning as much as possible about the illness, learning necessary skills, learning how to control their moods, learning how to cope with symptoms, learning how to manage their illness, and learning how to behave in ways that allow them to better accomplish their personal goals. Medication can help, but people also need to be active participants in their own recovery. Medications can help a person be a better problem solver, but the individual must still be the one to solve the problems.

The Role of Beliefs

> People make decisions based on their beliefs about the nature of the problem and their beliefs about the kinds of solutions that may help.

We all have beliefs about the nature of our own problems. Is John not working because he is lazy, because he is ill, because there are no good jobs around, because all of the employers in town have been talking about him and agreed not to hire him, because he is being careful about what job he takes, or because he does not need to work? Is Susan hearing voices because God talks to her directly, because everyone hears voices, because she has special powers of telepathy, because she is psychotic, or because she takes hallucinogenic drugs? Our belief about the problem will strongly influence what we decide is a reasonable solution to that problem.

For example, if John believes he is not working because he is ill, has trouble concentrating, and has trouble focusing, then he is more likely to accept the idea that a medication might help. If, on the other hand, the reason he believes he is not able to get a job is because there are no good jobs or because all employers in town are colluding with each other not to hire him, then is it is hard to understand, from his perspective, how taking a medication can possibly help. People take medication because they agree that they have the kind of problem that might respond to medication. Medication may make sense as a solution to one part of a problem, even if it does not seem to be a solution to other parts of the problem. For example, I might believe that the voices I hear are based on my telepathic powers, but I might also agree that medication could give me more control during times when these voices are too distracting. Medication may help my ability to focus, even if I believe that the source of the voices is not something that medication will ever affect. Medication may, or may not, help me get a job, depending on my beliefs about the reason I am not working now and the kind of help I think I will need to get a job. The potential solution to a problem depends, in large part, on my belief about the nature of that problem.

Not only are a person's beliefs about the nature of the problem important, but so are that person's belief about the nature of the potential solution. For example, I may believe that Valium will help decrease my anxiety, even if I believe that the

---

Why is John not working? Different beliefs about the problem:

- Lazy
- Stupid
- Waiting to start work
- Preoccupied with something else
- Looking for work
- Ill
- Conspired against
- Wealthy—doesn't need to

- Unmotivated
- Unskilled
- Stressed out
- On vacation
- In school
- Disabled
- Laid off
- Alcoholic

cause of my anxiety has to do with stress at work. My belief in the kinds of solutions that are likely to work are going to effect what treatment I am going to find acceptable. I may believe that my tiredness is caused by a vitamin deficiency. This belief will obviously motivate me to take vitamins. I may also be willing to exercise *if* I believe that exercise can help even if the primary cause for my tiredness is a vitamin deficiency. Someone with a different belief about the problem and the solution may be unwilling to try exercising as a solution for tiredness, believing that exercise could not possibly help if the problem were really caused by vitamin deficiency.

Some people are open to the idea that medication may help a wide variety of problems, whereas others cannot imagine how a medication could possibly help anything that is not definitely an illness. At times, staff members think that medication is a much better solution than does the client. At other times, clients continue to believe that there is a medication that will help if only they find the right one, while staff members are encouraging nonpharmacological solutions. We decide what to do, what solutions are worth trying, what medications we are willing to take, and even what side effects we are willing to tolerate based on our beliefs about what that medication is likely to do for us.

Not only does the client have beliefs about the nature of the problem and the kinds of solutions (treatments) that might benefit this problem, but so do the client's friends, family, neighbors, and extended support system. Prescribers and therapists also have their own beliefs. There is an entire "town meeting" of beliefs that impact the beliefs and decisions of the client.

Beliefs not only influence whether medication will be used but *how* it will be used. For example, if I believe that I should only take medicine when I am ill, not when I feel better, and I am now feeling great, I may logically decide that I do not need to continue taking it. Within this belief, it makes no sense to take a medication if there are no current symptoms of illness.

Other beliefs include the idea that "I need to give my body a rest from medication now and again, or I will get too dependent on it" or "I should be strong enough to control my thoughts or mood without medication." Such convictions run counter to the belief that medication continues to be needed, even if I am feeling good now, to keep from getting sick again in the future.

Effective Use of Medication

If medications are part of the solution, how can we use them most effectively? People understand that medication does not always work. It may not work because it is the wrong medication, applied to the wrong problem, or because the problem is not going to be helped by any medication. What is less obvious is that there are lots of things that the client, prescriber and therapist can do, working together, to make it more likely that the medication will be effective. Some of these things are more under the control of the client, some are more under the control of the prescriber or therapist, and some require the prescriber, therapist, and client to work together. It is important that the team understand and support the client's active involvement in all parts of his or her own treatment, including medication.

Medications are much more likely to work if:

1. *Clear target symptoms have been identified.* It is important to select and look for changes that the client and the rest of the clinical team have identified as important and that seem connected to a symptom that the medication might ameliorate. Medications are much more likely to be helpful if we are very clear about matching appropriate medications with specific target symptoms. This is part of a larger discussion about how the client, prescriber, and therapist identify such target symptoms.

2. *Everyone is optimistic that the medication will actually help, at least a bit.* Things that we think will work actually

work better. Our own mind has a lot to do with how well an intervention works, how well we push ourselves to work with the medication, how well we can tolerate side effects.

3. *The medication is part of our larger recovery plan.* Our overall recovery plan focuses on clients' own life goals—both short-term goals that clients want to accomplish soon and long-term goals that can keep them going through the hard times of a long recovery journey. Medication is only a part of what will help. If people are doing all of the other things that are needed to promote their own goals and their own recovery, then the medication will be much more useful to them than if they just sit and wait for the medication to do it all.

4. *The medication is part of a collaborative or "team process."* It is important that clients be an active part of decisions about their medication. The medication is likely to help them feel better, cause fewer side effects, and be taken much more regularly if people have a say in what is prescribed for them.

5. *The medication is taken regularly.* Many people taking medication—whether they are taking it for a medical or a mental illness, whether they are taking it for a minor illness or one that might kill them—do not follow the prescription. Often people think that taking the medication "almost every day" should be good enough. Many medications, however, work much better when taken daily than when taken more erratically.

6. *The medication is taken long enough.* Too often we expect a "miracle cure." People want medication to work right away. Unfortunately, most of the medications used for mental illness take multiple weeks to work. Taking one medication for a few days, then switching to another and another, does not allow time to find out if any of the medications will be useful.

Medications are much less likely to work if:

1. *The medication is not taken regularly or not taken long enough.* Some people never get their prescription filled. Others carry the medication around but never take a pill. Medication only works if it is taken consistently. This point seems obvious. Yet people often say that they have tried a particular medication and it has not worked—when they have not even given it a real chance.

2. *The dose is not correct.* If the dose is too high or too low, it may not work. Achieving the most effective dose requires working with the prescriber to balance side effects and positive effects. This may require a trial-and-error process, trying first one dose and then another, to find the one that works best for each individual.

3. *There is a concomitant use of drugs or alcohol.* Most street drugs and alcohol might feel good in the short term, but they generally increase depression and paranoia, make it more difficult for people to follow through with things that will allow them to get going in life, and make medication less effective. Alcohol can cause depression, sleep problems, and uncontrolled aggression in some people. Marijuana can make many people paranoid, often decreases motivation, and generally worsens the underlying illness.

4. *There is an unrecognized or untreated medical illness.* Being physically ill makes everything harder; being healthy makes everything a bit easier. Recovery, good mental health, and physical wellness are all connected.

5. *There is such overwhelming stress that it seems that nothing can help.* It is hard to feel better if one is homeless, arrested, or disconnected from all family and friends. Medication may enhance energy, focus, or sense of reality to help individuals cope with these problems more effectively, but the fact remains that overwhelming stress makes everything else more difficult.

6. *The person feels hopeless.* Hopelessness is one of the most difficult states of being to overcome. How can people work toward their own recovery if they have no hope that life can be better, that recovery is possible? Having goals, wanting things, tolerating medications, stopping the use of street drugs—all depend, in part, on having the hope that things can get better. One of the most important things that clinicians can do to help the recovery process is to *believe* that the client's life can improve, even when the client has given up hope. If clinicians truly believe that things could get better, then this sense of hope will be felt by the client. If the clinicians cannot imagine a person ever having a better life, then this sentiment, too, will be felt by the client. Recommending that clinicians convey belief and hope does not mean that things will necessarily get better, only that we can *imagine* the possibility.

7. *There are unrealistic expectations about what a medication can do.* If a person expects a medication to get rid of all of the voices, she may miss noticing that the voices are still there but are less bothersome and easier to ignore. If a client expects a medication to completely cure his depression, he may miss that he is now able to push himself to do more things, even if he is still not feeling great all of the time.

8. *Bottom line: Medications do not work for everyone.* At times, we must try a number of different medications before finding the best one for each individual. There is often no good scientific answer about which medication to try first. If a person is suffering from an illness that is causing serious problems, then continuing to try different medications is probably worth it. Unfortunately, some people do not respond to medications. All clinicians have to accept the fact that medications will help many people with serious mental illness, but they do not help everyone. The hardest question is often when to decide that a medication is not doing enough good to be worth continuing.

The Meaning of Medication

What does it mean to take medication? Even after people decide that they have a problem that might respond to medication, even after they are clear what they want the medication to do, they still have to decide whether or not to take it. Taking medication means different things to different people. For some people, taking medication means that they are really ill and it is not their fault that they cannot work. For other people, taking medication means that their problem is something that can be fixed. For still others, being told to take medication reinforces their sense that they are really damaged or even permanently disabled and will never be able to work.

These meanings are very important. If people have been told that they are not working because they are lazy, then having a diagnosis and being told to take medication might help decrease their sense of guilt and may decrease some of the pressure from their family or other people around them. In this case, taking medication is easy because it reminds them of things that help them feel better. On the other hand, if they are very worried about never being able to work again, taking medication may reinforce this concern. Every time a person takes a pill, it may reinforce concerns about being damaged, disabled, never able to work, and always being ill. Every pill can become a struggle because of all of the thoughts, feelings, and memories that are attached to taking it.

Similarly, people may take a medication because they want to take it, believe it will help, and have decided it fits into their own recovery plan. On the other hand, they may be taking it because someone else is pressuring them to take it. At times, we all have some pressure to do things, even things we might want to do anyway. I may be taking my blood pressure pill, in part, because my wife is worried about the risk of my having a heart attack, and she reminds me to take it every day. People with mental illness are often under more external pressures to take medication than are people who have some other kind of illness. Sometimes family, clinicians, other support people in the community and friends pressure people with a mental illness to take medication. This pressure is most obvious if the client is under a community treatment order with a court mandate forcing him or her to take medication. Often, these other people see medication as much more important than does the client. This focus on medication is sometimes helpful, but it can also lead some clients to feel angry about being pressured or forced to take the medication. Rather than the medication becoming part of their own plan, it becomes something that they are forced to do. Even if there is no legal coercion, clients often feel angry at all of the focus on medication and may think that everyone around them is more worried about their medication than about them.

It is important that clients take as much control over their own life as possible. Most people with a major mental illness have lost much of the control over their life. Struggles over medication just add to this sense of lost control. Too often, clients are "medicated" as though they are passive and the medication is done to them. It is important that clients and their support system learn what each medication is supposed to do and help develop clear targets to assess whether the medication is really helping. It is important that the client, prescriber, therapist, and other staff form a team so that the medication becomes a helpful part of the recovery process. Medication is a tool, a means to an end. Medication and medication adherence are never goals in and of themselves. The goal is to use medication as effectively as possible to support the client's own personal life goals.

CHAPTER TWO

The Therapist–Prescriber– Client Relationship

Mental health treatment is almost always more than just the relationship between a client and prescriber or between client and therapist. There is also a relationship between the therapist and the prescriber. This triangular relationship between prescriber, therapist, and client is complicated, often poorly defined, and rarely discussed directly. Therapists usually spend more time with the client and have a better sense of the client's own life goals. Therapists and prescribers each have special expertise, and each may have relatively more responsibility for some treatment decisions than others. The therapist and the prescriber may both be involved in overall treatment planning, but the former may be more involved in helping the client find stable housing, while the latter has more responsibility for medication decisions. These different decisions may be kept very separate, with the therapist and prescriber taking little responsibility for the decisions of the other, or there may be considerable overlap and blurring of responsibility. Often a shared sense of responsibility can lead to more comprehensive and integrated planning, but it can also lead to conflict between different clinicians who believe that they have overall responsibility for the same decision.

The Treatment Team

The *treatment team* in the world of mental health means very different things in different settings. Most narrowly it refers to the therapist and the prescriber. It also commonly refers to all of the mental health providers who work together in the treatment and rehabilitation of a single client. In this sense the team is a group of people who know each other and who are working together. This team can be rather large in some settings and include a therapist, case manager, job coach, residential staff, occupational therapist, peer support specialist, recreation therapist, rehabilitation specialist, the prescriber, and possibly a nurse and a drug alcohol counselor. More recently, the client has come to be included as an important member of this team, although too often the client is less than a full participant.

It has become increasingly evident that this narrow conception of the treatment team leaves out other professionals who play important roles in the treatment of many clients, especially those with serious mental illness. There are almost always other professionals involved in the client's life, treatment, and rehabilitation. The client's primary care physician can influence how the client thinks and feels about his or her treatment, medication, and quality of medical care. A vocational counselor can play a critical role in a client's reintegration into the community. In this sense, the treatment team can include professionals that may not know each other and may not be fully aware of the role or influence of the others. The treatment team may include people who do not realize that they are part of the team; they just know they are working with a particular client who has multiple problems.

The Support Team

Beyond the formal treatment team, there is also the support team: the array of important people in the client's life. These people may not know each other and may not be formally involved in treatment decisions. Nevertheless, their views, beliefs, and involvement have an important influence on the client's life, including his or participation in treatment, willingness to take medication, and ability to achieve life goals. Some of the people in this support team will have a direct influence, talking over decisions with the client and making suggestions about life issues. In contrast, other people may not even realize their influence. They may help the client cope with stress, participate in the community—in general, help make life worthwhile—and at the same time subtly encourage the client down one path or another. Whether formally involved or not, members of the client's support team are important parts of his or her treatment and recovery.

Although all members of the extended treatment team and the support team are important, for the purpose of this chapter, we focus on the relationship between the prescriber, the therapist, and the client, who formally make up the core team. The same relationship issues that are present between the therapist, prescriber, and client exist among the larger treatment team and the support team.

Collaborative Medication Management

The simplistic view is that each person on the treatment team has his or her own, clearly defined role. The role of the therapist/case manager is to provide and/or coordinate the nonmedical aspects of treatment, and the role of the prescriber is to make all medication decisions. However, this is rarely the best way to make such decisions. Although the final decision about which medication to prescribe is clearly the responsibility of the prescriber, the reality is that the therapist often has much more contact with the client, knows the client better, is more aware of his or her life goals, and is better able to predict how he or she will think and feel about a medication decision. The prescriber is likely to have a better overall view of what medication can or cannot do, what risks and alternatives to consider, and the medical complications associated with a specific medication. And, of course, it is the client's life, and the client has a central legitimate role in any medication decision. Collaborative medication management acknowledges these different roles and is based on the belief that the best medication decisions come out of collaboration between these members of the treatment team.

This kind of collaboration is very different from traditional psychiatric practice. In the past, clients with serious mental illness were not invited to contribute much input into the medications that they were expected to take. Nonmedical staff did not know much about psychiatric medication and were not expected to learn. The idea that a prescriber would not only listen to, but actively invite, input from a therapist is relatively new. Professional training of both prescribers and therapists rarely includes anything about collaborative prescribing. There are no courses on ways to help therapist, client, and prescriber work together to make the best medication decisions.

Patients are increasingly expecting to have input in medication decisions in the treatment of other medical problems. Physicians, for example, are expected to actively involve patients in decisions about the treatment of high blood pressure or diabetes. Spouses may also be involved, but typically there is no one in the role of therapist or case manager in the treatment of medical illness. Collaboration in other parts of medical care usually refers to collaboration between physician and patient. Collaborative medication management in mental health treatment extends collaboration to include the therapist and other members of the treatment team in addition to the client. At times this collaboration may also include key people in the client's support team.

Describing the Therapeutic Triangle

Unfortunately, collaboration and shared responsibility can cause complications as well as advantages. Within the triangle of relationships between prescriber, therapist, and client, it is often unclear who is responsible for what. Some of this confusion comes from the fact that different people have overlapping areas of responsibility. Some confusion comes from the lack of clarity about what is meant by *responsibility*. Some of the apparent lack of clarity is really based on disagreements that remain unresolved. And some of the lack of clarity is because the responsibility is truly shared and no one participant is truly the "responsible" agent. Although this sense of overlapping responsibility is most evident in decisions about medication, similar issues arise over all areas of treatment.

The prescriber–therapist–client relationship raises a number of important questions:

1. Who is responsible for what?
2. How do differences in power influence relationships in mental health?
3. What is an expert and what are the limits of this expertise?
4. How do personal values affect decision making?
5. What is the difference between compliance, adherence, and the effective use of medication?
6. How can collaboration between therapists, clients, and prescribers best be fostered?

Who Is Responsible for What?

The prescriber decides what medication is prescribed. Especially when the prescriber is a psychiatrist, he or she is often assumed to have responsibility for much more than just these prescribing decisions. The psychiatrist is often perceived, by other medical professionals and society, as responsible for the decisions of other staff on the team, even if the psychiatrist is not formally in charge of the team. For example, the prescriber is held legally responsible for the decisions of other members of the treatment team if there is a malpractice suit. Prescribers are often required to "sign off" on treatment plans that they may have had little input in developing. Prescribers may need to "prescribe" psychotherapy, admission, discharge, special transportation, or authorize use of other resources. The prescriber may even be held responsible for the client's behavior. If the client goes through a difficult period, and particularly if the difficulty leads to some kind of public event (e.g., becoming violent or having a car accident), it is often assumed that the prescriber should have done something to fix things before they got that bad. This sense of responsibility reinforces the notion that the psychiatrist is, or should be, "in charge" (Figure 2.1).

The therapist often knows the client much better than does the prescriber. The therapist is typically in charge of all aspects of a client's treatment and rehabilitation, even to the extent of coordinating medication and medical treatment. The therapist is the person first called if there is a crisis and often is in the best position to know what problems the client is facing, how medication may help, and what benefits or disadvantages seem connected to the medication. The mental health system may specify the therapist as formally "in charge" of developing, coordinating, and implementing all aspects of mental health treatment. It makes sense that the therapist would believe that he or she is the person "in charge" (Figure 2.2).

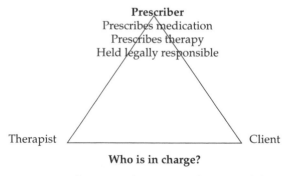

Who is in charge?

Figure 2.1. The prescriber's area of responsibility.

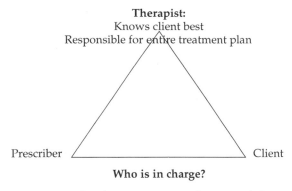

Figure 2.2. The therapist's area of responsibility.

With all of the potential dissension between the prescriber and the therapist about who is in charge of what, the client can easily be left out. But it *is* the client's life. This is clearly the ethical position. It is also the legal reality, unless a court has judged the client incompetent. The vast majority of people with severe, persistent mental illness have never been found incompetent by a court and have the same legal rights as anyone else. Even a client who may have some impairment in the capacity to make decisions still has preferences and can still weigh the pros and cons of what treatment makes sense to him or her. Although the prescriber decides which medication to prescribe, the client is going to decide whether or not he or she actually takes the medication (Figure 2.3).

It is surprisingly difficult to take responsibility for someone else who does not voluntarily cede or let go of that responsibility. A therapist can ensure that clients have food in their apartment, but they cannot really control what a particular client eats. A prescriber can decide which medication to prescribe but cannot control what a client actually takes. If a client is living in the community, even a court order will be ineffective without some degree of client collaboration; the client can decide not to take, or to cheek medication even if it is court

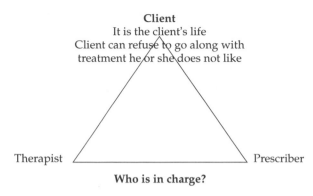

Figure 2.3. The client's range of responsibility.

ordered. If police show up to implement a pickup order, the client can decide not to open the door or not to be in the apartment at that time. Even the court-ordered imposition of long-acting injections requires that the client come in, as ordered by the court, be around when police show up, and go along with the authority of the court and the mental health system even as he or she may object to the proceedings. The client may be powerless to initiate ideas about what he or she wants, but the client can effectively block treatment proposals, including medication that he or she really wants to resist. So, although the client may believe he or she is powerless in this system, in some sense it is the client who is ultimately "in charge."

The bottom line is that prescriber, therapist, and client all have overlapping and often ill-defined responsibility for decisions. All are, to some extent, "in charge." The prescriber has direct control over what is prescribed and some control over what other resources are available. The therapist may be responsible for the overall treatment plan, including medication, housing, daily support, and benefits, but has little direct control over most of these areas. What a therapist can actually control are resources–how much time of specific sorts will the system make available for this client and how will this time be used. The client is going to decide what to go along with and what to resist. It is this overlapping sense of "taking charge" that leads to the complexity of the client, therapist, prescriber relationship.

Although the discussions about responsibility typically focus on medication decisions, many other decisions may be just as important to the client. For example, housing is a critical issue, connected to both stability in the community and quality of life. It is also a common area of disagreement between what the client wants, what the other members of the treatment team may recommend, and what is actually available. Who decides where a client lives? The psychiatrist may need to "sign off" on any housing referral and may have significant influence about what housing options are made available to a specific client. The therapist may have responsibility for arranging a client's housing and may have the most information about what housing options are available. The client may not be able to decide where he or she can live but can easily decide where he or she will *not* live by just staying away and living somewhere else.

This "power to block" is always the power of people with less formal power in a hierarchy, and it is used when more direct expressions of power and responsibility are not possible. Although the staff has the authority and responsibility to make decisions about the life of the client, the client has the power to block those decisions. It may be more difficult for a client to assert where he or she *does* want to live or what medication he or she *does* want to take. The client can always block decisions with which he or she strongly disagrees by refusing to use offered housing or refusing to take prescribed medication. For example, the prescriber and therapist may both believe that a particular group home is just the right placement for a particular client, but the client can always violate enough rules to ensure eviction, as demonstrated in the following example.

George has a very long history of both schizophrenia and substance abuse. He is constantly barraged with auditory hallucinations, often with a strong command component. He has bitten his arm down to the bone under control of the voices, and on one occasion he put his head through a window to try and escape from them. He has been institutionalized in a locked facility for months at a time, usually after "failing" at one or another group home. He has been evicted from group homes for staying out all night, smoking cigarettes or marijuana in his room, and having his girlfriend spend the night (against house rules and to the discomfort of his roommate). George kept saying that he wanted to live in his own apartment, but he was perceived as "too ill" to even attempt it.

Eventually an astute therapist noted that George was evicted from his group home for behavior that would not cause eviction from an apartment. He continued to use substances even in a group home, so substance use was unlikely to get worse. And, finally, since he wanted an apartment, maybe he would have some stake in keeping it if he got one. On the other hand, staff members expressed concern about liability if George were to hurt some person or property while living "unsupervised"; they were also concerned about supporting an endeavor that "had no chance of working," and about the amount of time they would need to provide to support George to help him handle having his own apartment. In reality, no one could prevent George from getting his own apartment. However, the therapist could decline to help George do the things that are necessary to help him get or keep an apartment.

In this case, George was supported in getting his own apartment, which he was able to keep, with help from staff. He continued to use drugs and be bothered by voices, but he also stayed out of the hospital and out of jail. Over time his behavior improved and the voices became less intrusive, and after several years he moved from his initial, somewhat disreputable apartment to one that was nicer.

Society increases the confusion over who is responsible. Often the prescriber, who may have the least contact with the client, is deemed the person ultimately responsible for all treatment decisions and held accountable for any bad outcome. This sense of legal and social responsibility pushes the prescriber into being responsible for areas that he or she may have little real expertise in, and little power to enforce. A malpractice case in Wisconsin held that the prescribing psychiatrist could be held legally responsible for the bad driving of a patient, even though the psychiatrist had not seen the patient for some time. The training of physicians that encourages them to "take charge" also promotes this sense of overall responsibility, as does the reality that psychiatrists are usually the people in the team with the highest social status. Physicians tend to be seen by all members of the team as "responsible," even the nonphysician prescribers, and they tend to take on this sense of responsibility.

The therapist also may have a sense of being "responsible for everything." The responsibility for all parts of a client's treatment plan is often an explicit part of the therapist's job. The therapist often spends the most time with the client and is most responsible for dealing with a crisis or disaster if one ensues. It is typically the therapist who is responsible for finding housing after yet another eviction. The relationship between the therapist and the prescriber is often complex. Some therapists are very knowledgeable about medication and involved in medication-related decisions. Others believe that medication is outside their area of expertise and provide little input into such decisions. Some therapists are very concerned about whether clients are taking their medication effectively, whereas others see no connection between what they do and anything concerning medication. Some prescribers believe it is appropriate for them to be involved in decisions concerning housing, work, and virtually all areas of the treatment plan, whereas others limit themselves to medication, as though medication issues could be divorced from other areas of the client's life.

And, finally, the client also has responsibility for his or her own life. Too often, mental health professionals, be they therapists or prescribers, talk about *their* responsibility and *their* need to make decisions about what should be done to maximize clients' quality of life, without sufficiently eliciting client input about those decisions. Much of the conflict and apparent lack of compliance between clients and their mental health workers occurs when clients' own views are not considered, when they do not think that the treatment plan is focused on meeting their own goals, and when there is a struggle for control that is framed in terms of their alleged "noncompliance" because they are unwilling to go along with the plan. Much of the noncompliance in the mental health system can be framed as an attempt by clients to take control of their own lives, over the objection of the other members of the treatment team.

There is no fixed way to orient the prescriber–clinician–client triangle. At one moment it may look as though the prescriber is at the top of the triangle, whereas from another angle it is equally clear that it is the client or the therapist who is at the peak. A more accurate perception is that the configuration of the triangle—the configuration of the relationship between the client, prescriber, and therapist—is always in a state of fluctuating equilibrium, changing not only the orientation of the triangle but also the perception of closeness or distance between the various participants. It is a flexible structure wherein each participant has a role that is defined in relation to the strengths, needs, preferences, and expertise of the others. The goal is to have a working relationship that is flexible enough to best meet the changing needs and preferences of the client. It is the goals and the needs of the client that are the paramount driving force in shaping these relationships.

How do Differences in Power Influence Mental Health Relationships?

Structural issues in the client–therapist relationship can foster the development of the relationship. Clients are, presumably, coming in for help, and the therapist's job is to provide that help. This idealization of the voluntary relationship is often very different from the realities initially encountered by people with more serious mental illness. These individuals often come into treatment under significant external pressure (e.g., from their families, friends, or even the police). Clients with serious mental illness rarely have much choice over what therapist they end up seeing or even the kind of treatment they receive. Even if a client's personal experience of the mental health system is positive, he or she will inevitably hear the stories of other clients whose experience is less positive.

One often thinks of coercion as either present or absent, but in reality coercion occurs along a continuum. We are all influenced by attempts at persuasion from friends and family and doctors who try to convince us to do things that they believe are in our best interest. At times, we experience pressure, a more insistent form of persuasion. This pressure can be increased by controlling resources: For example, we will give a client a ride to look for housing if he first comes in to meet with the prescriber. We may spend time helping a client get a job if she agrees to take medication. It is even further toward the coercive end of this continuum when clients with a financial payee are handed medication, with the expectation that they will take it, before giving them spending money from their own SSI check. A mental health commitment to a hospital is just one end of the continuum from full autonomy to legal coercion. Underlying all of these examples is a difference in power between client and therapist. Power is the ability to change the behavior of another person. Therapists tend not to think much about power and when they do, it tends to be prompted by the most coercive examples. We usually spend less energy thinking about all of the informal power that we wield: who gets to set the agenda of a meeting, who determines the frequency or length of appointments, etc. Power continues to exist as a force even if it is not used. In a graphic example, if I am pointing a gun in your direction, I have power that will dramatically influence our subsequent conversation even if I do not use the gun, and even if I indicate that I have no intention of using the gun. Just having the gun and the potential to use it is enough. If I have the power to hospitalize a client against his or her will, or the power to take control of SSI money, or the power to influence whether he or she will or will not get a wanted apartment, then this power differential will influence our subsequent relationship. It does not even require that I really have the authority to control these things, only that the client believe that I have such authority.

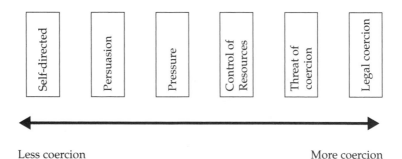

There are many sources of power. Some people exude power via the sheer force of their personality. Others have specialized knowledge. If you are the person who knows how to treat a heart attack or fix a broken air conditioner, anyone who needs to use that knowledge requires your help. Knowing how to apply for housing support or how to access the vocational system, or even the ability to address every other therapist in town on a first-name basis, constitutes an access that clients and other therapists might need. Control of resources, such as the person who schedules appointments or schedules transportation, is a form of power. Legitimacy, the perception of other staff and clients that you have power, is another form of power. Legal authority, having a title or a formal role, is also a form of power, but may not be the only, or even the primary, form of it.

Power is perceived very differently by the person who is "up" and the person who is "down" in the hierarchy. People who are "up" generally believe that they have very little real power over the person who is "down." However, the "down" person almost always believes that the hierarchy is much steeper. This differential perception characterizes the relationship between faculty professors and medical students, supervisors and employees, parents and their adolescent children, and therapists and clients. This difference of perception holds no matter what the nature of the relationship. For example, as faculty I can give a medical student a good grade or a bad grade, but few medical students are going to flunk out of school, and most medical students will become physicians whether they do well or poorly in my class. Students may believe I have a lot of power over their lives, but I believe that I have very little. Similarly, as a supervisor I can fire an employee, but this is a very rare event. I can fire someone only for clear cause—either clearly documented incompetence or a pattern of major infractions of agency policy—but over a range from just okay performance to stellar performance, there is little real power that I can impose. I can write good or mediocre performance evaluations, but these have little real impact on my employees' jobs. On the other hand, most employees believe that their supervisors have a lot of power over them.

Similarly, therapists generally believe that they have little real control over the clients with whom they work. Involuntary hospitalizations are very rare and are only an issue if the client is engaging in clearly dangerous behavior. Clients, on the other hand, are exquisitely aware that therapists can, at least potentially, hospitalize them, take control over their SSI money, and decide whether they will be able to move into their own apartment or obtain support to get a job. Remember that power is not only the actual imposition of control but the *perceived ability to exert control* if so desired. Therapists typically believe they have little power, and clients generally believe therapists have a lot of power.

Some kinds of power are specific to the clinical situation. Therapists have the power to label the clients' behavior. It is the therapist who decides whether behavior is "bad" or "ill." If a client decides to disagree with the therapist, the therapist decides whether this disagreement is rational or a sign of illness-related incompetence. The client is expected to accept the therapist's view of illness and behave in "acceptable" ways. It is the perspective of the therapist that goes into the clinical chart, becoming the history that will have a major influence on how other therapists later view this client. It is the therapists who most often set the goals for treatment, and the treatment team who decides which medication is needed, for how long, and for what purpose.

People who are "one up" and "one down" use very different mechanisms to maintain control, and there are significant differences in how people from different cultures deal with power. In mainstream American culture, one-up people assert power by being direct, making suggestions, and initiating change. One-down people assert power by deciding what change they want to block, and what change they want to support. These individuals do not announce that they are blocking change, and, in fact, their lack of power requires that they avoid being overt about what they are doing. Think of the example of dealing with a supervisor who has just come up with an idea for how you should completely reorganize your work. If you like the suggestion, you will go along with it. But if you strongly disagree with the suggestion, unless you really trust this supervisor, you will try to avoid it. You might say that you need to think about it, hoping that the supervisor will forget the suggestion. You might keep putting it off or start it in a very minimal way to indicate that you are working on it, but trying to make as little real change as possible. You may list all of the complications and costs of the change or start working on other projects that "must be done first." In short, you will become "passive–aggressive." *Passive–aggressive* describes how lower-power people cope with the suggestions of higher-power people. It is not an issue of personality style or diagnosis, but rather a structural issue of how people in different positions of a power hierarchy assert themselves. It is difficult and risky to directly tell the supervisor what you really think about his or her idea. It is safer–and more likely to keep his or her idea from intruding, uninvited, into your life–if you wait, hoping that it will eventually go away.

This style of behavior sounds a lot like what often happens between a therapist and a client. Often therapists make suggestions to clients, such as, "I think that you should . . . exercise more . . . get a job . . . stop smoking . . . take medication more regularly." Clients thank therapists for the suggestion, agree to do it, and then never follow through. Despite initial agreement, clients do not start exercising, do not get a job, do not stop smoking, and do not take medication any differently. Therapists then label this behavior as lack of motivation, resistance, or passive–aggressiveness. In many cases, clients' lack of follow-through has little to do with psychopathology and more to do with power issues. It is likely that in many cases a client copes with the therapist's suggestion in the same way that you might cope with a supervisor's suggestion. You verbally agree to everything because of the risk of overt disagreement, but you choose which parts of the suggestion that you really follow through with, hoping that the others can be put off as long as possible.

There is a range to such behavioral patterns. Some people are less sensitive than others to power hierarchies. Some people are so clear about their personal power or so secure in their position in the world that they are less bothered by the potential power of others. This is less an issue of how wealthy or powerful a person is than of his or her personal style and how he or she deals with the power of others. Hierarchal behavior around power is influenced by the range of choices available. Can the person easily find a new job or a new therapist? It also depends on the degree of emotional or objective dependence of the one-down person on the one-up person. How upsetting would a disagreement be? How might the one-down person be punished if the one-up person decided to do so? It also depends on the behavior of the one-up person: Is he or she open to ideas, critical of direct suggestions, abrupt in his or her style of dealing with subordinates?

A classic example of this response to a power differential is the way in which nurses in a hospital deal with doctors, especially resident physicians who are still in training, are temporary, and are unsure of their own role or power. A nurse can follow all of the rules and report to the on-call resident for every patient complaint, every request for a laxative or aspirin, every change in patient report of pain. If the nurse chooses to follow all of the rules precisely, then she can effectively make the life of the on-call doctor miserable, and there is nothing that the doctor can do about it because the nurse is just following the rules. On the other hand, the nurse can show some judgment about when to call the doctor, and when not. This exertion of judgment can dramatically improve the quality of life of the physician without in any way risking the patient's safety. This interaction depends, of course, on the personality style of the nurse. Is she someone who tends to follow rules exactly, or does she tend to allow for more flexibility? It also depends on the nurse's social context. Has he, or other nurses, been chastized for not following other rules? Such a reprimand would reinforce rigidity toward following all rules. The skill, attitude, and social role of the physician is yet another important contextual variable. Physicians who are friendly, well liked, and perceived as hard working tend to bring out a collaborative protectiveness on the part of nurses with whom they work. On the other hand, if the doctor is perceived as arrogant, lazy, or unavailable, then the nurses are more likely to assert themselves by using the power available to them—that is, by rigidly adhering to each and every rule available.

There are ways to improve communication between one-up and one-down people. These are, in fact, similar to the ways in which therapists and prescribers can improve communication with clients and each other. It helps enormously if the one-up person is friendly, accessible, respectful, available, and hard working. Communication becomes more difficult and leads to more passive–aggressive behavior, however, if the one-up person is rigid, condescending, disrespectful, and not perceived as listening. Improving such communication patterns takes time. There is no good reason why a client should automatically trust a mental health professional just because of a name on the door or an academic degree. In fact, many mental health clients have had personal experiences that might lead them to be suspicious of mental health professionals.

What Is an Expert and What Are the Limits of this Expertise?

• *Prescriber expertise.* The ambiguity about responsibility is connected to the complexity of issues surrounding expertise. Who is considered "expert" changes with specific issues and when examined from different perspectives. Even expertise of something as presumably straightforward as decisions about medication depends on the specific issue being addressed. The prescriber presumably knows most about the mechanism of medication, how medications are generally used, the scientific literature concerning medication, and the risks involved. The prescriber may also have expertise gained from experience with many other clients taking similar medication. This is important expertise, but it is not the only expertise relevant to medication decisions.

- *Therapist expertise.* The therapist, on the other hand, typically has much more expertise about a specific client. The therapist spends much more time with the client, often in different situations, discussing different aspects of his or her life. This additional time often leads to a more trusting relationship that allows the client to express concerns or mention potential side effects that may not come out during a brief "med check." The therapist may well be in the best position to understand the specific goal for a specific medication for this client, and how well the medication is actually working. This profile would suggest that the most relevant expertise for determining how well a medication is working or how well a new medication might work with this client would come from the therapist. From this perspective, more information about medication, in general, may be less important than specific expertise about this client.

- *Client expertise.* The client is the person who is most expert in reporting the subjective effects of the medication. Traditionally, professionals have dismissed clients' expertise, especially if it runs counter to that of the mental health professional. When a client says that a medication makes him feel worse or is not helping his symptoms or interferes with his ability to work, instead of believing him we are likely to assume that he is resisting taking the medication, and that this resistance is based on a lack of insight concerning his illness. Although this may be true in a particular case, the most optimistic research studies suggest that, at best, 70% of people with schizophrenia have a beneficial response to medication. This finding would suggest that at least 30% of people are reporting accurately when they say the medication is not helping them. It is extraordinarily rare for a client with active psychotic symptoms to be taken off antipsychotic medications simply because they are not effective for this client. Unfortunately, the situation is quite similar for people with depression, bipolar disorder, and other severe, persistent mental illnesses. In carefully structured research studies, subjects report many more side effects than are acknowledged in clinical practice. In these cases, the clients may have a more accurate assessment of the effectiveness and side effects of the medication than do the clinicians.

We all believe ourselves most expert about our own life; even people with mental illness believe that they are the best experts about their own life. The client has the most expertise in setting the goals for what constitutes "getting better." Is the goal of treatment stability in the community, avoidance of hospitalization, having friends, being able to work, experiencing less distress from symptoms, or having a sense of self that extends beyond the illness?

How Do Personal Values Affect Decision Making?

Different people have different views about what is most important for a good life, what is ethical and what is not, what should be addressed first and what should be postponed. Just as a client and clinician can disagree about what is most important, so to can the therapist and prescriber. Each member of the treatment team is likely to have his or her own values, and these differing values will influence the development of treatment goals. For example, even if the client does not seem to care, the therapist may believe that stable housing is better than living on the street, freedom is better than prison, being physically well is better than allowing medical illness to lead to disability or death. Prescribers may have values about the abuse of alcohol or other drugs, the value of work, or the possibility of how much life change is possible. Therapists also have their own views and values about how much people with disability should be given assistance, even at the risk of encouraging their dependence, and how much they should be encouraged to "stand on their own two feet." This value will influence not only how much a therapist is willing to support or "bail out" a client in trouble, but also what advice the therapist gives the client's family. We are all subject to these personal values, and they inevitably influence how we think about the world and what kinds of goals we will support or contend with.

Conceptualizing the Expert–Client Relationship

Whenever a person goes to an "expert," there is an understanding that the expert will know something that the person does not. Although possession of this knowledge gives the expert a kind of power, in most situations the client can just disregard the expert if the advice is not relevant, does not make sense, or requires too much time or effort. This is true whether the expert is a car mechanic, a doctor, or a mental health professional. If I take my car to my mechanic, I can follow his advice or not; it is my choice to decide what to do with the information he provides. I may be intimidated by his injunction that my car needs immediate repair, and this element of intimidation implies a potential element of pressure or coercion even in this completely voluntary relationship.

This relationship between expert and client is more complicated in the mental health arena. When a car mechanic recommends an expensive repair, it may be that the repair is really needed and the recommendation is made to help the client. It is also possible that the repair is not completely needed, and the recommendation is made to sell a service that serves the interest of the mechanic. Or both may be true: The recommendation is in the best interest of the client *and* in the best interest of the mechanic. In any case, most experts cannot make a decision or implement an action not approved by the client. No matter how much my car mechanic believes that I need new brakes, he is not legally entitled to put in new brakes over my objection.

Recognizing Our Own Paternalism

Experts in mental health are supposed to operate under very different rules. We are supposed to make recommendations purely based on the needs of the client and to largely disregard what is in our own (the expert's) best interest. Mental health experts, both therapists and prescribers, often make decisions in what they believe is the best interest of their clients, over the objection of their clients. This is called *paternalism*. Paternalism is sometimes thought to be a bad thing, but actually it just refers to any action that is done for the benefit of another person, without the consent, or over the objection, of that person. I am being paternalistic if I stop someone who is suicidal from killing him- or herself, or if I force someone who is dangerously intoxicated to stop drinking, or if I take control of a client's SSI check so that the rent gets paid and a potential eviction is avoided. At times, therapists may have loftier goals than clients can allow themselves to consider. A therapist may think that a client could return to school, get a job, or live independently, even if the client thinks these goals are so unobtainable that they should not even be sought. Paternalism can also refer to setting goals that the client says he or she does not want, even if most would consider them very positive.

Managing Conflicts between Autonomy and Paternalism

There are competing values around the issues of paternalism and autonomy. Ethical conflicts do not arise when there is a clear right course. They occur when there are competing goods—when it is the right thing to both do something and not do something. In the case of establishing treatment goals, there is an ethical value to support the client's autonomy—that is, supporting, as much as possible, what the client wants. There is also an ethical value to beneficence, to help the client have a better life, even if the client disagrees about some parts of the plan needed to make this happen. Although there are traditional platitudes that mental health professionals are supposed to be value neutral and not let their own values interfere, this is not possible. Personal values always enter in to decisions. Some therapists put more value on helping the client, even over the client's objection, whereas others put more value on supporting the client's own decisions, even if those decisions get the client into difficulty. The base for many clinical disagreements reflects this ongoing tension between beneficence—the obligation to do good—and autonomy—the obligation to support a person's own decisions.

Weighing Competing Values

Even ethical precepts that seem clear are, in fact, subject to competing values. Mental health clinicians generally hold that client confidentiality must be maintained, unless there is an issue of imminent danger that would override the requirement of confidentiality. It is generally held that confidentiality must be protected, even when the client's treatment is compromised. But in the real world, there are nuisances that complicate this apparent simplicity. There are times when paternalism—attempting to do good even over the objections of the client—may outweigh the need to support autonomy and confidentiality.

Rachel is a woman well known to the local mental health center. Although she has never been dangerous, she is often odd and inappropriate. A local police officer called the crisis team, saying that a woman identified as Rachel has been haranguing strangers downtown. The crisis team knows that if the police just walk away, they can be there in 20 minutes and likely calm her down without need for hospitalization.

They also know, based on past experience, that if the police attempt to bring Rachel to the local hospital emergency room, she will get more and more agitated, will probably end up in handcuffs, and by the time she gets to the hospital may well end up being involuntarily hospitalized yet again. In the background of this conversation with the police, the crisis staff can clearly hear Rachel shouting "Don't tell them anything—I forbid you to tell them anything!" Rachel refuses to pick up the phone to speak to the crisis staff, and the crisis staff is left with a decision to make. There is no suggestion that Rachel is now dangerous to herself or anyone else. Do they go along with her demand that they not say anything— which would mean that police would take her to the ER and a probable hospitalization—or do they breach confidentiality, tell police that she is known to the mental health system and is not dangerous, and that if they just walk away, the crisis team can be there in 20 minutes?

Acknowledging Our Personal Needs

Very separate from these issues of autonomy and paternalism, a therapist may also have goals that reflect his or her personal needs. If a client loses an apartment or gets into crisis, the therapist may be faced with a huge amount of extra work and frustration. If a client causes a major problem for the community, the therapist will likely to be held responsible and blamed. A therapist may make a decision that, in part, is influenced by these personal needs. A therapist who has just experienced a suicide of one client may be less able or willing to tolerate the risk of suicide in another client, and therefore force a hospitalization more readily. A therapist who is feeling emotionally burdened by the needs of other clients may be less willing to support the emotional demands that may occur if a client moves from a group home to an independent apartment. Note that these decisions may be framed as being in the best interest of the client, but they may have an unacknowledged component based on the staff person's needs. This is not to say that these needs are not legitimate. We all have such needs, and it is important to be as aware as possible when our personal needs are influencing us. This awareness makes it easier to look at them, hopefully with other members of our clinical team, including the client, and decide on when it is legitimate for staff needs to be part of the decision process, and when it might be better to find other supports and alternatives so that staff needs, as legitimate as they might be, do not interfere with the client's treatment.

There are also agency and society pressures that translate into treatment goals, if not for the client than at least for the staff. There is a need, experienced by staff members and agency administration, to keep both the community and the clients safe. There may be administrative needs to decrease the use of the hospital or decrease homelessness. The agency may have needs to limit risk. There will always be financial limitations that restrict what services may be available, even if those services are clearly needed and would clearly help. And finally, there are goals relating to poverty, race, or other issues outside of the mental health system, that clearly impinge on the client's life but may be outside the purview of the therapist.

Value Conflicts and Disagreement over Medication

One of the most common areas of disagreements is over medication. There are different ways in which the client and staff might disagree about the role of medication. The most common situation is one in which staff members believe that medication is more useful than does the client.

Susan is a woman who, most of the time, gets out of her apartment, enjoys spending time with friends, and is able to maintain a part-time job about which she feels good. These are all personal goals that she wants to maintain and even expand. She has gone through long periods, however, when she is too frightened of people talking about her to leave her apartment, gets too angry at supervisors to keep a job, and stops spending time with friends. During these times she has difficulty functioning, and she has been hospitalized several times for being unable to care for herself and for threatening neighbors. Staff members believe strongly that these periods correspond with, indeed are caused by, Susan's going off her antipsychotic medication. Susan believes equally strongly that the medication does not help and that the periods of difficulty have more to do with periods when the neighbors and the police target her in special ways.

It might appear that such situations are usually clear and that if only the client could think about the situation rationally, he or she would agree. What is less clear are all of the times in regular practice when medication has not been all that useful, when staff members have made assumptions about the effectiveness without careful review of behavioral data, or when the side effects outweigh the potential advantages. A medication may be effective, but the client may decide that the potential gains are outweighed by the risk of significant weight gain, sexual side effects, or other problems. A subtler disagreement occurs when staff and client espouse different kinds of "getting better." This topic was discussed in more detail in Chapter 1 and is at the core of many disagreements that appear irrational.

Vivian had been homeless after being evicted from many different apartments for such behaviors as stuffing up the toilets to try and stop the voices that were coming up from the drain. She responded very well to antipsychotic medication and, when taking it regularly, all of her psychotic symptoms disappeared. She was able to maintain housing and interact in fairly normal ways. At the same time she felt dead inside, out of touch with her "spirit side," which was very important to her. It was only after a very low dose of medication was tried that she could conform her behavior sufficiently to maintain an apartment while still being in touch with her "spirits." She had some disorganization, heard some voices, and was certainly eccentric on this lower dose, but she was also more comfortable and more willing to keep taking it than she had been on a full dose.

At other times, however, the client believes that medication is much more important than do staff members.

Eve is tormented by voices that are always critical and very difficult to ignore. She is now on two different antipsychotic medications, both in very high dose, an antidepressant, a mood stabilizer, a benzodiazepine, and a sleeping pill. Staff members are not very convinced that she is much better on this cocktail of medication than she had been before, but she is terrified that things will get even worse if any of the medications is stopped or even decreased. When any of the medications have been reduced by even very small amounts, she reports feeling more suicidal and a worsening of the voices within a day of the medication change.

Doug is extremely anxious and chronically depressed, and although he would like to have friends, he tends to avoid people. He spends most of his time alone, trying to write poetry. He often goes though periods of feeling very suicidal, and he has severe and chronic insomnia. He does not use either alcohol or other illicit drugs, but he has been taking very high doses of benzodiazepines and sleeping pills for many years. At one point, he was taking 80 mg a day fluoxetine (Prozac) for anxiety, panic, and depression; 12 mg a day of clonazepam (Klonopin) during the day for anxiety and panic, and two or three 10 mg tablets of zolpidem (Ambien) at night for sleep. He regularly requests an increase in his clonazepam, believing that just a bit more might really help. Both the therapist and the prescriber working with him have not seen much change as medications have been added, changed, or the dose has been increased.

At other times, neither the prescriber, the therapist, or the client believes that medications are very useful, but it may be hard to know how to stop them.

Ruth has limited cognitive abilities, constant complaints of auditory hallucinations, and a very long history of out-of-control behavior. When she gets frustrated, she becomes violent; she has kicked in doors, thrown objects, and, on several occasions, kicked or punched staff members. She has undergone long periods of hospitalization that seem to make things worse rather than better. She is now in an apartment that she shares with another client and a live-in staff. She has ended up on two atypical antipsychotic medications in addition to haloperidol deconoate (Haldol) and sodium valproate (Depakote). Neither the client, her family, nor staff members think that the medications have helped. Her prescriber believes that it would be difficult to taper down on the medications because of realistic concern that she is likely to have a period of violent behavior connected to the medication decrease. There is also the question that if she is doing this badly on all of this medication, would she be doing even worse if some of the medication was stopped?

What Is the Difference Between Compliance, Adherence, and the Effective Use of Medication?

The client who is going to take the medication, the prescriber who is ultimately deciding which medications are appropriate, and the therapist who has the most contact with the client and assists him or her with achieving personal life goals all need to work as a collaborative team. Unfortunately, such collaboration is not always the case. Traditional approaches to the use of medication start with discussions of compliance—how to get the client to *comply* with the decision of the prescriber. More recently, this behavior has been reframed as *adherence,* although the difference between these terms is often difficult to elucidate. Adherence or compliance refers to the degree to which the client's actions agree with medical advice. There is rarely discussion of therapist or prescriber adherence, the degree to which the actions of the clinical staff agree with the preferences or decisions of the client, or the extent to which the treatment system follows through on what it has promised. It may be more useful to focus on treatment concordance before addressing issues of adherence. *Treatment concordance* is the extent to which the prescriber, client, and therapist agree on treatment priorities, problems, goals, objectives, interventions, and the direction treatment will take. *Adherence* is the extent to which the treatment plan is subsequently followed.

Alliance between Client and Prescriber

> *"I have thrown away more prescriptions than I have filled, and I suspect that I'm not alone in this practice. I will tear up my doctor's prescriptions when I doubt that he has heard me. Why should I take his word, when he is not even paying me the courtesy of listening to mine?"*
> —Gutheil, 1977, p. 82

The relationship with the prescriber is a major factor in the client's decision to take or not take medication. If a client believes that the prescriber is competent, has the client's interest at heart, and knows and understand the client, the client is much more likely to take a medication. If the client believes that the prescriber is more concerned about cost or the clinic than the client and does not know or care about him or her, then the client is much less likely to take medication. This is true for all of us when we go in to see our own prescriber, and it is equally true for the person with major mental illness.

Does the client believe that the prescriber:

- Is competent?
- Listens to his or her beliefs, goals, and concerns?

- Has his or her interest at heart?
- Is on the client's side?
- Knows and understands the client?

How can clinicians move from a stance that seeks compliance to one that fosters concordance and alliance? The goal is to establish a collaborative relationship wherein client and staff work together to get the client's goals met. Certainly the skills and the attitude of the therapist can have a significant influence on how collaborative the network of contacts between client and staff members becomes. However, client symptoms, especially paranoia, grandiosity, or other psychotic symptoms, can make it more difficult to develop a collaborative relationship, as can the client's character style. "Fit" between client and therapist can be a factor. Lack of resources may make it very difficult for the therapist to offer real help. It also may be easier to get into a collaborative relationship if the client's life is going better. And, of course, substance use can make relationship building much more difficult.

Developing a trusting, collaborative relationship may take years. There is no clear reason why a client should automatically trust us just because we are mental health professionals. Clients may have had good experience with other professionals, or less good experience. In either case, it may take time for trust to develop on both sides. Trust develops from a history of being respectful, being reliable, following through on agreements, listening, and being genuinely helpful. It is based less on insight than on behavior.

Noncompliance of Mental Health System

We typically focus on the client's noncompliance, but there is also the issue of the noncompliance of the mental health system. Clients are sometimes told that if they would only take their medication, then they would be able to get a job, get their own apartment, or get help reestablishing contact with their kids, for example. Often clients do take the required medication for weeks or months or even years, but no job or apartment or contact with his kids is forthcoming. There are often very good reasons for this failure of follow-through. There are no jobs, or the budget for vocational supports has been cut, or the program is too short staffed to attend to this area right now, or the client is taking medication but still presents in a way that makes getting a job difficult. From the therapist's point of view the failure is justified, but from the client's point of view the system has not kept its end of the bargain. Sometimes this "bargain" was implied but never stated. At other times, there is enough ambiguity that the client can understand something very different from the therapist understands. "Take the medication for a while and then we will see what can be done" is a statement that may mean very different things to the person making it and the person receiving it. When clients decide to stop taking their medication, to become "noncompliant," it is useful to think about all of the ways that the system has been "noncompliant" first. What is perceived as a decision to stop treatment initiated by the client may, in some cases, be the client's response to a perception that the system has decided not to provide real help that was promised.

Effective Use of Medication

The therapist can have an extremely important role in the client's decision to take, or not to take, medication. It is not just an issue for the prescriber or the nurse, but should be an issue considered by all members of the treatment team. In Chapter 1 we discussed the connection between a client's willingness to take medication and his or her relationship with the clinicians connected with that medication. We have also discussed the importance of using medication as a tool to help the client achieve his or her own goals, developing clear target symptoms that allow the effect of each medication to be assessed, and enlisting medication as something the client can use to overcome illness, rather than something that is done "to" the client. There are a number of other issues that the treatment team can address to increase the effective use of medication.

People taking medication, be it for high blood pressure, diabetes, depression, or schizophrenia, are rarely completely compliant or noncompliant. Very few patients take all doses of a medication exactly as prescribed. Neither do most patients stop all medication. Rather most people who are prescribed medication are partially compliant. They take a few of the doses, or some of the doses, or most of the doses, or almost all of the doses. There is a continuum of reliability of taking medications. For some clients and some medication, "pretty good" is good enough. Vitamins or calcium are examples where pretty good compliance is probably sufficient. There are other medications, for example, birth control pills, where anything less than 100% reliability of use dramatically decreases the effectiveness of the medication. There is increasing data that for people with schizophrenia, there is a direct relationship between more psychotic symptoms and increased risk of relapse and increased gaps in their medication use. This data would suggest that partial compliance, which is the norm for virtually everyone, may keep antipsychotic medication from being as effective as it might otherwise be. The same is probably also true for antidepressants and mood stabilizers.

Educating clients about the importance of regular medication use can help, as can listening to the client's experience with the medication. Helping the client connect medication use to some other regular activity is something that most staff members do automatically. Clients may not come up with these strategies on their own, but they can be helped to develop similar structural contexts that support regular medication use. It is much easier to take medication if it is always taken along with morning teeth brushing, or along with breakfast, or connected to some regular activity. It is much easier to take a medication along with a meal (if the client eats meals regularly) or to remember to take a medication an hour before a meal. It can also be very helpful to suggest that a client use med boxes with a separate compartment for each day, so that he or she does not have to open a bunch of different bottles and can see, at a glance, if the medication has been taken that day or not. Finally, it is extremely helpful to simplify the medication regimen as much as possible. It is reasonably easy to take a medication once a day. It is much more difficult to take a medication twice a day, and very difficult to take a medication three or four times a day over a long period of time. Most medications used in mental health treatment can be taken once a day. A few really need to be taken twice a day. Very few require more frequent dosing than this. It is important to make the medication regimen as simple as possible.

People are not consistently compliant in another way. Most people taking medication for severe mental illness are on multiple medications, and it is common for a person to be much more reliable about taking one medication than another. The same woman who is very inconsistent with her Depakote may be absolutely reliable with her birth control pills. The same person who is very reliable about his antidepressant may be very erratic in his use of antipsychotic medication. There are a number of factors that influence why a person will take one medication and not another. Certainly side effects play a part, as does the person's belief about whether the medication is helping. If a person believes that the medication is causing weight gain or sedation, this belief may influence regularity of use. Similarly if the person believes that it is this medication that is preventing another hospitalization or behavior that would result in loss of a much-liked job, the medication is likely to be used more regularly. Others have learned that missing a couple of doses of an antidepressant may allow them to temporarily regain sexual function that has been impaired by the medication. These different experiences and beliefs will lead to very different medication use patterns.

The personal meaning of a medication influences how consistently a person will take that medication. If every pill reminds me that I am ill and unable to work, I will find it harder to take the medication regularly than if I believe that every pill is helping me overcome my illness and recapture my own life. People often think that if they take the prescribed medication, then they really have the diagnosed illness, and if they do not take the medication, then maybe they do not really have the illness. Some people assess how well they are doing by how much medication they are taking. It is important to help people focus on their own goals and how they are doing in their own terms. It matters little whether a person is taking 1 mg or 100 mg of a medication. What is important is how well the person is doing, how much distress he or she is feeling, and what side effects the medication may be causing. It is important to understand the client's beliefs about what the medication does, good and bad. It is also important to listen to the client's beliefs about would happen if he or she misses doses or discontinues the medication entirely. Obviously a person who is tormented by voices and unable to work, and who believes that all symptoms and problems would disappear if he or she could only stop taking the medication, is at high risk for discontinuing or missing doses of the medication. What happens, or what I believe will happen, if I miss a dose is also an important variable. Some people, sensitive to the withdrawal effects of antidepressants, have learned that missing even a single dose will leave them feeling irritable or headachy.

How Can Collaboration between Therapists, Clients, and Prescribers Best Be Fostered?

Improving collaboration between therapists, clients and prescribers starts with the development of trust. It requires honest and respectful sharing of information and a focus on the client's goals, as well as those of the prescriber and therapist. Developing a true collaboration takes time. It is not an instantaneous process, and the nature of the collaboration changes as the person's own view of his or her illness changes.

Improving Communication

Changing suspicion to trust takes time. Clients develop trust in therapists and prescribers in the same way any of us develop trust in people around us. It typically starts with small "tests." A client will "try out" a small disagreement or attempt to set the topic of a conversation or engage in other tests to see how rigidly the staff person is going to control the situation, and how assertions of power are handled. Developing trust requires reliability. Does the staff person follow through with commitments? If the therapist agrees to give the client a call, or find out about an apartment, or to talk with the prescriber about a potential medication change, does the therapist really do so? Trust requires an ongoing pattern of respect. The therapist does not always have to agree with the client, but the therapist does always have to be truly respectful. How often do we say or do something "just to put the client off," to finish a conversation or to keep the client from getting "too much information" that would "just confuse" him or her. It is a truism, but clients are not likely to respect us if we do not respect them, and they are not likely to trust us if we do not trust them. If we cannot trust a particular client, for a variety of good or bad reasons, then it is safe to assume that that client is very unlikely to really trust us.

Sharing information, respectfully, over time, is one of the better ways to establish a trusting relationship. Clients in most jurisdictions have legal access to their charts, but we rarely take this legality seriously, and most clients are socialized enough to know that they should not really ask for this access. If we really trusted our clients, however, we would be willing to let them see their charts. This shift would, of course, change what we wrote. We would not need to avoid saying things that are important, but we would need to say them in client-centric ways, using the client's own vocabulary and explanations.

Traditional note:
John has paranoid schizophrenia, and he continues to hold the delusion that people have stolen hundreds of dollars of cash from him. He has also engaged in dangerous behavior, leading to an involuntary hospitalization 18 months ago. He has been on court-ordered medication since that time, which has helped to decrease his delusions and decrease his previously frequent calls to the police.

Client-centric note:
John continues to be very upset because he cannot get anyone to believe that people have repeatedly broken into his apartment and stolen large amounts of cash. He was so upset about this that 18 months ago he got into a fight with the neighbor he believed was stealing the money, and was hospitalized after he slapped her and pushed her to the ground. Although she was not hurt, the police were called and took him to the hospital. Since then he has been court ordered to take medication, which he believes does not help very much and has not changed the thefts, but it has helped him feel less angry, and he has not called the police as much. He does agree that there are few side effects from the medication. Although he believes that the medication is not connected to these changes, I believe that the medication has helped him to make these changes.

The Importance of Focusing Treatment on the Client's Goals

Treatment, whether it is medication, skill training, or help with resources, should start with the client's goals: What does he or she want for his or her own life? This investigation includes identifying short-term goals that could be accomplished in a few weeks or a few months, and long-term goals that might take years. It includes realistic goals that might be attainable, and dreams that might never be possible but that keep all of us going through difficult periods. The client's goals should always be the bedrock of treatment. Unfortunately, this is not always the case, and disagreements about both goals and treatment are common. Although treatment should start with the client's goals, the therapist, the prescriber, and the agency may all have their own goals that either support or, at times, conflict with the client's goals. Supporting a client's goals is not a passive practice of automatically agreeing with anything the client says. It is, rather, the process of taking the client's goals seriously—perhaps at times more seriously than the client does.

For example, a client says that he wants a job, but he does not see his heavy use of alcohol as an issue and he does not want to talk about it. It is important, as a therapist, that I address the alcohol use, both my concerns about the client's use—how the alcohol use appears to be interfering with the client's goals—and my views of what I believe the client could do to begin thinking about his alcohol use. It is important that I not be moralistic in tone and not hold alcohol as the only thing we can talk about. On one hand, it is important that I not collude with the client to avoid substance use as an issue, but, on the other hand, I must also be willing to start where the client is, to invite him to speculate about the possible role of alcohol in his life, and to develop an active strategy to enhance his motivation to change.

Similarly, a client may have as a goal to discontinue medication. I do not need to share that goal, nor do I necessarily need to fight her about whether it is a good or bad goal. I can talk about other potential goals, the meaning of medication to that client, why getting off medication is so important, and encourage her to develop other markers for doing well. I can disagree with client's goals while taking them seriously and avoiding a fight over them.

The Developmental Course of Collaboration

Collaboration does not necessarily occur all at once. It is assumed that time is required to collect the important history and information about the client, but this is not the most time-consuming part of the treatment. Time is needed to develop an effective working relationship between client, prescriber, and therapist, to understand each others' values and styles, and to articulate shared goals. There is sometimes a bureaucratic need to have a treatment plan in the chart by the end of the first visit. However, a *real* treatment plan for someone with a serious, persistent illness is likely to take weeks or months to develop, and is constantly subject to revision and change.

In the first throes of the illness, such collaboration may be extremely difficult. In the panic and confusion of the initial onset of mental illness, a client may need help organizing what needs to be done. At times, especially with acute illness, therapists may need to provide more structure, offer limited choices, and provide accurate but simplified information. Much of the stereotype of the doctor–patient relationship is based on this model of acute overwhelming illness. Completely open-ended choices can, at times, be overwhelming rather than supportive. The management of persistent illness and coping with ongoing disability require much more initiative from the client and therefore require a very different involvement of the client in decisions.

Diabetes is sometimes used as a model for chronic illness that can be a metaphor for some parts of the treatment of mental illness. If diabetes presents as weight loss, tiredness, and the need to urinate frequently, then there is time to educate the patient from the beginning, discuss treatment options at length, and begin to talk about the major lifestyle changes that will be required to manage this chronic condition. On the other hand, if the initial presentation of the diabetes is an acute confusion caused by life-threatening keto-acidosis and delirium, initial treatment needs to be started at once, and options need to be presented as a set of more immediate and concrete choices (see Appendix 1). Understanding the developmental course of a person's relationship to his or her illness is critical. If the physician does not educate and involve the patient with chronic diabetes in his or her own treatment, then the patient will not participate in an autonomous and informed way in his or her own lifestyle changes. Giving too much information during the ketotic delirium will just add to anxiety and disorganization.

This difference between acute and chronic care is understood with medical illness but is often missed in psychiatric illness such as schizophrenia, major depression, and bipolar disorder. In the midst of an acute episode, client choice should be solicited but structure for those choices will be necessary. We sometimes want to support autonomy so much that we initially try to provide more information than the client can absorb at that moment, and present choices that require abstract consideration of how current decisions may effect things in the future. On the other hand, too often people who have persistent psychotic or mood symptoms are treated as though they have an acute illness, when in reality the focus of treatment must be to help them participate more actively in their own lives. There is a developmental course to serious and persistent illness, and our job is to help people with this illness navigate that course.

The relationship between the prescriber, therapist and client is complicated and constantly changing. It is a triangular relationship, the members of which interact in ways that are often difficult to explicitly describe. The participants have overlapping areas of responsibility, different kinds of expertise, and different styles of communicating. They sometimes have different goals and concerns, and they have different sources of power. Understanding the dynamic of this set of relationships is an important step that leads to more collaborative medication decision-making.

CHAPTER THREE

Collaboration in Medication Decision Making

Formal responsibility for deciding what medication to prescribe rests with the prescriber. On the other hand, although the prescriber decides what to prescribe, the client decides what he or she will actually take. The therapist also has an important role in working with client and prescriber to identify what "getting better" means and the role of medication in helping to improve the client's quality of life. For the best medication outcome, the prescriber, client, and therapist must work together in a collaborative relationship. This collaborative relationship also helps ensure that the client actually takes the medication. It is not the therapist's job to make medication decisions, but the therapist often works with both client and prescriber to "spark" the next strategy. Often the therapist has more time and more frequent client contact than does the prescriber and is able to help identify target symptoms for each medication, assess how well the medication is working to meet these targets, and initiate discussions about medication changes when necessary. This process leads us to the issue of how therapist, prescriber, and client can all participate in the decision-making process.

Issues of Language and of Style

Differences in language and communication style can be a barrier to effective, collaborative medication management. Recognizing and allowing for differences in communication style, developing a common vocabulary, and "hearing the meaning beyond the words" are all extremely important, and all can be a challenge even in long-term working relationships.

Vocabulary and Jargon

All of us fall into using a certain amount of jargon—specialized words that we use within our work setting or our discipline. Often we assume that because these words are so familiar to us, they are also familiar to everyone else. All professional disciplines have these issues, but physicians tend to use more jargon than others and often have trouble even knowing what is jargon and what is not. The terms *projection, countertransference, transference,* and *affect* are common language for some therapists but not for people outside of mental health. The most common form of therapist jargon is the use of acronyms or program names and assuming that the prescriber or other team members know what the therapist is talking about. "Yahara House," "Gateway," CSP, and ESU are program names or acronyms that can be thrown into a conversation at a rapid rate, completely obscuring effective communication.

The medical profession is, of course, famous for jargon; *distal, lateral, proximate, pathognomonic,* or *titrate* may be common language for a physician but equivalent to a foreign language to a nonphysician. A prescriber who wants to be in a collaborative relationship with his or her nonmedical colleagues must be sensitive to these issues. Unfortunately, it is sometimes hard to know which words are jargon and which are not. If I am used to using a particular word, it may be hard for me to always remember that this is not a word in common speech. It is easy for all of us to fall into our own use of jargon, even when we intend to avoid it. We are all much more sensitive to other people's use of jargon than our own.

We all use some words or terms that are unfamiliar to others. We also sometimes use words that we and the person to whom we are talking both understand, but understand *differently*. *Dangerous* may mean very different things to different people, who think they are communicating when they are not. *Delirium* has a specific technical meaning for a physician but may have a very different, less technical meaning to a nonphysician. If the meaning of a word is unclear or uncertain, it is okay for the listener to request clarification. In fact, it is not only okay, it is strongly recommended. Social workers, psychologists, and nurses all have their own technical jargon that each expects everyone in the world to understand. The client might use idiosyncratic terms for symptoms or side effects that can only be understood by asking for an explanation. All of us use words that we assume everyone can understand but may in fact lead to confusion instead of clarity.

Unfortunately, asking for such clarification can be difficult. None of us likes to reveal what we do not know or ask questions that might make us look dumb. In the midst of a fast-moving discussion, the moment for asking the meaning of some term may come and go in an instant, leaving miscommunication in its wake. We may think that our questions interrupt the flow of a conversation or take too much time. Asking questions about the meaning of some words is often awkward, and it is easier to let the confusion pass than to address it. It is important to remember that if we do not understand how a professional colleague is using a word, then the client is also likely to have some problem with that word. Asking a question about what a word means can clarify the information for yourself, clarify it for your colleagues (who may be even more reluctant to ask than you are), clarify it for the client, and inform the speaker that he or she is using a word that may not be in common usage. Taking the risk of clarifying communication and asking about the meaning of words is one of those difficult tasks that makes collaboration much more effective.

Depth of Detail

It is important to be sensitive and adjust to each other's information needs. Providing a wealth of information with rich detail when only a quick sketch or broad-brush strokes are needed and wanted can create communication obstacles. On the other hand, giving just the slightest details when specifics are needed can also pose collaboration problems. Often one member of the treatment team has more time than another. The therapist may call the prescriber when he or she is already running late seeing clients, or the prescriber may contact the therapist in the middle of a session. Traditionally, both because of time limitations as well as style, prescribers tend to use a more succinct, abbreviated way of communicating information. Therapists tend to provide more detail of the client and situation. These differences can easily lead to frustration on both sides. The therapist may believe that the prescriber is brusque and uninterested, whereas the prescriber may think that the therapist is unfocused and disorganized (see Chapter 2 for more discussion of this topic). One way to help minimize potential problems is to ask for the amount of detail you need. Examples:

- "I only have a minute, so boil it down for me."
- "I really need to understand this, so take your time and tell me as much as you can."

Style

Some of us tend to be brusque, talk rapidly, and allow little space between the end of one thought and the beginning of another. Other people have a more relaxed style, with longer pauses between the time that one person stops speaking and the next person starts. Some people interject with a rapid series of questions, whereas other people believe that questions are intrusive and rude. These differences in style can interfere with communication and can prompt a person to believe that the other person is rude, uninterested, too busy, or has little to say. Mental health professionals—be they therapists, nurses, or psychiatrists—must be sensitive to these stylistic differences and make sure they do not get in the way of a relationship. Much of what constitutes our personal style is actually part of our family culture. We tend to have the same communication style as do our own families. Our professional training can influence these styles, however. Physicians are taught, by their models in medical school and afterward, to be more direct and directive, to shorten pause length and speak a bit more rapidly. Therapists are socialized to listen, to be less directive. These differences in training can accentuate personal differences.

These differences can also interfere with communication and collaboration with clients. Serious mental illness, be it depression or psychosis, tends to increase pause length—the time gap between a question and answer, or between the time one person stops talking and the next starts in conversation. It is easy to "shut down" a client by not giving enough time for him or her to answer or respond. It is also easy to assume that a client is less intelligent or has impaired judgment just because his or her time to respond has become much longer.

The "Dance" of an Interview

When we have a conversation with another person, there is always a dynamic interaction on multiple levels. One level is the content of the discussion, be it about medication, symptoms, life goals, or personal history. Another level is the back and forth of control and collaboration. How much is one of the parties dominating the agenda, and how much is this a collaborative endeavor? Yet a third level is the dynamic of power: not only who is in control of this particular interaction, but what are the power dynamics that influence the interactions? All of these issues are part of the fabric of a clinical conversation between therapists and clients. Trained therapists are well aware of these issues, and yet when dealing with medication, they may find it all too easy to forget basic principles of interviewing. It is easy to get so caught up in the content that we forget that process is always equally important. Our job as clinicians is to make it as easy as possible for clients to share information and then to respect that information so that the client is not betrayed by the sharing.

The Use of Questions to Elicit Information

How can we best elicit important information from clients? There are times when direct, specific, concrete questions are a great way to get information. "Was the bus on time?", "Were you able to get your prescription filled at the pharmacy?", "Did you get to see your mother last weekend?" are just such questions. If this is the information desired, beating around the bush can be both condescending and inefficient. Most interesting questions in mental health, however, are either much more complicated, so that a simple answer is rarely enough, or have emotional overlay, so that a direct question may not be answered with a direct response. In fact, too many direct questions can start to seem like an interrogation to both client and clinician, and the client can easily respond by providing less and less information just when more information is needed. There are, of course, times when direct questions are extremely useful. There are often ways of asking questions that may increase the information flow while also increasing the sense of collaboration. The skill is in knowing when to ask a simple, direct question and when to use other ways to engage the client and encourage a sharing of information.

Open-Ended Questions

Open-ended questions do not have a predictable or correct answer. "What symptoms have you been experiencing?" is opened ended because the client can answer via many (infinite!) kinds of response. "Are you still hearing voices?" is a closed-ended question that encourages a "yes" or "no" response. A structured, yes-or-no question may actually help someone who is confused or disorganized because it is so straightforward and limited; no further information is requested. It is all too easy to fall into a pattern of interrogating clients with a series of specific, closed-ended yes-or-no questions. Clients often respond by providing less and less information—which, in turn, can provoke the clinician to ask more direct closed-ended questions.

Gentle Questions That Assume the Answer

Most people are very sensitive to the desirability of giving a socially appropriate answer. If I am asked about suicide and my belief is that only very ill people ever think about suicide, then I am going to be very reluctant to share my ideas about it than if I believed that both I and everybody else probably thinks about it, and the only issue is how much and when. To translate this point into the topic of asking questions, instead of asking "Do you ever think about suicide?", the clinician could ask, "How often do you think about suicide?", thereby asking a question that assumes that some thought about suicide is universal. Instead of asking "Do you ever forget to take your medication?", the clinician could ask, "How often do you forget to take your medication?" If the person always takes the medication without fail, he or she will correct your implied assumption that there are missed doses. Phrasing a question with a built-in expectation of a certain type of answer, broadly speaking, often encourages more information than would otherwise be the case. "What side effects have been bothering you lately?" assumes that there have been some side effects.

Assuming the Worst, Overstating the Issue, and Allowing the Client to Correct You

A third strategy is to ask a question that assumes a worse answer than you expect to be the case. For example, a question such as, "When is the last time that you went 2 weeks without medication?" gives permission for the client to answer with some lower amount—"I never miss more than 1 or 2 days at a time." We do not have to be endlessly creative in how we ask the questions. In fact, repetition and consistency will eventually acclimate our clients to what questions to expect. On the other hand, if a client does not seem to respond well to one way of obtaining information, switch to some other strategy. Make a conscious choice in your wording. *How* you ask is as important as remembering to ask.

Replacing Entrapment with Collaboration

Entrapment, in this context of eliciting information, is asking questions in a way that invites a defensive denial, a lie, or a partial truth. If we think we already know the answer to a question but ask the question in a way that invites denial, that's entrapment. An example of a common entrapment question is, "Have you been drinking?" when the therapist either smells alcohol on the client or has a reliable report of drinking from another source. Instead of using entrapment, we can help clients understand that secrets, withholding information, and telling partial truths or lies detract from, and can even derail, the goal of achieving optimal symptomatic recovery. How we ask questions and the approach we take to dealing with substance abuse relapse can be as important as what we ask. When medication nonadherence, substance abuse, or other lapses in recovery lifestyle are revealed, it may be tempting to respond with entrapment, shaming, blaming, "guilting," lecturing, or "got ya" tactics. Rather than falling into these common pit-falls we can choose to use collaboration and clinical sense. We can work collaboratively with the individual to explore lapses in recovery lifestyle habits and help him or her use the situation as learning and growing experience. A noncritical approach facilitates open and honest collaboration in ways that shame, criticism, and lecture do not. "It is pretty clear to me that you've been drinking. What were the triggers or events that led up to drinking this time?" The collaborative approach avoids en-trapment. We might go on to inquire about what the individual thinks he or she could do to handle a similar situation differ-ently in future. What knowledge, skills, or supports does the person need to be more successful next time?

Cultural Competence: The Skill of Working with Someone Different from Yourself

Therapists and prescribers are always in the business of working with clients who are different from themselves. This is most obvious if the client has a different skin color or gender or accent. Even a client who looks and talks like the therapist may have very different beliefs and communication styles. Each of us has beliefs about the nature of illness, how we are supposed to behave when we are sick, whether doctors are helpful or dangerous, and so on. We have ideas about the role of family and what kinds of information we share, and what kinds of information we keep to ourselves. One person's experience and belief is that pills can help many kinds of problems; another person's experience and belief is that med-ications rarely help and are too often oversold. One person as-sumes that family members should always be involved and are important sources of support during difficult times, whereas another person would never involve family. One person be-lieves that God and religion and connection with a higher power are very important parts of one's life, whereas another person has little interest in such matters. Although many of these beliefs are specific to each individual, a surprising number of our beliefs come from our families and our cultures. Our beliefs are heavily influenced by our culture, even when we are not aware of it.

We all have beliefs that make up our assumptions about the world. Too often we assume that our beliefs and assumptions are the correct ones, and that anyone with different beliefs is somehow wrong. It can be challenging to figure out whether a difference in beliefs is based on culture, individual differences, or a person's illness. "The government is dangerous and spies on people" may be a longstanding, culturally sanctioned belief of a group that has been persecuted by a present or past government. It may also be the belief of this individual based on personal and very real experience, or a concern that is connected with, and a potential symptom of, illness.

Differences can extend to more than beliefs. For example, some culturally supported patterns of communication include expansive body gestures, a loud voice, and intense emotion as a normal part of conversation. For someone from a different culture, this behavior can be interpreted as "obnoxious" or "out of control." A person whose culture supports subtler body movements and softer speaking may be interpreted as "shut down" or even depressed by a therapist from another culture. Direct eye contact is typically valued positively by the dominant European American culture in the United States, and mental status assessments include eye contact as a marker of how a client is doing. But there are some cultures, however, where direct eye contact is considered inappropriate. A Native American young woman, for example, is seen as sexually provocative if she makes direct eye contact with a man. Avoiding direct eye contact could easily be considered a sign of illness by a therapist from a different culture, but could be socially appropriate behavior for the client. Unless we are conscious of these complex issues, it is very easy to label cultural differences as psychopathology.

Other communication differences can lead not only to mislabeling but can directly interfere with effective communication. For example, the length of time that one allows between when another person stops speaking and when you start speaking is called "pause length." This varies from person to person, but also varies from culture to culture. Some cultures have a longer pause length, and others shorter. This kind of communication style can be passed down for several generations, long after all conscious awareness of cultural background has been lost. People with longer pause lengths tend to viewed as less intelligent by people with shorter pause length; similarly, people with shorter pause length are often considered rude by people with longer pause lengths. In a group, people with shorter pause length will talk more and have more chance to express themselves than people with longer pause length. In addition to cultural issues, people who are depressed or psychotic tend to have longer pause length. A therapist or prescriber with a very short pause length can get frustrated with the delay and may even ask a second or third question before the person with long pause length has time to answer the first. People with the longer pause length will often sense that they are being pressured or disrespected by someone with a much shorter pause length. The client with a longer pause length may interpret a therapist with a short pause length as rude and assume that the therapist does not really want to hear what he or she has to say.

Different ethnic backgrounds add to the complexity of working across differences. We all interpret the world through the lens our own experience. I will never have the experience of someone with a different ethnicity or gender or sexual orientation. If I am from a majority culture, I will never be as sensitive to issues of prejudice and stigma as someone who is from a culture that has been stigmatized and marginalized. All of us tend to react to "differentness." There is no way to avoid reacting to the ways that people are different from ourselves. *Cultural competence* refers to having the knowledge and skills to understand our own reaction to differentness, and know how to work most effectively across what could otherwise become a barrier. It is very important not to immediately assume that a view, value, or belief that is very different from our own is necessarily a sign of illness.

Measuring Medication Effectiveness

How do we know if a medication is working? How much symptom remission is enough? When do we "leave good enough alone"?

Identification of Target Symptoms

With some thoughtful discussion and exploration, it is usually possible to select key symptoms that can be used to measure the success of medication management. Medications do not cure any mental illness. Rather, the goal of a medication is to control symptoms so that they cause less distress, disability, and impairment. Some symptoms are salient because they are a problem for that client. The same symptom in another client may be much less of a problem, either because it is less distressing, less intense, or interferes less. For example, for one client voices are a problem because they are so intrusive that he or she can no longer enjoy reading. For another client, the voices cause little distress or problem. It is important to identify a set of "target symptoms" for each client that can be used to assess how well the medication is working.

The term *target symptoms*, however, does not encompass the entire picture. The goal is to work with the client to identify both specific symptoms and specific behaviors that are a target for the medication and that can be tracked over time to see how well the medication is working. To follow through with the example of voices, the intensity and frequency of the voices might be one measurable target; whether the client resumes reading as a pleasureable pasttime is another measurable target. Often, targeting the client's behavior and ability to pursue specific personal goals can be a very good way to judge the effectiveness of a medication.

The focus is on target symptoms and target behaviors that client, therapist, and prescriber believe are important. At times, the prescriber or therapist may focus on target symptoms that may be different from those of the client. It is important to be clear what the client hopes the medication will do, and what the therapist and prescriber hope the medication will do. The goal is to have these lists overlap as much as possible. If a medication does an inadequate job, it should be stopped and replaced by another medication that has a chance of doing a better job. To determine if a medication is doing a good job, we need to be able to measure how well it works. Consider the following questions and steps in conducting an evaluation of a medication:

• *Which symptoms bother the client the most?* Identify symptoms that the client finds most troubling. Track symptoms that are the most difficult to manage or that cause the most discomfort, disability, or impairment for the individual.

• *Which symptoms get in the way of the client's ability to achieve personal goals?* Choose symptoms that get in the way of accomplishing functional and role recovery. Help the client complete a sentence such as "If it weren't for *x* symptom, I would be able to..." or "If I could just get rid of symptom *z*, I could be a...."

• *Which symptoms are likely to be affected by medication?* Medications are more likely to help some symptoms more than others. For example, voices that have recently gotten worse or disorganized thinking are more likely to be helped by medication. Fixed, longstanding beliefs are less likely to be impacted by a medication. For example, medication is less likely to change a belief of many years that someone is hiding in the basement with a gun.

- *State the symptoms in specific and concrete terms.* Once specific symptoms have been selected as targets, to measure agree on the meaning of the words used to describe each one.
- *Make each symptom measurable.* Once the target symptoms have been selected, the next step is to establish a clear way to measure change in them. A useful target symptom must be simple enough to be easily assessed repeatedly over days or weeks or months, but still sensitive to any change that occurs. It is also important to be able to quickly and easily review the measure across weeks, months, and even years to determine long-term medication effectiveness. Choosing a method that permits efficient summarization and quick documentation makes evaluating the efficacy of medication management easier in the months and years ahead. *Frequency, severity,* and *duration* are often good choices for measurability. There are many good methods to choose from; the key is to select the method that is best suited to the client's target symptoms and individual capabilities.
- *Pay attention to behavior as well as symptoms.* What is the client now doing that he or she was not doing before? Is he or she going out to the store, going to a volunteer job, spending time with friends, reading, or talking more? Obviously this list must be based on personal goals for each client. Behavior is usually a better indicator of change, and more reliably rated, than symptoms. Whenever possible, the behaviors should be based on the client's own personal goals. What does the client want to be doing more of?
- *Pay attention to negative symptoms and cognitive dysfunction.* Most of the symptom scales now available for schizophrenia stress positive symptoms such as hearing voices or delusions. These psychotic symptoms are dramatic and easy to measure, but they are less correlated with ability to function and quality of life than negative symptoms and cognitive dysfunction. *Negative symptoms* refers to functions and states of

being that schizophrenia often takes away from the person: spontaneity, persistence, initiative, and motivation. *Cognitive dysfunction* refers to the problem that many people with schizophrenia, and other major mental illness, can having remembering and then using verbal information or making decisions that involve abstract reasoning. Clients can hold a job if they are hearing voices, but they cannot work if they are not motivated or cannot complete a task. Clients can survive in an apartment if they believe that they are god, but they cannot survive if their problem-solving and decision-making skills do not allow them to think through a menu for the week so that they can successfully go grocery shopping.

Assessment of Symptom Change

There are a number of strategies for assessing symptom change. These include using (1) an intensity rating scale, (2) a daily symptom checklist, (3) a client behavior checklist, (4) behavioral checklist based on observation of others, (5) mood monitor, or (6) an early warning sign checklist. Obviously not all of these approaches to assessment can be used at the same time. The point is to consider the range of assessment approaches available and then to work with the client to choose the strategy that seems most appropriate. All of these strategies are very straightforward, practical, and easily implemented.

1. *Intensity rating scale.* It is not unusual for symptom intensity (i.e., strength of the particular symptom) to improve before noticeable changes in frequency or duration. A person may still hear voices, but they may be less intense or less bothersome, even if they continue with their frequency unchanged. A severity measure can also be used globally to capture the total impact of symptoms. A simple rating scale allows the person to self-report global intensity or severity of each symptom:

"How depressed are you on a scale from 0 to 5?"
"How strong are the voices on a scale from 0 to 5?"
"How strong are the paranoid thoughts on a scale from 0 to 5?"

The specific symptom being monitored should be one that is important, impairing, disabling, or distressing to the client. The monitoring will be more accurate and more useful if the client collaborates in choosing the symptoms and the language used in the scale. (A free symptom tracker is available on the Web at www.recovery.bz. Scale: 5 = extreme; 4 = very severe; 3 = severe; 2 = moderate; 1 = mild; 0 = absent.)

2. *Daily symptom checklist.* For some symptoms, simply indicating presence or absence is preferable. A daily symptom checklist is used to record whether or not each symptom was experienced that day. This approach to symptom monitoring is best for symptoms that are not present every day, or symptoms that one hopes will go away as part of the recovery process. The best method is for the client to fill out the checklist on a daily basis. However, someone who has daily contact with the client could also complete a checklist if the symptoms are observable. As with the intensity rating scale, discussed above, this tactic will be most effective if the client is involved in setting up the symptom checklist and in deciding which symptoms to monitor.

3. *Client behavior checklist.* Another approach to monitoring symptoms is to use observable behavior that the client wants to do more often. The client's use of a monthly calendar that hangs on the wall or the refrigerator can be useful. The client puts a checkmark every day that he or she goes out for a walk, has a social conversation, or goes to the library. This calendar provides a way for the client to track his or her own behavior and to rapidly get visual feedback on how well he or she is doing over time. (To experience the power of this kind of behavioral feedback system, take some behavior that you want to do regularly, such as exercise or keeping to a healthy eating habit, hang a calendar where you will see it every day, and put a

checkmark every day that you do the activity. You will rapidly see how much such a system can help you modify your own behavior, as long as it is behavior that you yourself want to change.) Obviously, this will be most effective if the client can identify behavior that he or she wishes to increase.

4. *Behavior checklist based on observations of others.* Behavioral monitoring can be helpful when done each day by people who have regular contact with the client, such as a caregiver, residential staff, inpatient staff, day program staff, or family member. When several people share the responsibility for marking a behavior checklist, it is important that the target behavioral symptoms be clearly defined, observable, and understood by everyone. It is all too easy to come up with behaviors to measure that may be important to staff or family but of much less importance to the client. Whether the client takes a shower every day, or cleans up his cigarette butts, or makes it to breakfast may be important for staff/family and may even be important for the client's progress, but the client may not agree. Staff should think carefully before monitoring client behaviors that the client does not agree are important. Although doing so may be necessary in some situations, it is to be avoided whenever possible. Many of the behaviors that staff/family believe are important may, in reality, make little difference to the client's stability, recovery, or quality of life. On the other hand, a collaborative list of behaviors can be a valuable tool in monitoring progress toward agreed upon goals and objectives.

5. *Mood monitor.* When depression, mania, irritability, or mood instability is the primary target symptom, a daily mood monitor can prove helpful in measuring medication effectiveness. Sometimes it is helpful to have two people rate mood: the client and someone who has daily contact with him or her. It is not unusual for clients to score periods of mania lower than the people around them would score the same symptoms. The goal is not to argue over which score is more accurate, but simply to note the differences in perceptions and monitor for

improvement, over time, as medication strategies are employed. The rating scale that we use follows:

4. Extremely Manic, High
3. Very High, Manic, Elated
2. Somewhat High, Manic, Elated
1. A Little High, Manic, Elevated
0. Good, Normal, Regular
−1. A Little Down, Slightly Depressed
−2. Somewhat Depressed, Down
−3. Very Depressed, Down
−4. Extremely Depressed

6. *Early warning sign checklist.* Schizophrenia and most other major mental illnesses are persistent, relapsing disorders. For most people, the disorder gets better, then worse, then better over time. One of the primary purposes of treatment, both pharmacological and psychosocial, is to help the person maintain as much stability and quality of life as possible throughout the up-and-down vicissitudes of the disorder. Detecting a developing problem before it becomes severe is essential to achieving this baseline stability and quality of life. An early warning of impending relapse can help reduce the risk of complete relapse. If there is warning, medication can be adjusted, additional social supports can be added, outside stress can be reduced, and risk-reduction strategies can be employed.

Typically, most people experience the same early warning signs each time a relapse occurs. Including several of the individual's internal and external or behavioral early warning signs on a daily checklist helps the client and therapist watch for, and quickly respond to, the first indications of relapse. For most clients, the earliest signs of impending relapse are not psychotic symptoms but rather changes in typical behavior. One person may stop sleeping before a relapse; another may stop calling his parents, although normally he calls every day; yet another person may stop leaving her apartment or stop going to her volunteer job because she now finds the noise at the job too bothersome. Determining what behavioral changes occurred before the client's previous relapse can help start interventions early, even before there are any changes in psychotic symptoms. As with all such monitoring lists, the client him- or herself is often in the best position to help figure out the early behaviors warning of relapse and the range of interventions that would be useful in helping to prevent the relapse.

Discussing Medication Issues: Role of the Client, Therapist, and Prescriber in the Collaborative Relationship

A small number of clients come into a medication assessment able to explain their hopes and goals to the prescriber, ready to discuss side effects, able to articulate what they want from a medication, and already prepared to be a full partner in medication decisions. Most clients, however, come into the session experiencing some anxiety as well as difficulty expressing themselves clearly. Clients are often confused about why they are supposed to take medication, unclear about what they want the medication to do, and disorganized in their expression of thoughts during the brief period of a medication assessment. The therapist can play an important role in helping the client to think about medication issues ahead of time. The therapist can help clarify important concerns with the client, preparing the client to talk with the prescriber directly or acting as a "cultural translator" so that the prescriber has a better sense of what the client wants.

Preparing the client to talk with the prescriber may involve discussing his or her hopes, dreams, and beliefs; role-playing the interaction so that the client can practice what he or she wants to say to the prescriber; and helping the client develop written lists so that questions are structured and not forgotten. It also involves teaching the client how to be a more effective participant in the medication assessment. The prescriber, as the high-status member of the team with the most direct control, must actively invite and support collaboration or it will cease to exist. A prescriber cannot be passive about collaboration. The prescriber must actively support the role of the therapist and client as participants in the medication management process. The following suggestions can help the client, therapist, and prescriber become more effective collaborators, better able to work with each other in making medication decisions.

Suggestions for the Client

We realize that more clinicians than clients are likely to read this book. It is still important to think about suggestions we would make to the client, rather than just making suggestions to the staff. This segment of this chapter, in which we directly address clients, could be used for psychoeducation with clients.

• *Be honest.* It is important for you to be as accurate as possible about whether you are really taking the medication, how often you miss doses, and what happens when you do miss doses. It is also important to be open about problems, symptoms, what is working well, and what is not. Finally, it is important to be honest about substance use.

The problem is that being honest requires a great deal of trust. There is always the fear that such honesty and openness will be used to somehow "punish" you. You may worry that being honest will lead to a withholding of help or to you being blamed, lectured, or criticized. Staff may immediately respond negatively to your honesty, and their reaction to your disclosure may seem very much like punishment. If you do acknowledge not taking medication or using drugs, staff may step in by taking more control, providing more supervision, or doing something to convince you to change your behavior. At times, money may be controlled to limit drug use or family may be involved to encourage medication use. What is intended to be helpful by staff may seem like punishment to you as the client. This is a real dilemma that is not easily solved. It will help if the clinicians at least acknowledge the risk that you are being asked to take when you are asked to be honest.

Real trust requires trust on both sides of the relationship as well as real respect on both sides. Too often therapists ask that clients trust them without doing the work that provides the foundation for such trust. Trust develops over time, by following through with agreements and understanding the other's point of view. An honest relationship requires that the therapist and prescriber be honest with the client. Honesty and respect are always a two-way street. We realize that it is a bigger risk for the client to trust the staff than it is for the staff to trust the client.

- *A conversation between client and prescriber needs to consider six areas.* Not each can be fully discussed at each visit, but it is important to make sure that all are discussed at some point during a period of treatment. It can seem like an overwhelming list of topics and questions. Discussing these topics and questions with your therapist may help you figure out what is most important to talk about with your prescriber:

1. Goals and dreams
2. Symptoms and impairments
3. Prescribed medication
4. Adherence
5. Substance use/abuse
6. Side effects

Goals and Dreams

- *Goals.* It is important for the prescriber to know your personal life goals and how medication might help you better achieve these goals. It is also important to share your concerns about how medication might get in the way of these goals.

– *Short-term goals* are concrete things that you could start working on now, such as taking a walk every day or signing up for a couple hours a week at a volunteer job.

– *Long-term goals* are things that you are actively working on that may take longer to achieve, such as getting a part-time job or finishing school.

• *Dreams.* We all have dreams, ideas that may not necessarily be realistic but that keep our hope alive. Some ideas that started off as dreams and did not really seem possible at first, have become reality for many of the clients that we know. Getting a full-time job or earning a graduate degree may be the kind of impossible dream that sometimes happen.

Work toward your goals and dreams. What else are you doing, besides taking medication that is helping you to achieve your life goals? Remember, medication is never a goal in and of itself. Medication is a tool that will hopefully help you to meet your own life goals. Medication alone is never enough, and besides taking medication, you and the rest of your treatment team must figure out what is needed to make life better in ways that are important to you.

Symptoms and Impairments

Be clear what symptoms you have and how they get in the way of being able to do things that you want to do.

• *Target symptoms.* Which symptoms have been bothering you the most? Which symptoms get in the way of being able to do things that you want to accomplish? From that list of symptoms, what are the specific target symptoms that would enable you, as the client, the people closest to you, and the staff working with you to know if things are getting better or worse? It is helpful to be very concrete, clear, and specific in the identification of these targets:

— How would you know that things are a bit better?
— How would you know that things are a lot better?
— How would you know that things are a bit worse?
— How would you know that things are a lot worse?

• *Improved symptoms.* If your symptoms have improved, how are they better? For example, symptoms might be happening less often, be less intense, or perhaps do not last as long as they used to. Perhaps they are still there, but they are not getting in the way as much as they used to.

• *Remitted symptoms.* If you are not experiencing any symptoms, tell your therapist which symptoms that used to be a problem are now gone.

Prescribed Medication

You may be taking medication for a variety of medical as well as psychiatric problems. It is very easy to get confused about what medications you are taking, and what each is supposed to be doing. That is why we recommend the following:

• Know the name of each medication that is prescribed for you.
• Know how much of each medication to take.
• Be clear about the purpose of each of your medications.

Having a written list of your medications can be very helpful. Writing each one down or asking your doctor or a nurse or your therapist to write each one down can help you keep track of them. At times, the pharmacist can give you a list of your medications, with some basic information about each one.

Adherence

Talk with your therapist and your prescriber about how you are actually taking your medication. Even more than in other areas, this discussion requires trust and sensitivity for you, your prescriber, and your therapist. There are a several problems that are likely to happen if the people working with you do not know how much medication you are really taking. The medication is less likely to work well, it will be much harder to figure out the right dose, and it will be difficult to decide which medicine is best for you.

- *Missed doses.* How many doses have you missed in the past week? Focusing on this time period will give you and the people working with you some idea of how consistently you are taking medication. People miss doses for many reasons: people fall asleep without taking them, forget, run out, lose them, or just decide not to take every dose. Is there any pattern to when you miss a dose of medication? Is it when you are particularly tired, or upset, or when you have been drinking alcohol? Discuss what happened that you missed those doses. What is the longest that you go without medication? Do you notice any difference?

- *Changes in amount.* Have you made any changes in the amount of medication you are taking?

   - *Decreased dose.* If you decreased the dose of your medication, how much have you really been taking? What were your reasons for making the decrease? If you are still taking the medication, but at a lower dose than is prescribed, talk about your decision to take less than prescribed.
   - *Increased dose.* If you increased the amount of medication you take, how much are you taking and what were the reasons that you decided to increase the dose? What did you want to accomplish by taking more medication? Is the higher dose working for you?
   - *Stopped medication.* If you decided to quit taking one or more of your medications, which one(s)? What were your reasons for this decision? How long has it has been since

you have taken the medication? What differences have you noticed since you stopped?

Substance Use/Abuse

How much caffeine, alcohol, marijuana, and other drugs are you now using? What drugs are you using that you buy at the drug store? What about drugs that are illegal? Do you use every day or just now and again? What do these drugs do for you, both good and bad? How do they help? What problems do they cause? How do you afford them? Even if you do not think they are a problem, do your family or friends think they are a problem? How much of information about your drug use are you willing to share with your therapist or prescriber?

Side Effects

What medication side effects do you have? How big a problem are these side effects? Do they bother you a lot or only a little? Do they keep you from doing things you would like to do? Are they there all of the time or only now and again? Your prescriber is more likely to be able to help you do something about the medication side effects if he or she knows about them and how much they bother you.

• *Discuss the next medication strategy.* If you have a specific medication request, it is suggested that you tell your prescriber what you would like to take. Your prescriber may agree or disagree with you, but at least this begins a discussion of what you would like and what your prescriber thinks would be best. It also allows you and your prescriber and your therapist to talk about the reasons for the decisions that are being made.

If you think a medication increase might help get your symptoms under better control, it is a good idea to say that to your prescriber.

Example: "Since I'm still having a lot of symptoms, I'm wondering if we could increase my medication?"

If you'd like to switch to a different medication that might be less likely to cause a specific side effect that is bothering you, it is important to say that to the prescriber.

Example: "Since I'm having so much trouble with *x* side effect, I'd rather take something else. Is there another medication that might work for me that is less likely to cause *x* side effect?"

Of course, it is your prescriber's job to listen to you, to take your questions and concerns into consideration, to think through all the options, then to work with you to make a decision about what needs to be done. Although it is up to the prescriber to make the final decision about what to prescribe, it works best if these decisions can be jointly made by you, your therapist, and your prescriber whenever possible. Sometimes the decisions that are made about medication may not be exactly what you anticipated or wanted. Even if you cannot get the medication change that you would like, you should be included in the decision-making process and be informed about why a particular decision was made.

• *Ask about the prescriber's decision.* Depending on what the prescriber decides, you might want to ask some questions that help you understand his or her decision. The prescriber may decide to do something totally different from what you asked for or expected. Do not assume he or she did not listen. Getting angry may be natural, but it will probably not help you understand the decision. It will not help you know what you need to do to get your prescriber to come up with a decision you like better in the future. When your prescriber goes in a totally different direction than you expected, it is important to understand how that decision was reached. Ask questions to help you understand the decision.

Example: "I was hoping you would decrease my medicine, but instead, you added something new. Help me understand your decision."

• *Ask about your medication.* Regardless of whether or not the prescriber makes a decision that you expected or hoped for, asking questions will probably still be a good idea:

— *Type.* If you are uncertain, ask the prescriber what type of medication is being prescribed. Knowing if it is an antidepressant, antipsychotic, mood stabilizer, or side-effect medication will help you understand what the medication is expected to do for you.

— *Purpose.* Find out what the new medication is expected to do for you. Ask which symptoms are expected to improve as a result of taking the medication. Whether you are beginning a new medication or your current medication is being increased, ask the prescriber which specific symptoms are likely to improve if the medication works well for you.

— *Amount.* Ask what the typical target dose is and what the usual dosage range is. Ask whether or not there will be room for a medication increase if you need a higher dose to control symptoms in the future, or whether a lower dose is possible if there are side effects.

— *Special instructions.* Ask the prescriber if there are any special instructions for taking the medication with meals or at certain times of the day. Find out what the prescriber wants you to do if you miss a dose—take it when you remember it or skip it and wait to take the next scheduled dose? Find out if you can simplify how often you take the medication. It is much easier to take medication once a day, along with some other regular activity. If the prescriber suggests taking a medication two or three times a day, you might want to ask if you can take it all at once.

– *Side effects.* Ask the prescriber to talk with you about the most common side effects. Ask if the side effects usually go away after a while or if they are likely to continue no matter how long you take the medication. Find out if there are any side effects to watch for that would be a problem and would require immediate attention.

– *When to expect improvement.* Ask the prescriber how long you can expect to wait until you will begin to notice an improvement in the target symptoms. Ask when you might expect the medication to reach peak effectiveness–that is, to help you as much as it is likely to at the dose prescribed.

Suggestions for the Therapist

Too often, therapists and prescribers talk with clients about which medication they should take or how much to use. However, it is important to start with a discussion of the *reasons* to take a medication. What is the problem that medication could help solve? This discussion requires beginning with what the client wants. What are the client's goals and dreams, and what does the client hope that medication could do?

Therapist's Work with Clients

• *Ask about the client's goals and dreams.* Start with a discussion of the client's goals and dreams, including short-term goals that can be worked on now, longer-term goals that may extend over years, and dreams that may be unrealistic but that serve to inspire. Be specific and detailed. Use the client's own words to describe these goals and dreams. If you have goals that are different from those of the client, be clear which are your goals and which are the client's. Connect medication to these specific goals: How will medication really help? And be clear what else, besides taking medication, is being done to support the client's achievement of these goals. Talk about readiness to pursue personal life goals, steps taken, and progress made.

• *Highlight the client's accomplishments.* It is important to include, early in the conversation, a discussion of what is going well and what the client has been able to accomplish. Learn to help the client celebrate even small achievements. It is easy to talk about failures and disappointments and what has not worked. Clients are usually well aware of what is not going well. Focusing on everything the client has done wrong or has not been able to do is not a useful way to motivate him or her to work toward goals. For example, if a client has lost a new part-time job after just a week, the therapist can focus on the job loss or on the reality that the client got the job and was willing to take the risk, go in, and work for a while. It is far preferential to focus on what has been learned and how to best support the client taking this risk again.

• *Ask about symptoms.* Ask what symptoms the client is experiencing, what kinds of problems are caused by these symptoms, and how they interfere with the client's life. Symptoms are not necessarily problems. They are problems when they cause distress or in some way interfere with the client's life. Just asking about the presence or absence of symptoms may miss important changes in the impact of these symptoms on the client. For example, a client may still hear voices, but these may interfere with reading less than they used to. Or a client may still be afraid that the Nazis are after him, but not so afraid as to avoid leaving his apartment.

– *Target symptoms.* Work with the client to be clear on how you and he or she will know things are getting better or worse. Write down the target symptoms, with examples that are as concrete as possible. Follow these targets to assess how well the client is doing. Encourage the client to follow these same, collaboratively developed target symptoms so that he or she can better learn to assess his or her own status and progress.

Encourage the client to talk about the target symptoms that he or she has been experiencing lately. Determine frequency, intensity, and duration of symptoms. Discuss and document symptoms in measurable terms as much as possible. Discuss how the symptoms impair everyday functioning and limit ability to achieve personal life goals. Also discuss strategies the client has used to overcome the impact of these symptoms.

- *Improved symptoms.* If symptoms have improved, determine how much improvement has occurred. Discuss and document improvements in frequency, intensity, duration, and impact using measurable terms whenever possible. What is the client now able to do that was previously impossible or more difficult?

- *Remitted symptoms.* If the client reports an absence of symptoms, inquire about which specific symptoms are in remission. What has this symptom remission allowed the client to do? What is new in the client's life because of the symptom remission? Determine if there are any residual impairments and whether they may impact achievement of personal life goals.

• *Gently, respectfully, and directly ask about substance use.* How much caffeine, alcohol, nicotine, and marijuana is the client using? How about other drugs and over-the-counter medicine? Is the substance use regular or episodic? What problems does the drug use seem to be causing? Is it causing any financial problems?

• *Explore and monitor your client's prescribed medication.* What medication is prescribed, what side effects are present, and what medication is the client actually taking with what frequency? The therapist has an important role in helping to ensure that the best medication is prescribed, that side effects are recognized and treated as best as possible, and that the client is encouraged to use medication in a way to maximize the likelihood that it will be effective.

There are three parts to inquiries about medication:

1. Make sure that both you and the client understand what medication is prescribed and, if more than one, what each is supposed to do.
2. Ask about the side effects that the client associates with each medication.
3. Ask about client's adherence—that is, what medication the client is actually taking.

1. What medication is prescribed for the client? Clients often do not know which medications are prescribed for them or what each is supposed to do. It is hard to take medication as prescribed or believe that medication is really important if you do not even know what medications are prescribed for you.

Several different doctors may prescribe medications. Some medicines may have been discontinued a long time ago and yet are still in the client's medicine cabinet. Others may have been added recently. If it is hard for the therapist to figure out what medications are prescribed for the client, it may be even harder for the client to do so. Even a physician or nurse may not have an accurate and complete list, because several doctors may be prescribing for different disorders. It is important for both the therapist and client to know the name of each prescribed medication.

• *What is the name of each medication?* This information may be available from the psychiatrist, nurse, medical record, or from the client's primary care doctor. It may also be most easily available from the client's pharmacy. Pharmacies are a great source of information about medications, purposes, and side effects.

• *What is the dose of each medication and how should it be taken?* How much, how often, how, and when is each medication to be taken?

• *What are the common side effects associated with each medication?* What side effects does the client associate with each medication? The client's experience may be very different from what the books say about side effects.

• *What is the purpose of each medication?* What is each supposed to do? Which target symptoms are expected to be reduced or controlled as a result of taking each of the medications?

• *What will happen if the client stops taking each medication?* What symptoms or problems are likely to return or get worse without each medication?

It is important for the therapist to listen to and understand the client's beliefs about the purpose and importance of the medication and what the client believes would happen if each were stopped. Beliefs about health, illness, and treatment are prime determinants of what any of us will do with treatment that is prescribed. These beliefs are also an important focus for psychoeducation rather than lecture, debate, or criticism.

2. What Side Effects Is the Client Experiencing? How big a problem are those side effects? How often does each side effect occur? What is the client's perception of tolerability, and what the client has been doing to manage each side effect?

The more specific your questions about side effects, the more likely the client will be able to share useful information. A general question, "Do you have any side effects?", will elicit less information than "Does the medication make you feel tired?" or "Does it ever make you feel 'antsy' so that you can't stop moving?" Typically, open-ended questions are better than closed questions. "What side effects have you been experiencing lately?" is usually more productive than "Are you having any side effects?" On the other hand, too many questions can end up seeming intrusive rather than supportive.

A side effect may be a much bigger problem for the client than for the therapist. "A slight hand tremor" may be "slight" for the therapist, but may be a much bigger concern to the client who has to live with it. "Minor weight gain" may seem far more minor to the therapist than to the person who is actually gaining the weight.

Be sensitive to the risk of frank disclosure for the client and treat any information with respect. A client's statement "I don't want to take that medication because it makes me tired" can be a chance to listen to the client's concerns, or it can provoke a lecture from the therapist about why the medication must be taken anyway. As with all discussions about medication, it is extremely important not to be critical or punish the client for information that he or she has shared with you.

3. Determine Actual Pattern of Medication Use
• *Missed doses.* How many doses has the client missed in the past week? Although it may be more than a week since you have seen the client, it is often difficult for people to accurately remember adherence beyond the past week. Asking about the previous week will give you some idea of the degree of medication adherence. Work with the client to estimate the total number of doses that were accidentally forgotten, inadvertently missed, and intentionally skipped. How often does the client miss medication, and what happens when misses occur? If the client stopped medication for a couple of days or longer, what are the reasons that the client decide to restart the medication?

• *Changes in amount.* What changes has the client made in the amount of medication he or she is taking?

– *Decreased dose.* If the client cut back on medication, how much has he or she been taking? What are the reasons the client decided to make this reduction? If he or she is still taking the medication, but at a lower dose than prescribed, what led to the decision to take less than prescribed?

— *Increased dose.* If the client increased the amount of medication he or she is taking, how much is being taken and what are the reasons for the dose increase? Encourage the client to talk about what he or she wanted to accomplish by taking more medication and determine whether or not the higher dose is helping.

— *Stopped medication.* If the client quit taking any prescribed medications, find out which one(s) and the reasons for stopping. Ask about the motivation behind the client's decision to stop taking the medication. Find out how long ago he or she quit taking it and what changes have been noted in symptoms and side effects.

Discussion, monitoring, and education about symptoms, side effects, substance use and medication are an everyday part of clinical work, whether we do individual, group, or family therapy, psychoeducation, case management, or assertive community treatment; inpatient or outpatient; residential, psychosocial rehabilitation, or day treatment.

Therapist's Work with Prescribers

Although we have stressed the importance of a collaborative relationship between client, therapist, and prescriber, the reality is that the prescriber often has very limited time and is outside many of the discussions around medication. It is therefore important for the therapist to be able to fill the prescriber in on what has been happening with the client so that all can be involved in the collaboration.

The issue of trust has already been discussed. This is an important issue in the relationship between therapist and prescriber, just as it is between client and prescriber. If the prescriber uses information provided by the therapist to blame or punish the client, then the client will be less likely to share more information with that therapist. On the other hand, not sharing known information with the prescriber would be unprofessional and would certainly interfere with the therapist's relationship with the prescriber. Ideally, this and other issues should be discussed between therapist and prescriber. At the very least, the therapist sharing sensitive information that has been provided by the client should stress the need to respect this sensitivity with the prescriber.

Briefly present the facts. It is usually very important to be brief and to the point when talking with the prescriber. Details, depth, embellishments, and complexity are *not* generally signs of competence in this situation. Being succinct, concise, and to the point are priorities with most prescribers. Less is more. Prioritize and condense the most important points and say them only once.

Six areas need to be covered as part of the collaboration between therapist, client, and prescriber. The information from all six areas is needed to make an informed medication decision. Any combination of client, prescriber, or therapist can bring up these areas. The topics can be covered in any order, and not every topic needs to be covered at every visit, but they must all be considered in decisions.

1. *Goals and dreams.* A focus on the client's personal goals and dreams should always be at the forefront. It helps all of us stay connected with what we are hoping the medication will help achieve.

2. *Symptoms.* Mention one to three primary target symptoms briefly and succinctly. Focus on symptoms that cause problems, impairments, and distress rather than those that might be most dramatic.

3. *Prescribed medication.* Make sure that you and the prescriber, and hopefully the client, are clear about the name and total dose of all current medications.

4. *Adherence.* Summarize the consistency with which the medication is being used and the reasons for the client's use pattern if known.

5. *Substance use/abuse.* Make sure that the prescriber is aware of current substance use/abuse, including alcohol, street drugs, and caffeine.

6. *Side effects.* Identify side effects observed or reported. Also identify how much of a problem these side effects are for the client in terms of tolerability, distress, and impairment.

Here is an example of a therapist's report to a prescriber:

"John's goal is to be actively involved at church again, and he dreams of being a preacher. He is still very depressed and continues to wake about 2 A.M. and is unable to get back to sleep. He continues to hear some voices in the background, but he says these are not much of a problem and he can pretty much ignore them most of the time. They are certainly much less of a problem then they were 3 months ago. He continues to be unmotivated, and despite wanting to go to church, has not been able to actually get up and get there. His family continues to be supportive and he gets over to his parents once a week or so for dinner, although otherwise he is socially isolated. He has nothing to do during the day and no regular structure of activities. There are no major life stressors, except for the chronic issue of not having enough money. He's taking 15 mg of *x* and 20 mg of *y*, which he says he takes consistently, as prescribed. He reports no substance use and an absence of side effects."

Discuss the next medication strategy. This discussion includes not only the therapist and prescriber but usually also the client. A discussion about a medication change can be initiated by the client or the prescriber, but in reality it is often initiated by the therapist. Often it is the therapist who is in the best position to recognize subtle medication side effects, assess how well the current medication is working or not working, and help identify target symptoms that can be a focus for the next medication decision. Although the prescriber makes the formal decision, the therapist can have an extremely important role in framing that decision. The therapist's job is often to provide the social and historical contexts that can lead to an informed medication decision. It is formally the prescriber's job to consider all of the available input, to think through all the options, to select the next strategy, and make the prescriptive decision. Actually, all members of the treatment team should have input into this process. Often it is the therapist who spends the most time with the client who is in the best position to suggest the most effective medication strategy.

To have an effective role in the medication decisions, therapists must do their homework by taking time to talk with clients, thinking through the options, doing medication histories, and then bringing this information into the medication discussions. How the therapist makes suggestions or provides input is going to vary depending on a number of factors. Ideally, in a well-functioning prescriber–therapist relationship, direct suggestions and opinions of the therapist are welcome and openly considered. In other prescriber–therapist relationships one or both prefer that the therapist's input be phrased as questions to acknowledge and respect the authority and expertise of the prescriber. Some therapists are uncomfortable with "telling the prescriber" what to do about medication, especially if phrased as a direct suggestion or opinion. Some prescribers are offended if a therapist suggests a medication strategy instead of asking about such a strategy. The need for such indirect communication is unfortunate, because it can easily interfere with the full and easy exchange of information that leads to the most effective decision. A direct suggestion from a therapist who knows a client well does not need to usurp the authority of the prescriber. The suggestion can be taken as welcome and respected input into the decision, and the prescriber can always make a decision in agreement or at odds with this suggestion. In this area, in particular, it is important to know the members of your treatment team, preferred communication styles, and relationship boundaries. In all cases, the suggestions are likely to be much more useful if they are based on data that are shared along with the suggestion. Following are examples of direct and indirect suggestions made by therapists to prescribers.

Direct suggestions:
"I think that an increase in Jack's medication might help get his symptoms under better control. He was doing better last year before his dose got decreased, and nothing else has really changed."
"JoAnn has been on the top dose for 2 months now, and I think that it is time for us to consider a switch."

Indirect suggestions:
"Do you think an increase in Jack's medication might help get his symptoms under better control? He was doing better last year before his dose got decreased and nothing else has really changed."
"JoAnn has been on the top dose for 2 months now. Do you think it's time for a switch?"

Direct communication between colleagues may be the best choice in some instances, but we realize that this is not always possible. At times the hesitation comes from the therapist, who is concerned about encroaching into the authority of the prescriber. At other times, it is the prescriber who is concerned about keeping prerogatives of decision making clear.

Understand the thinking behind medication decisions. It will be difficult for the therapist to help the client understand medication decisions if the therapist does not understand them first.

Understanding the decisions may require asking the prescriber to explain the reasoning behind the decision and then asking follow-up questions if necessary. Understanding the reasoning behind a decision is particularly important if the prescriber makes a decision that is very different from what the therapist had anticipated. An open and direct relationship between therapist and prescriber allows differences over prescribing decisions to be openly discussed. If the relationship does not support a direct discussion of differences over medication decisions, the therapist may need to be content with understanding the decision. The job of the therapist is to bring as much information as possible into the decision process, not to determine the end result. Framing questions in a way that clearly seeks understanding without challenge may be an important part of facilitating both information and relationship. Questions that start with *why* often invite a defensive response. Asking a client or a prescriber "Why did you do *x*?" is more likely to raise defensiveness than asking "What were some of the reasons you decided to do *x*?".

Suggestions for the Prescriber

Everything suggested for the therapist applies to the prescriber. This includes starting discussions by asking clients about their goals and dreams is also as well as talking about the clients' recent accomplishments—what has gone well, not just what has gone badly. The prescriber's main job is to help the client understand how medication could help him or her achieve his or her goals. As part of this discussion, the prescriber needs to know those goals as well as the target symptoms and what it would mean to the client for those symptoms to get better or worse. It is, of course, important to know what the client knows about his or her medication, what side effects the client is experiencing, and what medication the client is really taking. The prescriber is also responsible for knowing all of the medications a client is taking, even those prescribed by other physicians, and all medical problems, both because of their direct interaction with behavioral problems and because medical illness impacts all areas of the client's life.

The prescriber must also understand the client's beliefs about illness and medication. None of us take medication because of research or because someone else thinks that we should. We take medication because *we* believe, based on the advice of our doctor or what we have read or what friends have said, that this medication will help. It is our belief that determines whether or not we will take a prescribed medication. Clients, too, take—or decide not to take—medication based on their belief about the nature of the problem with which they are trying to cope and the role of the medication in helping them overcome this problem. The prescriber must have a clear understanding of the client's beliefs about the nature of his or her problems and about the role of medication in addressing those problems. Understanding these beliefs will help the prescriber more effectively convey the importance of medication to the client and increase the likelihood that he or she will take the medication.

Being honest is an important suggestion for the client. It is equally important for the prescriber. Clients often avoid mentioning important issues because of concern about how therapists or prescribers will react to this information. Clients typically think "If my prescriber knew I missed some doses of medication..." or "If my therapist knew I had smoked a couple of joints of marijuana..." then they would be criticized or punished in some way. The concern is that clinicians will react or overreact to this information. Prescribers have exactly the same dilemma. If a prescriber believes that it is very important for a client to take a particular medication, then too much honesty about side effects or too much information about how the medication typically only helps with part of the problem may discourage the client's use of it. The prescriber may be tempted to omit some information in an attempt to "nudge" the client toward making the correct decision. The problem is that, in the long run, these strategies do not work. The issue is not just to get the client to take a medication now, but to develop a respectful and trusting relationship with the therapist and prescriber. Any kind of dishonesty will inevitably get in the way of this relationship. This does not mean that every conceivable piece of information needs to be shared with a client all at once, or that a client who is currently confused and frightened needs to get an hour lecture on side effects. It does mean that information should not be withheld because of concerns over the client's reaction. Honesty is an important element on all sides of the relationship between client, prescriber, and therapist. It is unreasonable to expect clients to be more honest with prescribers than prescribers are with clients. If a client is to function as a true partner in his or her own treatment, then it is important for the client to have accurate knowledge about both the benefits and the problems associated with all parts of treatment, including medication.

One of the more complicated skills required of the prescriber is how to best use the therapist's information and relationship with the client. The therapist will typically know the client better than the prescriber, will almost always spend more time with the client, and will not infrequently have a more trusting, or at least more comfortable, relationship that will allow the client to share certain kinds of information more easily. The therapist may know more about how the client's symptoms interfere with life goals, the pattern of substance use, or even what most concerns the client. The ability to work in a collaborative relationship with both client and therapist will make the prescriber much more effective in assessing the goals of medication and the impact of medication on meeting those goals and on increasing the chance that the client will be willing to take the medication in a more consistent way.

The effectiveness of the relationship between the therapist and the prescriber depends on both parties. Both parties must recognize the importance of the relationship for the best interest of the client. The prescriber, who has formal authority over what medication to prescribe, and the therapist, who often knows the client better, must collaborate to ensure that as much information as possible can be brought to bear on this prescribing decision.

Dealing with Medication Side Effects

Unfortunately, side effects are common. All medications have side effects for some people. Some medications have more common side effects, and others may have less common ones. Some side effects may be more distressing for one person and less of a problem for another. A client's first reaction to a side effect is often to stop the medication that is believed to be causing it. Too often a staff response to this client report is that the side effect "is not that bad"—thereby dismissing the client's discomfort. At times, the identified "side effect" may have nothing to do with the medication. At other times, especially if the medication is working well or the problem the medication is hoped to help with is significant, it is important to do as much as possible to decrease the problem caused by the side effect before simply stopping the medication.

An important part of the collaboration between client, prescriber, and therapist is learning how to talk about difficult issues, and talking about side effects is at the top of this list. Discussing potential side effects at the beginning of each medication change can help minimize the risk that a client will decide to stop taking his or her medication, or take it only erratically. Knowing that a client is experiencing a side effect is the first step toward figuring out ways to manage the side effect. If the therapist or prescriber does not start the conversation, either the client may suffer from a side effect that could be treated, or the client may just stop taking the medication.

It is necessary to actively look for, and directly inquire about, medication side effects. Some side effects are observable, others are not. Clients may have a side effect that they will only rarely bring up. For example, few clients will spontaneously report sexual side effects, even if they are a significant problem. At times clients will report side effects, at other times they will respond to a direct question but would not report the same problem spontaneously, and at times the clinician who is looking for it can directly observe a side effect. Motor restlessness and tremors may be obvious if the clinician is looking for them, but could be missed otherwise.

Often the most effective way to deal with a side effect is either to change the dose of the medication or change the timing of when the medication is taken. The best response is not always lowering the dose. What to do depends on the specifics of each medication and each side effect. For example, if a client experiences motor restlessness (akathisia) on risperidone (Risperdal), decreasing the dose may help considerably. However, this decision depends on whether the client needs the current dose and whether a dose reduction would be prudent. If a client gets anxious or agitated on ziprasidone (Geodon), increasing the dose may help; ziprasidone is more activating at low doses than at higher doses. If the problematic side effect is tiredness caused by olanzapine (Zyprexa), then taking it at night rather than in the morning might help, even without a change in dose; on the other hand, decreasing the dose of olanzapine is unlikely to help deal with the common side effect of weight gain. Because this side effect is not dose related, psychoeducation about weight management strategies might be used to help individuals who are otherwise benefiting from the medication.

Sometimes there is a medication than can help with a specific side effect. For example, the tremor that people get from lithium often responds to propranolol (Inderol). However, not all side effects can be treated with a side effect medication, and side effect medications themselves have side effects. Sometimes the side effects of the side effect medication are as troublesome as the side effects it is intended to manage. For example, benztropine (Cogentin) can help to control the stiffness and tremor caused by some antipsychotic medications, but it also may cause dry mouth, constipation, and some memory problems. At times, the best way to handle a side effect is to change behavior. For example, some medications cause a blood pressure drop and dizziness if a person stands up quickly (i.e., orthostatic hypotension). Simply getting up a bit more slowly may help avoid dizziness. Using sugarless gum or sugarless candy can help alleviate dry mouth.

Prescriber to Client

As noted, some clients are reluctant to mention side effects. Alerting the client to the most common side effects is more helpful than hoping none will occur or assuming that the mention of side effects might discourage adherence. Initiating the topic by asking "What medication side effects have you been experiencing?" is usually more effective than asking "Are you having any side effects?" It is also helpful to mention side effects that may otherwise go undisclosed or a few of the most frequent side effects as a prompt. "Some people who take this medication have trouble getting an erection or difficulty urinating. What side effects have you noticed?" Weight gain, tiredness, and motor restlessness are common side effects of medications that may be particularly uncomfortable.

At each medication change point, it is important to initiate a discussion about potential side effects. Let the client know about the transient side effects that could occur as well as the persistent side effects that are likely. Offer suggestions for how to cope with persistent side effects and mention any rare but potentially serious side effects. It is useful to develop a regular pattern for discussing side effects. Typically, a discussion about side effects should occur when:

- Starting a new medication
- Increasing the dose
- Switching medications

- Stopping a medication
- Or every year or so during a regular review of medication with the client.

In any discussion of side effects, replace or define all medical terms. *Urinary retention, akathisia,* and *dystonic reaction* are just a few of the many medical terms that are a common part of the prescriber's vocabulary but are usually unfamiliar to clients. Explain side effects in everyday terms, using words that are within the typical vocabulary of the client. If a medical term is preferable, explain the meaning in everyday words the client can understand.

Client to the Prescriber

Each time the client meets with the prescriber, it is important to review medication side effects. Sometimes it will be just a quick review of existing side effects that are minimal, well tolerated, and effectively managed. Other times it will be a problem-solving discussion focused on getting the best results from medication while minimizing troublesome side effects. There are also times when side effects are such a big problem that a medication change needs to be considered, even if the medication otherwise seems to be working well. Some side effects are more obvious and easier to talk about, such as weight gain. Others are potentially embarrassing, such as loss of sexual interest or function.

The client can prepare for appointments with the prescriber by making a list of his or her current medication side effects and any specific questions about them. In the short period of a medication review appointment it is very hard to think of all of the important things about which a client may want to talk. It may not be possible to get through all of the important issues. Making a list and then prioritizing the items so that the most important issues are mentioned first, can make the appointment time much more useful.

It may not be possible to eliminate all side effects. The goal is to figure out a medication strategy that works as well as possible to decrease symptoms that cause the client problems, while keeping the burden from side effects as low as possible. Achieving this goal requires an open discussion between the client, the therapist, and the prescriber.

To prepare for a meeting with a prescriber, clients can consider the following questions:

What is the purpose of this medication?
• What are we hoping this medication will do for me?
• Why do you think it is a good idea to make this medication change at this time?
• How long will it take this medication to work?

What are the most common side effects of this medication?
• Which of those side effects are likely to disappear with time?
• How long is it likely to take before the side effects go away?
• Which side effects are less likely to disappear in time?
• Are there any dangerous side effects that I need to watch for?
• Are there any long-term side effects?

What are the most common, persistent side effects?
• What can be done to make these side effects less of a problem for me?
• What other medication might help me AND be less likely to give me these side effects?

Therapist to Client: When and How to Inquire

It is important to revisit the issue of medication side effects on a regular basis. At times, this discussion can be connected to visits between the client and prescriber, or it may arise based on a comment from the client, on an observation of the therapist, or as a routine component of services. If the therapist is informed and interested in medication issues, the client may be willing to share information about medication concerns and side effects that might be harder to share with the prescriber. Side effects that may not be apparent in a brief office visit may become obvious to an experienced therapist in other settings. Discussions of issues seemingly unconnected to medication may suggest that unrecognized side effects are a potential problem. The therapist may learn that side effects are very bothersome, yet have not been discussed with the prescriber.

• *Teach clients about side effects.* Clients need to learn a number of things about side effects to be confident and competent participants in collaborative medication management. Education about medication is often a critical part of daily services provided by all members of the treatment team, including the therapist. There are several key pieces of knowledge that clients need:

1. *Symptoms versus side effects.* It is important for clients to understand the differences between symptoms and side effects. Although this distinction may seem obvious, many people confuse the two. "Symptoms come from the illness, side effects come from medication," is one approach to explaining the distinction. It can be useful to work with clients so that they can identify a few personal examples of each.

2. *Transient versus persistent side effects.* Some side effects will go away with time, whereas others are likely to continue regardless of how long the medication is taken. It is not unusual for clients to tolerate side effects that they would otherwise not be willing to put up with, if they realize that the side effects will probable be temporary.

3. *Predicting side effects.* When predicted and discussed ahead of time, side effects can be understood as an indication that the medication is getting into the brain and beginning to work. Side effects can be a sign that something good is beginning to happen, rather than a sign that something is going

wrong. A discussion of side effects before they occur is likely to increase the willingness of the client to tolerate the medication, especially if the side effect is likely to be temporary. Without this anticipatory discussion, many clients tend to interpret transient side effects as an indication that they are on too much medication or the wrong kind of medication. Talking with clients about possible side effects before they occur will increase consistent medication use much more often than it will interfere with this use.

4. *Coping strategies.* Some side effects can be managed and tolerated by the client. Coping strategies do not eliminate the side effects but may help the person compensate for some of them and diminish the impact of others. Identifying, discussing, and encouraging the individual to learn about, and then use, coping strategies help put the person in control. If a medication is sedating, taking it about an hour before bedtime may be beneficial. Doing aerobics and showering in the morning can help reduce daytime sedation and is usually preferable to ingesting a large quantity of sugar and caffeine. Learning how to stand a bit more slowly may reduce the dizziness that can come with orthostatic hypotension. Chewing sugarless gum or sucking on sugar free candy and increasing intake of high fiber foods can help alleviate dry mouth and constipation. Walking 15–30 minutes a day, paying attention to serving size, and choosing lower-calorie foods and beverages can help minimize weight gain from increased appetite. Cutting back on caffeine, doing aerobic exercise, and taking medication in the morning may help cope with any activating side effects. Helping the person choose and use specific strategies is typically more effective than a more general recommendation or suggestions. And often, it takes more than a passing mention of coping strategies to incorporate them in the client's behavioral changes and habits.

5. *Potentially dangerous side effects.* It is important for clients to know which side effects are merely troublesome and which

are potentially serious. It is also important for clients to separate side effects that are more common and less dangerous (even if very bothersome) from those that are more serious and likely cause for greater concern. This comparative approach alerts the client to side effects that may be rare but that require immediate attention if experienced.

• *Work with the client to choose when medication is changed.* There are some instances when the timing of a medication change may be important. It is best to involve the client in selecting the best time to increase medication or begin a new medication. This approach encourages the client to take an active role in the process, and timing the change according to the client's preference can help him or her manage transient side effects. For some clients, initiating a medication change on Friday gives them the weekend to adjust to it without the demands of work, day treatment, school, or rehabilitation services. For others, the weekend would be a less desirable choice due to social plans, family obligations, or investment in regular attendance at religious services. Sometimes a medication change is so urgent that it is not feasible to time the change to minimize the impact of transient side effects. However, if the client can be included in the decision-making process and have input on the timing of medication changes, the scales may tip toward successful medication management.

• *Immediately respond to bothersome side effects.* Sometimes a medication side effect is perceived by the client as intolerable. No matter how common or manageable the side effect may be from the clinician's perspective, it is the client's perception that counts. When an individual reports an intolerable side effect, quick action, rather than minimizing, reassuring, or lecturing, is required. Failure to act quickly almost invariably leads to the client's discontinuation of the medication or to his or her taking it erratically. The prescriber should be rapidly involved to consider alternative medication strategies. Even telling the person to wait a few days until the next available appointment is likely to be a prelude to covert or perhaps announced discontinuation of the medication.

• *Monitor side effects.* Monitoring target side effects along with target symptoms may sometimes be helpful. If a crossover switch is being done with the goal of improving symptom control while also minimizing or avoiding specific side effects, a combined symptom and side effect checklist may prove useful. Simply adding the target side effects to an existing symptom monitor is relatively easy to accomplish and can help determine if all the switching goals are accomplished.

Therapist to Prescriber

Become knowledgeable about side effects. A therapist is much more likely to observe a side effect if he or she knows what to look for. A therapist is much more likely to hear a client identify something that might be a side effect if the therapist knows which side effects are more common. And a therapist may be able to recognize dangerous side effects earlier if dangerous side effects are known. The therapist typically sees the client in more varied situations and discusses more aspects of the client's life than does the prescriber. The therapist will often have information about side effects and their impact on the client's life, earlier and with more contextual information than will the prescriber.

Any use of medication involves a balance between efficacy and tolerability. We are always asking the questions "How troublesome are the side effects compared to how effective the medication is?" and "How big is the problem that the medication is targeted to help solve?". It may be worthwhile to put up with side effects from a medication that works exceptionally well for a problem that is huge. However, even minimal side effects may not be worth tolerating from a medication that is only marginally effective or that is focused on a problem that does not cause much distress or impairment. The ultimate goal is to maximize both efficacy and tolerability—to use a medication that works well without side effects—but that is not always possible. Sometimes it is necessary to tolerate some persistent side effects in order to stay on a medication that works well. However, it is the client's perception of tolerability that matters. If a side effect is intolerable from the client's perspective, then the cost is too high. If side effects can be managed, minimized, or coped with, then we can get the best results from the medication while reducing the risk of relapse.

• *Discuss all side effects.* It is important to discuss all side effects, even if they are considered transient, mild, or well managed by the client. Side effects play an important role in the medication management decision-making process. Relying on the client to mention side effects, or on the prescriber to observe side effects, can lead to side effects being missed. Discuss observed side effects even if they have not been mentioned by the client; do not discount an observed side effect just because the client is unaware of it. Similarly, do not discount a client's reported side effects simply because you cannot confirm them with your own observations.

• *Be brief and to the point.* As with most communications with the prescriber, whether written or oral, brevity is usually a good choice. For example: "Client reports no improvement in resting hand tremor since starting 1 mg of Cogentin 4 weeks ago." In most instances, going into rich, descriptive detail is unnecessary, unwanted, and undesirable from the prescriber's perspective.

• *Convey urgency about intolerable side effects.* If the therapist believes that a client is likely to stop taking a medication due to side effects, it is important to explain the urgency of the situation to the prescriber. For example: "John is having trouble playing guitar because of an active tremor. It didn't improve with Inderal, and I'm concerned he'll quit taking his mood stabilizer medication. Do you think a higher dose of

Inderal might help or do you think it would it be better to switch to another mood stabilizer?" Simply reporting a side effect without indicating that the client perceives it as intolerable may negatively impact both the client's use of the medication and therapeutic rapport and trust.

• *Immediately report potentially dangerous side effects, even if you are not sure.* Promptly discuss potentially serious side effects, whether merely suspected or clearly confirmed. It is better to give false positive report than to overlook a serious side effect. Err on the side of caution without sounding frequent or unwarranted false alarms. When in doubt, be clear about both the observation and the uncertainty of knowing exactly what is going on. For example: "I'm not sure if it is serious or not, but I'd like for you to see John and evaluate *x*."

A collaborative relationship between the therapist, prescriber and client is the foundation of effective medication management. An effective medication is more likely to be selected, side effects are more likely to be minimized, and medication is more likely to be consistently used if therapist, prescriber and client are all working together toward common goals.

CHAPTER FOUR

Medication Management Strategies

Discussions about how to manage or make decisions about medication often start with a discussion about which medication to use or how much to use. Before we can discuss how to manage medications, however, it is important to think first about what we want medications to do. Only then can everyone discuss how medication may be useful to help solve those problems. Prescribing or taking medication is never a goal in and of itself. Rather, as noted throughout this book, medication is a tool that can be used to help solve some problems. The client may complain that she feels tired all of the time, or cannot get a job, or continues to be bothered by voices in her head that interfere with concentration, or that her thinking is blocked in some uncomfortable way. The therapist may be concerned that the client is impulsive, yells at neighbors, and does not shower or take care of herself. The client and/or staff may see the medication as either the potential solution to the problem or the cause of the problem. In either case it is very important to clearly identify the problem, identify as much detail about the problem as possible, discuss all possible solutions to this problem, and then discuss the potential role of medication. The client's view of a problem and the staff's view may be very different. Both need to be clearly understood. Disagreements about medication often arise because client and staff are talking about very different problems. Other disagreements arise because of conflicting beliefs about how effective medication could be in solving a specific problem.

Medication use is often focused on positive symptoms such as hearing voices or paranoia. Although it is understandable why clinicians tend to focus on these symptoms, in many cases they may overestimate their importance to clients. Hearing voices is a problem only if it causes distress or interferes with something else that the person wants to do. For example, if the voices interfere with the person's ability to read, follow and participate in conversations, or stay at a job, then the voices are a problem. If the voices are friendly and help the person deal with boredom, then they may not be a problem. Medication is most likely to be taken when it is perceived as being potentially useful in helping solve problems that have been identified by both clients and staff as being important. Improvement is not just improvement in the symptom, but improvement in the underlying target connected to that symptom. For example, a person may be given medication because "voices" interfere with his ability to study or work or read or even watch TV. Medication may help decrease the frequency or loudness of the voices or may eliminate them completely. More commonly, the client may report, when asked if the voices are still there, that they are but do not cause as much distress, do not intrude as much, or do not interfere with other activities as much. Asking the correct question is important. If the question is "Are the voices still there?" or "Are the voices as loud as before?", it may appear that the medication has not been very effective. It is much easier to gauge the effectiveness of the medication if the question is "Do the voices interfere with your life as much?" or "Is it easier to concentrate on work or follow a favorite TV show?"

Medication is a tool that helps the client cope more effectively with a problem or a set of problems. No discussion of medication can be very productive without a clear understanding of the problem that medication is intended to help solve. This discussion includes a history of the problem, the degree to which this problem intrudes into the client's life, what else has been tried to solve or alleviate the problem, what has worked and what has not. How important is this problem for both client and staff, and how much in the way of risk or side effects does each think reasonable in trying to treat it? If a client agrees that the problem is huge and that nothing else has helped, he or she may be willing to tolerate a side effect that would be intolerable if used to treat a smaller problem or one that may have other possible solutions. Before discussing a medication change, it is important to have a clear understanding about what it is hoped the medication could do, clear target symptoms so that both client and staff can follow whether things are getting better or worse, and a sense of the time that it may take for the medication to take effect.

Overview of Medication Strategies

It may seem that there are millions of possible decisions that one can make about medication. In some sense, given the possible medications and combination of medications, this complexity is real. It is useful to simplify this complexity to make it easier to think about and easier to talk about. There are only eight actions or strategies that one can implement concerning medication: increase, switch, wait, decrease, add, combine, subtract, or continue. Be clear on the concrete problem that you are hoping the medication will help to solve. Then work within the structure of these eight strategies to organize the discussion and guide the development of a medication strategy.

Unfortunately, outcomes of such discussions are not always that positive, and sometimes agreement and even a collaborative sense of participation is hard to achieve. It may be that the client is so fixed on a particular solution that is hard to be collaborative. For example, a client may believe that there is, and has been, no problem with mental illness, that the past reports of symptoms can be explained in some very different way, and the discussion starts and ends with a demand that all medication be discontinued. Actually, these discussions are relatively rare. Even as such a client may demand to discontinue all medications, he or she is often willing to explore past history, talk about problems, and talk about attempted solutions to those problems. Team members do not have to agree about everything, rather, they just find some area where some agreement is possible.

Eight Medication Strategies

1. Increase
2. Switch
3. Wait
4. Decrease
5. Add
6. Combine
7. Subtract
8. Continue

Preliminary considerations

Before making any changes to the current medication regimen, think about the potential reasons that it may not be working. These include the following possibilities:

• *Substance abuse among people with major mental illness is the rule, not the exception.* It is very common for people who already suffer from schizophrenia, bipolar disorder, major depression, or the other major disorders to abuse street drugs, alcohol, or large amounts of caffeine. It is possible that no medication strategy will overcome these impediments to recovery. Lectures about the evils of drug use are rarely useful. Rather, it is often helpful to get clients to identify the effect of street drugs, alcohol, and caffeine on their own life. It is important to focus the conversation on the client's own goals and the impact of drugs and alcohol on these goals. Once a client has identified what he or she wants a medication to do, it is easier to point out how drugs and alcohol use can keep medication from working and make symptoms worse. If drug and alcohol abuse continues to be a problem, changing medications may not lead to further improvement.

• *Medication is often not taken consistently.* Medications are only useful if they are taken consistently, and we know that in most chronic illness, from schizophrenia to high blood pressure, erratic medication use is the rule rather than the exception. It is important to be clear about why we are prescribing the medication, why the client would want to take the medication, and develop strategies that support taking medication consistently.

• *Social and psychological stress can destabilize a person, even if he or she is taking medication.* It is difficult for any medication to overcome hopelessness, lack of support, lack of stable housing, or all of the other issues that people with major mental illness often face.

• *Unrecognized medical illness can exacerbate or cause behavioral symptoms.* People with major mental illness are much more likely than the general population to have a chronic medical illness, much more likely for this illness to go unrecognized, and much more likely for this illness to be poorly treated.

• *Unrealistic expectations can interfere with recognizing what the medication is able to do.* As clinicians, we want to adjust medications, as well as all other aspects of treatment, to work as well as possible to help clients have the best possible quality of life. Many major mental illnesses, including schizophrenia, often have fluctuating courses: periods of doing better, and periods of more severe symptoms. One of the most challenging clinical problems is when to adjust medications during these periods of difficulty and when to focus on providing extra support to help the client get through the periods as easily and rapidly as possible. There is sometimes a magical expectation that adding or changing medication will provide the solution.

Sometimes a medication change might really help, but other times it just allows staff members to believe that they are "doing something," whereas it is the natural cycling of the illness, rather than a medication change, that will lead to return to baseline.

Medication adjustments are often the first treatment change that is considered if a client is not doing well. Often a medication change might help, but all of the treatment issues that too often interfere with a client's life should be considered first.

There are a number of strategies to develop respectful, collaborative relationships. Empathy, listening to the other, finding areas of agreement are all very important. Another kind of strategy is to structure the conversation, keeping it to logical "chunks" that can be considered one at a time. When thinking about the various possible changes that can be made with a medication, "chunking" is a very helpful way to share information, decrease personal confrontation, and initiate a give and take in the conversation that may help all participants consider which options are possible.

1) Increase

The first medication strategy is to increase the dose of medication. Each medication has a therapeutic dosage range, that is, the amount of the medication that is usually needed to be most effective. The medication history charts in Appendix 4 show the usual therapeutic dose range for many commonly prescribed medications used with people who have severe, persistent mental illness. Although most clients will do best if they take medication within this dosage range, some people are very sensitive to medications and may feel better if they take less than what is normally considered a full therapeutic dose. Other clients may need a higher dose than the chart suggests. To avoid intolerable side effects, the prescriber will often start a new medication at or below the bottom of the therapeutic dosage range, although with some of the new medications there may actually be fewer side effects if the medication is started at closer to a full dose or increased more rapidly. Many medications are started at a low dose and, gradually stair-stepping the dose up, titrated up to the therapeutic dose. The specific strategy and the reason for that strategy can be discussed with the prescriber.

Once the therapeutic range is reached, further medication adjustments, up or down, may be required to achieve the best possible response. If a person experiences severe or persistent distress, symptoms, or functional impairment, the first question to ask is whether the person is taking the medication consistently and whether substance use or medical illness could be interfering with the medication. It is also a good idea to go back to the original medication target and review whether this is a target that is likely to respond to medication. Finally, it is always worth considering what else, in addition to medication, might help. Once a decision is made to adjust the medication due to an incomplete response, it is worth considering an increase in the dose. Although this is formally a question for the prescriber, in a collaborative relationship this is an issue that actively involves the client, therapist, and prescriber.

In general, it is better to consider adjusting the dose of the current medication before switching or adding medication. Too often, people switch before they have had a chance to find out if the original medication would work. If the top dose has not been reached and side effects are not a big problem, it is generally better to increase the dose, rather than switch, add, combine, or decrease. Switching medication carries the risk of making things worse and usually takes longer than a dose increase to find out if the change is going to help. Changing to a new medication too rapidly or before trying a full dose of the current medication leaves everyone on the team asking whether the current medication might have worked if it had been tried a bit longer or at a bit higher dose. Unless there are significant side effects or a significant worsening of a person's condition, maximizing effectiveness of the current medication should be done before anything else.

Maximizing the effect of a medication requires that it be taken long enough to have an effect, in high enough dose, and without complicating drug or alcohol use. Almost all of the medications used in psychiatry take at least 3–4 weeks to see if they will work. Some take much longer (e.g., clozapine). Stopping a medication after a few days gives very little information about whether the medication would have worked or not. How the dose of a medication is adjusted—whether it is raised or even lowered—depends on the specific medication, the person's side effects, and the person's history. For example, if a person becomes more agitated after starting a new antipsychotic medication, the agitation might mean that the dose should be increased, or it could mean that the person is experiencing a motor restlessness called akathisia, and that lowering the dose of medication or treating this side effect might be a better course. More is sometimes—but not always—better.

At times, clients spend a long time on a very low dose of a medication without getting much better and without being willing to have the dose raised. The issue is not how many milligrams of medication a person is taking, but is it the right dose to do the job? If the medication is not at a full dose, is not causing major side effects, and the symptoms are still causing a lot of distress or impairment, then raising the dose may make more sense than having the person risk a medication switch without using enough of the current medication to see if it would really work.

Whereas some clients end up on too low a dose of medication to be effective, others end up on a higher dose than they probably need. This dosage imbalance is a common problem with any relapsing disorder that tends to get better and then worse. It is not unusual for a person with schizophrenia who has been stable for some time to go through a period when symptoms worsen. Increased stress in the person's life, an increase in substance use, or merely the episodic nature of the underlying illness may be the cause. It is common for the dose of the person's medication to be increased, and if the person improves over the next few weeks it is assumed that the increased dose of medication made the difference. It may be that the temporary increase in the dose of medication really helped, but the dose could be decreased to the old baseline after the crisis has passed. In other cases, the exacerbation just "ran its course," and although everyone might believe that the medication was responsible, in reality it may have had nothing to do with the person returning to the previous level of function. In either case, the person is very likely to continue on this new, higher dose of medication until a year or so down the road when he or she experiences yet another period of exacerbation, and the dose of medication is again raised. If a person continues to be unstable, it may be difficult to find the right time to decrease the dose of medication. If the person is having a difficult period every few weeks, whenever the medication is decreased it can be predicted that within a few weeks the person will again go through a more difficult period. It is very difficult not to attribute this worsening of symptoms to the last medication decrease, even if it is completely unconnected. Over a period of years it is easy for someone with this kind of pattern to end up on a very high dose of a medication—much more than is needed and enough to cause an increase in side effects.

At times, it is fairly clear what dose adjustment is needed. If a person continues to have distressing or impairing symptoms on a very low dose of medication—for example, on 1 mg of risperidone (Risperdal) or 5 mg of aripiprazole (Abilify)—then increasing the dose almost always makes sense. On the other hand, some people metabolize these medications very slowly. In these "slow metabolizers" a relatively low dose may build up in their body to a normal level, and a normal dose may cause more side effects than it would in most people. The research that is available pertains to "most people." Although there is some science in adjusting a medication dose and the research can help guide a decision, it is also a bit of an art that can be best guided by a discussion between client, prescriber, and therapist. Even the officially approved dosage ranges are only an approximate guide for how a particular individual will respond. The dosage ranges approved by the Food and Drug Administration (FDA) are not always the same as those suggested by the most recent research. For example, the upper-FDA-approved dose of risperidone (Risperdal) is 6 mg/day, and relatively few people will respond to a higher dose if they have not responded to several weeks at this dose. On the other hand, the upper-FDA-approved dose for ziprasidone (Geodon) is 160 mg, but there is a growing consensus that a significant number of people may do better on a higher dose.

Adding another medication from the same class of medications complicates the dosing schedule, increases the risk that one medication may interact with the other in unpredictable ways, risks new side effects, and increases cost. Monotherapy—the use of a single medication instead of a combination of medications—is preferable when effective. Decreasing the dose in the face of severe, persistent symptoms is likely to make symptoms worse, not better. So unless side effects are a significant issue, a medication increase may be the next logical medication strategy if problems persist, especially if the person is not already on what is normally a full dose of that medication. Potential exceptions to the strategy of increasing the dose are listed in Table 4.1.

When considering medication strategies for most medications, comparing the client's current dose to the normal dosage range is useful to decide whether a dosage increase is both safe and likely to be helpful. For most of the medications used in psychiatry, blood levels provide very little information. There is no way to find out from a blood level whether olanzapine (Zyprexa) or quetiapine (Seroquel) should raised or lowered. However, for some mood stabilizers such as lithium and di-

Table 4.1. Checklist to Evaluate Medication Increase

Consider a Medication Increase	Consider Something Other Than an Increase
☐ Client is experiencing symptoms with moderate–severe distress or impairment.	☐ Client is experiencing mild symptoms with little distress or impairment.
☐ Symptoms and impairments are distressing and match the purpose of the medication.	☐ Purpose of the medication does not match the symptoms and impairments.
☐ Medication is below maximum dose.	☐ Medication is at maximum dose.
☐ Side effects are either absent, transient, mild, manageable, or tolerable.	☐ Side effects are persistent, moderate–severe, or quite bothersome and cannot be managed.
☐ Medication has not been increased recently, and full effectiveness has been achieved at the current dose.	☐ Medication has recently been increased, and more time is needed to reach full effectiveness.
☐ Medication is consistently taken daily, as prescribed.	☐ Medication is not consistently taken, as prescribed; doses are forgotten, skipped, or reduced.
☐ Client does not use or abuse street drugs or alcohol and does not drink large amounts of caffeine.	☐ Client continues to use or abuse street drugs and/or alcohol and/or consumes large amounts of caffeine.

valproic acid (Depakote), blood level, rather than dose, is used to determine therapeutic range and top dose. When considering an increase of lithium or divalproic acid, a recent lab report indicating the client's blood level will rapidly reveal whether an increase is possible. If the blood level is already at the top of the therapeutic range, then a medication increase is a less likely option. For other medications such as clozapine, a blood level can provide some guidance, although the correlation between blood level and clinical response is only approximate. Appendix 3 includes information about therapeutic blood levels for the older mood stabilizer. In summary, a recent blood level can be an important part of the discussion for some medications but is less useful for others.

2) Switch

There are times when a medication switch might be a better strategy than a dose increase. If an individual continues to experience moderately or severely distressing symptoms and impairments after 4–6 weeks at the top dose of a medication, it is probably time to consider a medication switch. When a person has been taking a medication consistently for 4–6 weeks, it is likely that the depression, mania, or positive psychotic symptoms such as hallucinations and disorganization would at least begin to respond. It may take medication longer to show maximum improvement on cognitive and negative symptoms; however, there should be some initial significant improvement even in negative symptoms within 4–6 weeks at full dose. If the person continues to have problems with symptoms, as always, consider whether he or she is really taking the medication, whether the dose is correct, and whether substance use is interfering. Switching is a good option if the client has taken a high enough dose of medication for long enough, and is still having distress or impairment from symptoms that should respond to the medication.

It is important to remember that although switching medications may make things better, it may also make things worse. The suggestion to switch medications is based on the data that the various medications work differently (have different "mechanisms of actions") and have different side effects. Research can provide information about effectiveness and side effects of medication for populations of people, but it is not possible to entirely predict how any given individual will respond to any new medication. This unpredictability means that the timing of a switch is critical. If the switch is elective, it is usually best to do it when there are adequate supports in place and stress levels are at baseline (e.g. the client is *not* about to start a new job or move into a new apartment). Often, the push for a change in medication occurs at the same time as many other changes are occurring in the client's life. This can represent a push toward recovery. At times, the push to switch medications serves as a distraction from some other major issue, such as a change in clinician or illness of a close family member. Whenever possible, the goal is to change one thing at a time: change one medication, not two; start a new job, not start a new job *and* switch medications. If the switch improves things, then great. But the switch may makes things more difficult or causes a temporarily bumpy period—which is why it would be preferable to time the change so that other problems can be minimized.

Better Is Not Sufficient

Often, a person improves on a medication but is still left with symptoms that are causing significant distress and dysfunction. Even if there has been notable improvement, a client may still be left with impairments that interfere with his or her ability to achieve desired goals. Once the maximum dose has been sustained for a sufficient period of time, it is important to talk with the client about how much improvement has been achieved. Review medication target symptoms, persistent side effects, and severity and degree of impairment. If moderately to severely distressing symptoms and impairments persist, it could be time to consider a medication switch. Different medications, even within the same class, work differently. If a specific medication is only partially effective, another medication, even in the same class, might work much better. A different medication might work better than exceeding the top dose of the current medication. There is, of course, the risk that a different medication may not work as well, but this may be a risk worth taking.

Baseline Is Not Good Enough

It may be tempting to "leave well enough alone," especially if the person had a symptom exacerbation during a past medication switch or if the persistent symptoms are "baseline" for this person. It is easy to give into the myth of chronicity and believe that the person will never get any better as a way to justify the choice not to pursue further symptom reduction. If the symptoms and impairments are longstanding, it may be tempting to settle for the level of recovery the client has achieved, however modest, and discount the potential for improvement, and stop short of the next switch. While people can recover their life despite ongoing symptoms, decreasing the distress and problems caused by symptoms will make the recovery process much easier. Optimal functional recovery and role recovery are made easier by symptomatic recovery. When we settle for moderate–severe, persistent symptoms and impairments, we risk settling for custodial care instead of continuing to pursue recovery-oriented treatment.

Review Medication History

It is important to know the person's medication history before making a decision about a possible medication switch. Information about past medication trials can be obtained from the client, the client's family or caregiver, and the client's past medical record. All of these sources are important and are likely to provide different kinds of information. It would be best to know all the medications the client has taken, the top dose taken of each, how well each one worked, what side effects occurred, and reason(s) the medication was discontinued. Even partial information can be helpful. Sometimes clients or families will remember particularly noteworthy medication trials in which medications worked particularly well or poorly. Often the client and family can provide background that supplements the formal medical record. For example, a client may explain that he or she was using drugs during a particular medication trial or that his or her mother's death may have been a better explanation for a relapse than the particular medication. Sometimes clients or families report that a particular medication was not very helpful—despite the fact that this particular period coincided with the person's holding a job or doing well in school for the first time in years. It is important to be as specific as possible, both about the medication, the response to that medication, and what else was happening in the client's life, good or bad. Sometimes it is helpful to go over a list of the names of the medications within a medication class to help the client/family/caregiver identify which ones the client has already taken. Pharmacies are often an excellent but ignored resource and can provide a printout of all medications dispensed to the client.

The medical record may help identify maximum dose taken, side effects that were experienced, and the prescriber's reasons for making medication changes. Unfortunately, medical records are commonly incomplete, illegible, and less useful than one might desire. Nevertheless, they are still an important resource and can be integrated with the chart description of how the client was doing and the client's own recollection of how he or she was doing to develop as complete a picture as possible.

When constructing a medication history, the main questions are:

- What has been tried and worked?
- What has been tried and not worked?
- What has never been tried?

These questions help guide the decision about which new medication is the best one to try next. As discussed previously, in a formal sense it is ultimately up to the prescriber to decide whether or not to switch, and if so, which medication might be next. However, this decision is likely to lead to a more effective outcome and to more consistent and effective medication use by the client if the client and therapist are actively involved in the decision. Although it is the prescriber's responsibility to organize the information about past medication trials, the therapist has an important role in helping to collect this information. Client, therapist, and prescriber all have active roles in decisions about which goals should be pursued and what risks are worth taking.

When Repeating a Past Medication Might be a Good Choice

Simply because a medication was prescribed in the past does not mean that it cannot be tried again. Trying a medication again might be worth considering if the medication:

- worked in the past but was stopped anyway.
- was never tried at an effective dose.
- was stopped before transient side effects had a chance to get better.
- effectiveness was blocked by drug use or other lifestyle habits.
- was never taken consistently enough to have a real chance of working.

When Medication Was Effective in the Past

Sometimes, a medication is stopped in spite of, or even because of, symptomatic improvement. It is not unusual for a client to stop a medication "just to see what happens," to test the need for long-term medication, or because of doubts about the need for medication. In these instances, lack of medication effectiveness is not the issue, and, in fact, effectiveness may paradoxically contribute to the decision to stop taking the medication. "Take medication the right way, every day, even when symptoms go away," is a rhyming reminder of the importance of continued medication use after symptomatic recovery is achieved. Unfortunately, it is difficult for most of us to follow this sage advice.

> *Example*: While reviewing Barry's medication history, we find out that he took medication *b* about 2 years ago. He remembers doing well on it, does not recall any specific side effects or problems, but does not remember what dose he took. He tells us that he quit taking medication *b* because he thought he didn't need it anymore. He relapsed, was hospitalized, and was started on medication *c*. In this example, repeating medication *b* might be an option for a medication switch. Because it was effective in the past and there were no known troublesome side effects, it is quite likely that medication *b* would prove effective the second time around.

When Medication Was Not Optimally Dosed

Occasionally we may find that a person took a specific medication in the past, but only at a relatively low dose. If the medication was abandoned without increasing the dose, in the absence of documented or remembered troublesome side effects, repeating the same medication might be an option for a medication switch. Sometimes there is a plan to increase a medication over time, but the medication is discontinued before a full dose is actually taken for any substantial period. There may even be a hazy recollection that the medication was ordered at a full dose, and only careful checking with both client and records clarifies that a full dose of the medication was never actually ingested by the client. In a situation where a full therapeutic dose was never tried, the medication may still be a reasonable option for a medication switch.

Example: While discussing his medication history, Harry reports that he took medication *d* but was not on it very long and does not recall why he quit taking it. A review of his chart shows that he started on medication *d* in the hospital but when he returned to his usual prescriber and reported severe, persistent symptoms, the decision was made to switch him to medication *e* instead of increasing the dose of medication *d*. There is no indication in the chart of troublesome side effects, and the dose of medication *d* prescribed in the hospital was on the low end of the therapeutic range. Perhaps Harry was having problems unrelated to the medication, or perhaps his usual prescriber overreacted to Harry's casual report of side effects. Neither Harry nor his family remembers much in the way of side effects with medication *d*, and both agree that he was not on it long enough to know if it would work or not. Harry is willing to try it again. In the absence of evidence to the contrary, repeating medication *d* might be an option worth considering if it is time for a medication switch.

When Medication Was Abandoned Due to Transient Side Effects

Sometimes people become alarmed, discouraged, or troubled by transient side effects. It is not unusual for people to experience some initial side effects when starting a new medication or when a medication dose is increased. If common medication side effects were not discussed in advance, were troublesome, or were misinterpreted, the client may have stopped the medication or a requested a switch. Unfortunately, this request for a switch can happen even if the side effect is expected to be transient. Sometimes people will tolerate transient side effects if they know what to expect and how long it may take for the side effects to subside. Sedation is an example of a transient side effect of some medications that can be anticipated, discussed, and temporarily tolerated or compensated for. If side effects are not discussed ahead of time, clients might misinterpret common transient ones as a sign that they are on too much medication or that the wrong medication has been prescribed. The person who was prescribed a starting dose of a medication but abandoned the medication in response to transient side effects may be willing to wait out the adjustment time if the side effect is anticipated and discussed in advance. In this case, repeating that medication may be an option for a switch. Often, depending on the specific medication, side effects can be minimized by starting the medication at a lower than normal dose and then increasing it to a full dose over time. If the medication side effect was perceived by the person as intolerable, then repeating the medication is less likely to be a good option.

Example: Kate explains that she was prescribed medication *f* in the past but only took it for a few days. Because it made her sleepy during the day, she decided it must be "too strong" for her and she quit taking it. She wasn't scheduled to see the prescriber again for 6 weeks, so she just decided to "take a drug holiday" until her next appointment. Not too surprisingly, she was acutely symptomatic at the next appointment, and the prescriber started her on medication *g*.

After a discussion of the advantages and disadvantages of medication *f*, Kate seems to understand that sedation is a common transient side effect that usually gets better after a few days, and that it does not mean the medication is "too strong" for her. She tells us that she is willing to tolerate the side effect if she knows to expect it, if she could take the medication in the evening rather than in the morning, if she could start the medication on Friday, and if she could be switched to a different medication if the sedation does not go away. After discussing the problem, Kate, the therapist, and the prescriber also agreed that it would make sense to try and minimize initial sedation by restarting medication *f* at a lower than normal dose and increasing it to a full dose over 2 weeks. Under these circumstances, repeating medication *f* might be one option to consider if it is time for a medication switch. Repeating medication *f* would probably not be a reasonable option, however, if Kate says that she would stop taking any medication that causes sedation, regardless of whether or not the side effect is transient.

When Medication Effectiveness Was Impeded by Drug/Alcohol Use or Lifestyle Habits or Life Events

Street drugs, alcohol, large amounts of caffeine, huge amounts of over-the-counter medicine, and stressful life events can all override the ability of medication to control symptoms. Abuse of street drugs, alcohol, and even caffeine often worsens the problems caused by the underlying illness and can block the therapeutic effects of medication. The higher the intake of substances, the lower the chance of symptomatic recovery. Even at a relatively low threshold, substance abuse can worsen problems, regardless of what medication is prescribed, no matter what dose is achieved, and in spite of consistent medication adherence. Substance abuse can so increase mood instability, impulsivity, and other symptoms that even an otherwise effective medication has much less chance of being helpful. Once the problems of street drugs and alcohol are resolved, there is a chance that almost any psychiatric medication may be more effective. Under such circumstances, it may be reasonable to repeat a trial of a previously prescribed medication once the person is no longer abusing drugs.

> *Example:* Although Lloyd has a history of drinking alcohol and smoking pot, he has been clean and sober for the past 6 months. He tells us that he took medication *h* during the time he was drinking and getting high. Even at top dose, medication *h* did not do a good job of either controlling

his symptoms or helping him work toward his life goals. Because Lloyd is now clean and sober, it's possible that medication *h* might be much more effective than it was during his period of substance abuse. If it is time for a medication switch, medication *h* may be worth considering as an option, in light of Lloyd's improvement in recovery lifestyle habits.

When Medication Was Not Taken Consistently

Medication must be taken consistently, every day, to be most effective. When a medication is not taken consistently, the chances of it helping the individual work toward life goals is greatly reduced. Skipping doses, cutting down on the amount taken, running out of medication for 1 or more days before getting the prescription refilled, taking the medication "only when needed," and forgetting to take doses will all decrease how well the medication works. If medication is not taken consistently, it may seem to not be working, and the prescribed dose may be increased. The actual amount of medication the client is taking may be uncertain and may increase or decrease based more on how consistently it is taken than on how much is prescribed. Under such circumstances, it is hard to determine whether the medication itself was ineffective or if symptomatic recovery was hampered by consistency problems.

Example: Jason was prescribed medication *j* in the past. The dose was gradually increased to the top of the therapeutic range, but symptoms causing significant distress and dysfunction persisted even after 3 months. Clinical staff working with Jason had a sense that medication adherence may have been a problem. When Jason was asked about this, he acknowledged that he was living alone at the time and frequently forgot to take the medication. Now, however, he is committed to taking medication to see if it will really help. He has learned and mastered several strategies that enable him to take his medication consistently. For example, he always eats dinner at about the same time, and he has learned that it is easier to remember to take the medication if he takes it as part of his regular pattern of preparing and eating dinner. His prescriber also has helped by simplifying Jason's medication regimen so that he needs to take medication only once a day. Medication adherence is now one of Jason's recovery lifestyle habits. In addition, he is now lives in a supervised apartment, and medication adherence is a frequent topic of discussion. In this context, if it is time for a medication switch, repeating medication *j* may be worth considering.

It is a good idea to ask clients what medication they are actually taking, then ask what happens if they miss a day or two, and how often this happens. Assuming some degree of inconsistent use opens the door to the topic and makes it easier for a client to acknowledge what he or she is really doing. It is important not to punish a client who acknowledges partial adherence. Almost everyone misses medication now and again. The point is not to "trap" a client into an acknowledgment of wrongdoing, but rather to open up the discussion of how the client decides to not take a dose, his or her perspective of what happens when some doses are missed, and what happens to prompt him or her to start taking the medication again.

When Repeating a Past Medication May Not be a Good Choice

Sometimes it is not the best idea to repeat a medication that was previously prescribed. Two of the most common examples are (1) a medication that did not work well and (2) one for which persistent side effects were a problem.

Medication Did Not Work Well

If the medication was not very effective, even at maximum dose, then repeating it is probably not a good choice. If the person continues to experience bothersome symptoms and impairments on a high dose of medication, repeating it would probably not be an attractive option. Assuming consistent medication use plus an absence of alcohol or street drugs the first time the medication was prescribed, the medication will probably not be effective the second time around.

> *Example:* Lily took medication k for about a year. The prescribed dose was at the top of the therapeutic range for the last 3 months she took it. Lily continued to experience very bothersome and persistent symptoms and impairments in spite of the maximum dose. There was no indication of substance abuse, and medication use was reliably consistent. Lily is clear that at the time of her trial of medication k, she had limited her caffeine intake to two cups of coffee a day and did not drink soda or tea, and notes in her chart confirm that at the time she told this same thing to her therapist. There is no documented evidence of significant life stressors at the time. Medication k did not achieve an adequate degree of symptomatic recovery in the past, so switching back to it would probably not be a logical choice. It is unlikely to be any more effective now than it was previously.

Problems with Persistent Side Effects

If a medication taken in the past caused persistent side effects that the person perceived as troublesome, intolerable, or stigmatizing, it would probably be unwise to repeat the same medication at the same dose, especially if the problem resulted in the client stopping the medication or taking it erratically. It is quite likely that the person will experience the same side effects the second time around. Unless there is a way to minimize or resolve the problem with side effects, the client is likely to stop the medication or not take it consistently. If a medication worked well in the past and if previously bothersome side effects can be minimized or managed, then repeating the medication might be worth considering. At times, depending on the specific medication and the specific side effects, it may be worth considering trying a lower dose of a medication that in the past seemed to be effective but had been difficult to tolerate.

Example: Patrick tells us that he experienced an active tremor taking medication *l*, in spite of also taking side effect medication. He was embarrassed about the hand tremor and said he didn't want to "look like an addict." The tremor also impaired his ability to play guitar and write music, hobbies he's enjoyed for the past several years. Rather than quit the medication abruptly, he explained the problem to his prescriber and was switched to medication *m*. Even though medication *l* was improving John's persistent symptoms and there had been room for further medication increases to optimize symptomatic recovery, the problems caused by side effects outweighed the potential for symptom remission. Repeating medication *l* again is likely to result in reemergence of an active tremor. In light of these problems, medication *l* would probably not be selected for a medication switch unless there was an effective way of treating this side effect or avoiding it by trying medication *l* at a lower dose.

Identify Medications That Work Differently

Sometimes there is no way to know in advance which medication might work best for an individual. However, once the options have been narrowed by reviewing the person's medication history, it may be possible to prioritize the remaining possibilities. Although it may seem as though there are hundreds of different medications, there are relatively few within any one group. For example, there are only five first-line atypical antipsychotic medications, and they are all somewhat different, but some are more different from one another than others. Within the class of antidepressants, some work in similar ways and are likely to have similar side effects, and others work through different mechanisms and are likely to have different side effects.

All of the medications, even those that seem to work similarly, are different enough that some people will respond to one and not another. For example, selective serotonin reuptake inhibitors (SSRIs) are a very common kind of antidepressant. Even though all of the SSRIs work through a similar mechanism (i.e., the reuptake of serotonin is blocked, leaving more available), a person may respond to one of these and not to another. On the other hand, there are also antidepressants that are not SSRIs and have very different ways of working. The first question when switching is whether to switch to a medication relatively similar to the old medication or to switch to a very different kind of medication.

There is enough variability in individual response that in some situations it may make sense to try several medications from the same class before moving to another subgroup of medications. The important point is to not give up. A person may need to try one medication after another until he or she finds one that works well and does not cause intolerable side effects. There is enough difference between medications, even between those of the same type, that it is worth going through a number of different ones before assuming that no medication will work.

Example: Charlotte has been taking medication *n*, one of the SSRI antidepressants. She is taking a high enough dose that a further increase is unlikely to be any more effective, yet she continues to experience symptoms causing moderate to severe distress and impairment. A review of her medication history indicates that she has taken one other SSRI with about the same degree of symptomatic recovery. Switching to an antidepressant with a different mechanism of action—one that is not an SSRI—may be worth considering. There are several different kinds of antidepressants. It is important that the prescriber talk with both the client and therapist about the various options, so that they can be an informed part of the decision-making process. An important question with any medication switch is whether to change to a medication that is relatively similar or to one that is relatively different. Table 4.2 summarizes these decision-making concerns.

Discussing Options with the Prescriber

Taking a careful medication history is often time consuming, and, although a medication history may be collected by the prescriber, it may also be collected by a therapist. Once the historical information is gathered, it can be part of the discussion that involves all members of the team. The review of what medication has been tried, what has worked, and what has not can help point to the most reasonable medication strategies. Switching medications is always a bit trickier than just adjusting the dose of an existing medication.

How to Switch

One question with a switch is how fast to do it. It is usually unwise to simply stop the old medication one day and start the new one the next. A crossover approach tends to minimize problems with both side effects and relapse. Once there has been a decision to switch medications and the next medication to try has been selected, the next decision is how to switch. There are three ways to switch medications: crossover, stop and start, and taper and titrate. As with all other medication decisions, the formal choice of how to switch medication is ultimately up to the prescriber, but it is much more likely to work out well if there is a collaborative decision involving prescriber, client, and therapist. A decision that involves the therapist and

Table 4.2. Checklist to Evaluate Medication Switch

Consider a Medication Switch	Consider Something Other Than a Medication Switch
☐ Client continues to experience symptoms with moderate–severe distress and impairment.	☐ Client is experiencing symptoms with little distress or impairment.
☐ Symptoms and impairments match the purpose of the type of medication.	☐ Purpose of the type of medication does not match the symptoms and impairments.
☐ Medication is already at, or above, upper end of the normally recommended dosage range.	☐ Medication dose has not been optimized; the dose is still lower than normally recommended upper limits.
☐ Side effects are persistent, moderate–severe, and bothersome.	☐ Side effects are either transient, mild, or tolerable.
☐ Medication has been taken at a full dose for some time, but symptoms continue to be a problem.	☐ Medication has recently been increased, and more time is needed to reach full effectiveness.
☐ Medication is consistently taken as prescribed.	☐ Medication is not consistently taken as prescribed; doses are forgotten, skipped, or reduced.
☐ Client does not use or abuse street drugs or alcohol.	☐ Client has continued to use or abuse street drugs and/or alcohol within the past 30 days.
☐ Client does not consume large amounts of caffeine.	☐ Client consumes large amounts of caffeine.
☐ One or more medications of the same type have not been prescribed or have not been taken at maximum dose for 4–6 weeks.	☐ Every medication of the same type has been taken at top dose for 4–6 weeks and proven no more effective than the current medication.

client may help reduce the number of problems encountered. One client may be very anxious about stopping a medication that she has come to trust, and would prefer a very slow transition. Another client may find the side effects of the current medication intolerable and want to stop it immediately and try something else. Prescribers, like clients and therapists, typically have their own preference about how to switch. Although some of this decision may be guided by research, there is very little research on the best way to change from one medication to another. If a particular prescriber does not normally invite the client's or therapist's participation, it may be useful for the therapist to open the discussion to consider alternatives and concerns before a decision has been made. It is important for the prescriber to make a decision that the therapist and client can support. Asking the prescriber to reconsider a decision that a client will not follow or that the therapist has strong concerns about, is preferable to remaining silent and then having to address the problems that occur later.

Cross Taper

The main focus of the cross taper is to reduce the risk of relapse and of side effects by making sure that all changes are gradual. Nothing is done rapidly, withdrawal effects from the first medication are minimized, and there is a therapeutic dose of the combination of medications, even if there is not a fully therapeutic dose of any one medication. Depending on the specific medication, this is often one of the safest ways to switch medications. For most medications, a cross taper is preferred whenever possible. The first medication is gradually tapered down in stairstep fashion as the new medication is titrated up in a corresponding stairstep manner (Figure 4.1). This cross taper can occur over days or, in some cases, may extend over many weeks or even months, depending on the medications involved, the preference of the client, and side effects being experienced.

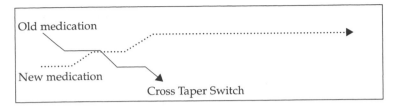

Figure 4.1. The old medication is gradually tapered off while the new medication is gradually titrated up to full therapeutic dose.

If stopping the current medication is not urgent, due to intolerable or dangerous side effects, and speed of the medication switch is not a priority, the cross taper may be the safest way to accomplish a medication switch.

One problem with a cross taper is that it is complicated; it requires a number of coordinated medication changes, decreasing the dose of the old medication in stages at the same time as the new medication is increased in stages. It is important to make sure all of these changes are written out.

Crossover Switch

For some medication changes, the best way to switch is to start the new medication, increase it to a full dose, and then slowly decrease and stop the first medication (Figure 4.2). In a crossover switch, the new medication is at a full therapeutic dose before the first medication is gradually reduced and then discontinued. This method ensures that there is always a therapeutic level of medication. Whether this is a good strategy depends on both the reason for the switch and the specifics of the medications involved.

For example, when switching from another antipsychotic to aripiprazole (Abilify), a crossover switch is usually suggested. There are usually no significant increases in side effects if aripiprazole is added to one of the other antipsychotic medications;

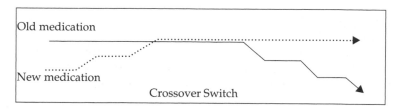

Figure 4.2. With the old medication at full dose, start the new medication, slowly increase it to full dose, then taper off the old medication.

specifically, there is no increase in sedation and no apparent increased risk of motor restlessness (akathisia) or other motor side effects (EPS, extrapyramidal side effects). On the other hand, if a sedating medication such as olanzapine (Zyprexa) or quetiapine (Seroquel) is stopped too rapidly, there may be a rebound agitation that may make it appear as though the new medication is the cause of the problem. For example, switching too rapidly from quetiapine to aripiprazole will frequently lead to increased agitation that will make it appear as though the aripiprazole is not working, whereas in reality the agitation may be a reaction to the withdrawal of the first medication. The aripiprazole can be started at 10 mg for a week, then increased to a full dose of 15 mg; only then is the first medication decreased slowly over weeks or even months. If a person is switching from olanzapine (Zyprexa) to ziprasidone (Geodon) to decrease weight-related side effects, getting the dose of the ziprasidone to a therapeutic level and only then very slowly backing off the olanzapine may decrease the potential risk of the switch.

On the other hand, for some medications a crossover switch is likely to lead to an increased risk of side effects. For example, motor restlessness or akathisia may be a risk if a full dose of risperidone is added to a full dose of haloperidol. In a haloperidol to risperidone switch, a cross taper will often be preferred over a crossover switch. Similarly, if a full dose of olanzapine is added to a full dose of quetiapine, sedation is likely to become a significant problem.

The crossover switch is often preferable because it lessens the chances of breakthrough symptoms and relapse. A crossover switch is one of the safest ways to accomplish a medication switch if:

1. stopping the current medication is not urgent and there are no intolerable or dangerous side effects
2. additive side effects are not a concern because of the specific medications involved
3. speed of the medication switch is not a priority.

Stop and Start Switch

In this method the first medication is stopped and the new one is started. Because this approach to switching has the highest risk of breakthrough symptoms and relapse, it is primarily used when a rapid switch is required due to intolerable side effects or time constraints. It is most often employed when clients have already stopped a medication on their own or are unwilling to continue taking it. The older medication is immediately stopped (or has already been stopped by the client) and the new medication is started and titrated to a therapeutic dose (Figure 4.3). Stopping the older medication without tapering is safest when only a low dose is being taken or when rebound side effects are unlikely. Immediate stopping of a medication increases the risk of rebound or withdrawal effects. It also increases the risk of relapse because there is a potential gap between the withdrawal of the old medication and the time it will take for the new medication to start working.

As a general rule, it is much safer to make slower, gradual changes than big abrupt ones. If a client wants to stop or change a medication, doing so more slowly is almost always safer than doing it abruptly.

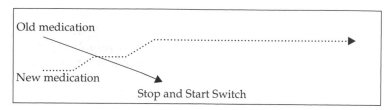

Figure 4.3. The old medication is stopped and the new medication is started and titrated to a therapeutic dose.

3) Wait

Wait between medication changes: Be patient. Do not get pushed into making too many changes too rapidly. Psychiatric medications do not work like pain relievers. When dealing with a headache, pain pills work in under an hour, and the headache is gone very quickly. Psychiatric medications usually take weeks or months, not hours or days, to reach full effectiveness. If a medication is increased too rapidly and the person then improves, it can be impossible to determine whether the higher dose was really needed or just more time was needed. Increasing a dose too rapidly can lead to a higher does of medication than really needed and a greater risk of side effects.

It can take 3–6 weeks for an antidepressant or antipsychotic medication to reach full effectiveness in treating positive symptoms or depression. It may take even longer to see full effects on cognition or motivation. Mood stabilizers tend to work more quickly and are likely to help stabilize acute mania in under 2 weeks. Table 4.3 summarizes the conditions that suggest waiting versus other actions.

4) Decrease

Sometimes a medication may be started at a high dose when there is pressure to "do something" as fast as possible, for ex-

Table 4.3. Checklist to Evaluate Waiting vs. Other Actions

Consider Waiting	Consider Something Other Than Waiting
☐ Symptoms and impairments match the purpose of the medication.	☐ Purpose of the medication does not match the symptoms and impairments.
☐ Medication has recently been increased and there has not yet been enough time to see how effective it will be at the current dose.	☐ There has been enough time to see if the current medication at the current dose will be effective.
☐ Side effects, whether transient or persistent, are mild, tolerable, manageable.	☐ Side effects are severe, intolerable, or dangerous.
☐ Medication is consistently taken as prescribed.	☐ Medication is not consistently taken as prescribed; doses are omitted or reduced.

ample, for someone who is acutely ill and in a hospital. In other cases, a medication dose may be rapidly increased over a few days to a high dose, without allowing time to see if the person would respond to a lower dose. If a medication has been started at a high dose or the dose has been rapidly increased, then it may make sense to reduce the dose once there has been some decrease in the person's symptoms.

With only a few exceptions, there is little research to indicate that starting a medication at high dose actually leads to a faster response than starting, or titrating a client up to, a normal maintenance dose. Nevertheless, despite little research support for the practice, it is a strategy that is commonly used. It may make more sense to start some medications at high dose than it does for other medications. For example, aripiprazole and olanzapine can be started at a higher than normal maintenance

Table 4.4. Checklist to Evaluate Decreasing the Medication vs. Other Action

Consider Decreasing the Medication	Consider Something Other Than Decreasing the Medication
☐ Client is experiencing complete symptom remission or has symptoms with little distress or impairments.	☐ Client is experiencing symptoms with moderate–severe distress or impairment, and previous attempts to very gradually lower the dose have made things worse, not better.
☐ Medication was initiated at a high dose with plans to decrease the dose once acute symptom control was achieved.	☐ Medication has been increased, recently, and full effectiveness has not been achieved.
☐ Side effects, whether transient or persistent, are difficult to tolerate and dose dependent.	☐ Side effects, whether transient or persistent, are mild, tolerable, or manageable.
☐ Medication has gradually been increased to a dose above normal limits, the client is still very symptomatic, and it is unclear if the past increases have really helped.	☐ Medication is not consistently taken as prescribed; doses are omitted or reduced.

dose with little increase in side effect burden. Starting risperidone at too high an initial dose can substantially increase risk of side effects and may decrease the client's willingness to continue the medication. Whether a medication is started right from the beginning at a high dose or rapidly increased, some clients get discharged from the hospital at a dose that is higher than a normal maintenance dose. There may be little interest on the part of either therapist or prescriber to decrease the dose to a more normal level. If the person is doing well, everyone may prefer to not change anything that could make things worse. If the person continues to have severe, persistent symptoms and impairments, the therapist and prescriber may fear that decreasing the dose will make a difficult situation worse.

With medication, more may be better, but more also may not be better. At times, a slow, gradual decrease with close monitoring of target symptoms may help the client optimize his or her dose of medication, especially when recent increases have exceeded normal limits, with little or no additional benefit. The goal is to adjust the dose of medication to achieve the best possible effect with the minimum of side effects and risk. Table 4.4 summarizes the conditions that suggest decreasing medication versus taking some other action.

5) Add

When all medication options with the one medication have been exhausted, it may be helpful to combine two medications from the same class. Most experts consider monotherapy (the use of a single medication rather than a combination) preferable. Despite this preference, virtually all prescribers use additions or combinations for some clients. If a single medication is enough to achieve symptomatic recovery, then monotherapy is ideal; it is also less expensive, less complicated, and may result in fewer side effects. Whenever multiple medications are used, there is the potential for complicated and sometimes unpredictable interactions. There is also very little research to guide the use of multiple medications. Despite all of these concerns, if an individual continues to experience moderate–severe symptoms, distress, and impairment, in spite of an adequate trial on each of the available options within the medication group, then adding two medications together may be the next logical step. It is important to give the first medication time to work before adding a second, and it is important to have clearly identified target symptoms so

Table 4.5. Checklist to Evaluate Adding a Medication
vs. Other Action

Consider Adding a Medication	Consider Something Other Than Adding a Medication
☐ Client is experiencing symptoms with moderate–severe distress and impairment.	☐ Client is experiencing symptoms with little distress or impairment.
☐ Medication dose has not changed in some time, and further dose change seems unlikely to help.	☐ Medication has been increased recently, and full effectiveness has not yet been achieved.
☐ Side effects, whether transient or persistent, are mild, tolerable, or manageable.	☐ Side effects are severe, intolerable, or dangerous.
☐ Medication is consistently taken as prescribed.	☐ Medication is not consistently taken as prescribed; doses are omitted or reduced.
☐ Client does not use or abuse street drugs or alcohol.	☐ Client has used or abused street drugs or alcohol within the past 30 days.
☐ Several medications of the same type have been taken at maximum dose for 4–6 weeks and proven no more effective than the current medication.	☐ One or more medications of the same type have not yet been taken or have not been taken at maximum dose for 4–6 weeks.

that the client, the therapist, and the prescriber can all tell if the addition of the second medication has really helped.

Often the prescriber will use the medication that was most effective as the primary treatment and then supplement it by adding another medication from the same group, but one that is pharmacologically most different from the first medication. Within each class of medications—whether antipsychotic, antidepressant, or mood stabilizer—there are medications that are more similar and those that are less similar to each other. The premise on which using combinations of medications is based is to use two medications that work through somewhat different mechanisms. Effectiveness as well as side effects are both important considerations. At times the best options are readily apparent. However, a review of the person's medication history is often helpful when identifying medication options. Hopefully a comprehensive medication history is already available, but often it must be constructed as completely as possible. Without a good medication history, it is easy to overlook medications that might help and that have never been tried. Table 4.5 summarizes the conditions that suggest adding a medication versus taking some other action.

6) Combine

Sometimes persistent symptoms that continue to cause significant distress and impairment may be most effectively treated by combining different types of medication. When the primary target symptoms are well controlled, but symptoms in a different domain are distressing or impede functional and role recovery, it may be helpful to combine medications from different groups. For example, a client's psychotic symptoms have improved significantly, but he or she continues to be very depressed; or, the client's mood stability has improved by hallucinations continue. It is possible that when one symptom area is prominent, another domain of symptoms goes undetected until the first area improves. Combining medications from different groups may also be helpful to augment or enhance partial symptomatic improvement. Sometimes a mood stabilizer is used to augment an antipsychotic medication, or vice versa. Table 4.6 summarizes conditions that suggest combining medications versus taking some other action.

Table 4.6. Checklist to Evaluate Combining Medications
vs. Other Action

Consider Combining Medications	Consider Something Other Than Combining Medications
☐ There is little distress or impairment associated with the primary target symptoms, but symptoms in a different domain are distressing, impede functional and role recovery, and combining may augment partial symptomatic improvement.	☐ Client is experiencing symptoms with little or no distress or impairment.
☐ Medication dose has not changed in some time, and further dose change seems unlikely to help.	☐ Medication has been increased recently, and full effectiveness has not yet been achieved.
☐ Side effects, whether transient or persistent, are mild, tolerable, or manageable.	☐ Side effects are severe, intolerable, or dangerous.
☐ Medication is consistently taken as prescribed.	☐ Medication is not consistently taken as prescribed; doses are omitted or reduced.
☐ Client does not use or abuse street drugs or alcohol.	☐ Client has used or abused street drugs or alcohol within the past 30 days.
☐ Switching to another medication of the same type is unlikely to target the domain of symptoms that may be improved by combining medications.	☐ One or more medications of the same type have not yet been taken or have not been taken at maximum dose for 4–6 weeks and are likely to improve the targeted domain of symptoms.

7) Subtract

Unfortunately, there are instances when a medication that was added or combined proves to be of little or no benefit, even at the upper end of the normally recommended dosage range. If new medications are gradually added or combined without subtracting any medications, the person may eventually end up taking three, four, five, or even more medications, some of which may not be particularly beneficial. Sometimes stopping a medication that has not added much benefit will help decrease side effects and will certainly decrease cost and risk. Sometimes stopping an ineffective medication will work better than continuing a medication that is not helping. Once a client is on several different medications, stopping a medication may be a better strategy than starting yet another. If a client has been on a particular medication for some time, a gradual taper is usually safer than an abrupt discontinuation. If the current medications do not appear to be working very well, stopping one or more of them and simplifying the entire medication package may be an important step before yet another new medication is added. Multiple medications piled on top of each other, if they are not clearly helping, can increase side effects and the risk of drug–drug interactions and make the actions of each of the medications less predictable. Table 4.7 summarizes the conditions that suggest subtracting a medication versus taking some other action.

8) Continue

When the current medication strategy is working well, it is usually a good idea to continue the current medications without making any changes. Once the individual has achieved a reasonable level of symptomatic recovery, is not distressed by symptoms, is not troubled by side effects, and is capable of working on functional and role recovery, then no further medication changes are required. Energy can be invested in achiev-

Table 4.7. Checklist to Evaluate Subtracting a Medication
vs. Other Action

Consider Subtracting a Medication	Consider Something Other Than Subtracting a Medication
☐ Client is experiencing symptoms with moderate–severe distress or impairment.	☐ Client is experiencing mild symptoms with little distress or impairment.
☐ The dose of the medication that was added or combined has not changed in some time, and further dose change seems unlikely to help.	☐ Medication has been increased recently, and full effectiveness has not yet been achieved.
☐ The remaining medication is likely to be sufficient to prevent an acute worsening of symptoms.	☐ The remaining medication is unlikely to be sufficient to prevent an acute worsening of symptoms.
☐ Side effects, whether transient or persistent, are moderate–severe, difficult to tolerate, or hard to manage.	☐ Side effects are severe, intolerable, or dangerous.
☐ Medication is consistently taken as prescribed.	☐ Medication is not consistently taken as prescribed; doses are omitted or reduced.
☐ Client does not use or abuse street drugs or alcohol.	☐ Client has used or abused street drugs or alcohol within the past 30 days.

ing functional and role recovery while maintaining symptom control by continuing medication. The old saying "Don't fix what is not broken" is often worth following.

Unfortunately, some clients go through a period when they believe that they no longer need medication just when they are doing very well. It is frustrating for families (and for clients, once they experience the consequences) when clients discontinue or change medication just when they are doing really well. It is important to listen to the client and understand his or her motivations and needs. At times it is possible to work with the client to avoid a high-risk medication change just when things are going well. At other times, the client will insist on a change or even a discontinuation, and the clinician's job is to work with the client to develop target symptoms so that everyone can identify early indicators that things are getting better or worse. At times clients will insist on a medication change that clinicians find risky or irrational. Our job is to work with the clients and do our best to make these client-initiated "experiments" as safe as possible. The concern is not just for how a decision will effect clients over the next week or month, but what we can do to improve clients' decisions about medication over the next year and the next decade.

Of course, there are times when it is reasonable for a client to consider discontinuing a medication that he or she has been on for a long time. Often there is no way to be sure that a medication is still needed, unless one tries stopping it. Unfortunately, discontinuing medication can lead to relapse even after long periods of stability. Often this relapse does not occur right away but months after the medication has been stopped. Stopping medication very slowly and having clear target symptoms about when medication should be restarted are both ways to decrease the risk of discontinuing medication. It is also clear that most people with schizophrenia, bipolar disorder, or recurrent depression are going to have more stability and a better quality of life if they stay on effective medication for several years. It is hard to say if a person will need to stay on medication forever, but it is fairly easy to identify clients who are likely to need medication for the foreseeable future. Table 4.8 summarizes conditions conducive to continuing medication versus taking other action.

Table 4.8. Checklist to Evaluate Continuing Medication vs. Other Action

Consider Continuing Medication	Consider Something Other Than Continuing Medication
☐ Client is experiencing an absence of target symptoms or mild symptoms and impairment that do not interfere with pursuit of personal life goals and dreams.	☐ Client is experiencing moderate–severe symptoms, distress, and impairment.
☐ Side effects, whether transient or persistent, are mild, tolerable, or manageable.	☐ Side effects, whether transient or persistent, are moderate–severe, difficult to tolerate, or hard to manage.
☐ Medication is consistently taken as prescribed.	☐ Medication is not consistently taken as prescribed; doses are omitted or reduced.

Focusing on these eight medication strategies can help simplify and structure medication decision making. In addition, it is also important for the client, therapist, and prescriber to develop and practice communication skills that facilitate collaboration. The combination of logical strategies and collaborative decision making is needed to optimize effective medication management.

CHAPTER FIVE

The Pros and Cons of Medication: Why Take It, and Why Not

It is sometimes assumed that a client who is prescribed a needed medication will take it, consistently and reliably and without complaint. This is not the way most of us would react if we were on the receiving rather than the giving end of the treatment suggestions. Most people have mixed thoughts and feelings about taking medication. There is concern about the underlying illness, about whether the diagnosis is accurate, about whether the medication is the correct one and will work, what the side effects might be, and what this will all mean for the future. There is often a jumble of thoughts swirling around the idea of taking a medication. The degree of confusion and ambivalence varies from one person to another and from one illness to another. There are also different thoughts and feelings commonly connected to different kinds of medication.

Why Medication? What Does Medication Do?

How can a medication change how someone feels or thinks? Actually, all thoughts or feelings or moods are connected to chemical changes in the brain. Just as a computer works by electrical impulses flowing through silicon chips, the brain works due to an extremely complicated interaction of electrical impulses and chemical messengers. Nerve cells communicate with each other primarily by the release of neurotransmitters, which are specialized chemicals that are released from one nerve cell and picked up by a nearby cell. These chemicals interact to make it more or less likely that the nerve cell will "fire," which will, in turn, release other neurotransmitters that will affect other cells. The brain is much more complicated than any computer.

There are very elaborate control mechanisms that balance how much of what chemical is released when and how fast. There is never an "on" switch in the brain without some kind of "off" switch, and both are influenced by many other nerve cells that make complicated feedback networks. Whereas a computer is made up of binary transistors that are either "on" or "off," much of the brain's complexity comes from nerve cells that are influenced to be "toward on" or "toward off" or "prepared to fire" or "reluctant to fire." These chemical processes are not just unidirectional. Not only does a neurotransmitter influence how we feel or think, how we feel or think will influence the production and release of neurotransmitters. Doing something enjoyable will cause a release of certain neurotransmitters that will fire cells in the brain associated with feeling pleasure.

Two people engaged in the same activity may experience very different amounts of pleasure. Presumably the two people experience different degrees of stimulation of the pleasure centers of the brain, either because of genetic differences other biological differences, different life experiences, or any other factor that affects brain function. Not only is the brain more complicated than can be comprehended, the brain is always interacting with what we do and with what others do around us, further complicating the situation. No one has just a "brain" operating on its own. We have brains that are reacting to stored experience, current activities, and even future hopes. We can influence our brain by deciding what we are going to think about—and when you realize that it is the brain that is involved in making this decision, you can see that the situation with feedback systems and everything influencing everything else rapidly gets complicated.

Mental illness involves a complex interaction between a biological predisposition and social stress factors. *Biological predisposition* refers to all of the things that influence the biology of the brain, including genes and past infections and even chemicals such as smoking or alcohol that a mother uses while pregnant. Alcohol and substance use and medical illness can lead to biological changes. We now know that experience can change biology. Severe traumatic events can lead to long-lasting and even permanent brain changes.

These biological effects interact with social effects. There is now research demonstrating that some people are genetically much more likely to become depressed if they end up in stressful life situations. If they do not experience stressful life events, their risk of becoming depressed is not much different from anyone else. This particular genetic change in a specific enzyme does not cause someone to become depressed, but it does make the person more sensitive to social situations causing depression.

A person can have more or less of a biological predisposition, similar to many medical problems. If you are very prone to developing diabetes, you will get it no matter how well you take care of yourself. On the other hand, there are many people who will not develop diabetes even if they become obese, eat lots of sugar, and never exercise. In the middle are people who can either prevent the development of diabetes or delay its onset until much later by eating right and exercising.

What all this means is that even a pure "brain disease"— something that is primarily caused by biological factors—could be helped by psychological treatment. Cognitive–behavioral therapy is a specific technique that is useful for many people with depression, even though we know that depression has a significant biological component. We also know that medications can affect a psychological process, whether that process was caused by a biological change or not. If someone goes through an extremely anxiety-provoking situation, Valium (diazepam) will help him or her feel less anxious—but no one suggests that the anxiety is caused by "Valium deficiency."

Medication as Treatment

Scientists have learned a lot about the brain, how it works, and what goes wrong to cause mental illness. For example, anything that increases the neurotransmitter dopamine in a particular part of the brain, the limbic system, will cause a person to experience psychotic symptoms. The person with too much dopamine in the limibic systems will hear voices, become paranoid, become disorganized, and appear to have many of the symptoms of schizophrenia. Any medication that decreases dopamine in this part of the brain acts as an antipsychotic. Unfortunately, the brain is much more complicated than just this limbic system. Too little dopamine in the frontal part of the brain causes a person to feel apathetic, unmotivated, flat, unable to feel pleasure, and unable to display spontaneity. Many drugs of abuse, such as cocaine and amphetamines, are taken because they increase frontal dopamine. Older antipsychotic medications such as haloperidol (Haldol) and chlorpromazine (Thorazine) blocked dopamine all over the brain. These medications decreased psychotic symptoms but caused many other side effects and worsened the "negative symptoms" of schizophrenia. The newer antipsychotic medications attempt to block dopamine in the limbic part of the brain and, at the same, time increase dopamine in other parts of the brain.

Note that this discussion is about anti*psychotic* medications, not anti*schizophrenia* medications. Although the current medications are very helpful in assisting people with schizophrenia to cope with some of the symptoms, they do not cure the underlying disorder. Antidepressants or mood stabilizers can be very useful in decreasing symptoms and helping the person cope more effectively, but they rarely work so well as to take away all signs of the underlying disorder. Indeed, few medications cure the underlying illness. Medications for diabetes, high blood pressure, high cholesterol, and many other physical disorders help decrease symptoms, maintain function, and keep things from getting worse. Psychiatric medications are similar. Even if they do not cure, they can be very effective in helping a person better manage his or her illness. However, medications alone are rarely enough. There is research support that cognitive–behavioral therapies and other talk therapies can help decrease symptoms of psychosis, depression, anxiety, and insomnia. Presumably these talk therapies work by changing brain chemistry and helping people manage persistent symptoms. Many people with major mental illness continue to have symptoms, even with medication and other kinds of treatment. Many people are left with some degree of impairment that makes it more difficult for them to work, to live where they want, to be part of a support system. Therapy, case management, vocational support, and other kinds of assistance are all important parts of treatment. While medications are often a very important part of treatment, they are rarely sufficient.

If the medications only decrease symptoms, and do that only partially, why do they seem to be such an important part of psychiatric treatment? Symptoms can be a significant problem for many clients with mental illness, causing distress and making day-to-day functioning more difficult and less enjoyable. A medication that helps to decrease distressing symptoms can be very useful. Medications are also important in helping people maximize their ability to function. For many people with depression, the nonmedication therapies do not work well enough to allow them to go to work or stay in school. Antipsychotic medications can help a person control symptoms, avoid hospitalization, keep an apartment, or get a job. Effective medication may make it more likely that a person will be able to stay in touch with family and friends. Of course, not all medications work for all clients. For some, medications may help, but not in a way that is important to them, or not enough to be worth the side effects or other problems. For a medication to be considered effective, it must increase functioning in a way that is important to the client.

The ability of medication to decrease symptoms and improve functioning is very important. A person who has been hospitalized several times in his or her 20s is going to have more difficulty "catching up." A person who goes years without being able to work is going to find it more difficult to get and keep a job. Medication can help a person function better, cope with symptoms more effectively, and maintain stability in the community. The research is not completely clear, but medication may also change, for the better, the ongoing course of mental illness. There is increasing concern that being psychotic, being manic, or being severely depressed may be bad for the brain. There is some evidence that every manic episode may make it more likely that a person will have another manic episode. There is also evidence that psychosis may cause death of neurons. There is also some evidence that medication can be protective. The data supporting these ideas is far from conclusive, but they support the need to make effective treatment available as rapidly as possible, and to create conditions that maximize client willingness to consistently take a medication.

Ambivalence about Taking Medication

Most people who take medication are ambivalent about it. Most people go to a doctor because they recognize that they have some kind of illness or are concerned that they might have an illness. Often they want to get a diagnosis (knowing is better than not knowing). Having a diagnosis means that they can *name* the problem. A diagnosis means that the problem, whatever it is, is known, can be understood, and hopefully can be treated. Having a diagnosis can give people a sense of control over the problem, whatever it may be. A problem that cannot be diagnosed is a problem that is unknowable and uncontrollable. There is often a significant need to name a problem, and clients will search for someone who can come up with a name for what ails them.

Naming the Problem: Coming up with the Correct Diagnosis

Of course, some names and diagnoses are more acceptable than others. A client may believe that a problem is religious or moral and object to a medical name or diagnosis. At other times a client may believe that the problem is medical and may search for a medical diagnosis while rejecting psychological or other explanations. A person may agree that he or she keeps getting evicted from apartments, but strongly disagree that it is caused by his or her own behavior. Outsiders may label the problem as the person's false beliefs or mental illness. The person may label the problem at the landlord's racism or the FBI's persecution of him or her. The first step in coming up with a solution to a problem is finding areas of agreement about the nature of the problem. Obviously, if the client and clinicians disagree about the basic nature of the problem, they will likely also disagree about the solution to the problem.

Not only is it important to name the problem but also to decide how big or serious it is. Being homeless, hearing voices, or not having friends may be a much bigger problem for one person than for another. The client and clinician may have very different views of the seriousness of the problem. How far one is willing to go and what risks one is willing to take to solve a problem depends on how big the problem is. However, determining how big a problem is may be more complicated than it might initially seem. Some problems are so scary that they cannot be faced. A client who is convinced that he or she is dying or that things will never get better may do everything possible to just avoid thinking about it. This is not the solution that everyone would choose, but for some people, it may seem to be the only option. A clinician may think that a problem is huge and immediate, whereas the client may disagree that there even is a problem. A person may be at risk of imminent eviction but refuse to acknowledge it. This refusal may be labeled as the product of a delusion or poor insight, but it may also be connected to how the person copes with something that is too overwhelming to acknowledge. Clients, too, may be much more concerned about a problem than is the therapist, and much more anxious.

At times, partial agreement can be enough, but not always. A depressed women in an abusive marital relationship may want to focus solely on her depression and refuse to address the marital issues that seem to the therapist to play an important role in the depression. In this case, medication may be readily accepted. Another women in a very similar situation may want to focus exclusively on the impact of the marital issues. Although she may agree that she has had a longstanding history of recurrent depressions unrelated to this marriage, and acknowledge that this history of depression runs strongly in her family, she may believe that accepting medication would place the problem within herself and keep the focus off her husband and their marriage.

Agreeing on the Solution to the Problem

Once there is some agreement on the nature and seriousness of the problem, one can discuss the range of possible solutions. A client and therapist can agree that the client's depression is connected to his or her immoral behavior, but then they must agree on a solution from a range of choices: from praying more frequently, to doing good works, to seeking forgiveness from the person wronged, to working through the psychological issues involved. Both therapist and client may agree that the client's intrusive nightmares, startle reaction, and unwillingness to get into relationship with other people are all caused by past trauma, but then they must agree on a solution from a range of choices: from individual or group psychotherapy, to confronting the abuser, to working in a shelter for other victims of abuse, to taking medication. Just as client, therapist, and prescriber can disagree about the nature of the problem, there can also be disagreement about the kinds of solutions that might help.

At times, there are costs or problems with some solutions that are not immediately evident. For example, the woman with depression and marital issues sketched above may be concerned that accepting medication will give her husband ammunition to use in their marital warfare. Her anger and irritability and lack of productive activity could be attributed to her biological depression rather than to the issues relating to the husband's abuse. This concern over how a particular solution will impact the definition of a problem is very common. A person refuses to take an antipsychotic medication because doing so would mean acknowledging that he has schizophrenia and will never be able to hold a job or finish school. A person refuses to accept a mood stabilizer because doing so would mean that she really has a bipolar disorder and will have more episodes in the future. Certain solutions make the problem definition implicit, and with this definition comes associations that may be incorrect and even destructive. A person could be taking antipsychotic medication for many different problems than just schizophrenia. Many people taking antipsychotic medication for schizophrenia do finish school and get jobs. Accepting the solution will hopefully make the goal more likely rather than less likely. At the same time, for the client, accepting certain solutions may be connected to accepting specific problem definitions that may have very real psychological costs.

A woman in her mid-20s had had three clearly manic episodes, although two of them were connected to cannabis use. She was extremely erratic about taking her prescribed

mood-stabilizing medication and was extremely ambivalent about whether her psychotic episodes were part of a
bipolar disorder or just bad drug trips. When asked what it
would mean if she were bipolar, she said that being
bipolar would mean that she would never have or keep a
good job, would never have a stable marriage, and would
never have kids. Accepting the idea that she was bipolar
was simply too high a price to pay, even if it would help
stabilize her life. It was only after she was able to change
her ideas of what it meant to be bipolar that she was able
to take the medication consistently.

Common Concerns about Taking Medication

Medication is a tool that can be used to help a person cope
more effectively with a problem. Even if there is agreement on
the nature of the problem and agreement on the potential effectiveness of medication in helping with the problem, there
may still be considerable ambivalence about taking the medication. Although medication can be greeted by a client as a way
of solving a problem and reestablishing control over symptoms,
it can also raise many concerns. Common concerns about taking medication include:

- Risk
- Side effects
- Dependency
- Control
- Cost
- Embarrassment
- Reminder of illness and loss
- Disbelief that medication is needed

Risk

All medications involve a certain amount of risk. At least a
few people die from aspirin every year. How big a risk is too

much? There is no simple answer. How much risk is "too much" depends on the nature of the problem, the seriousness of the problem, the alternatives available, and how well the medication is likely to work. It also depends on the values and characteristics of the people involved. If the problem is huge and serious, such as a near-fatal cancer or a depression that is causing the person to be dysfunctional and very suicidal, more risk may be justified than if the problem were minor anxiety or a vague sense that the world is not all that enjoyable. There is always a process of weighing the risk of taking this medication at this time against the hoped-for benefit of taking this medication at this time.

Alternatives also matter. If cognitive–behavioral therapy is available, this might be an excellent initial treatment for a mild to moderate depression or anxiety disorder. This treatment may have fewer risks and side effects than medication; but it is also likely to take longer, involve the client in doing more of the work, and may not be readily available. At times, effective alternatives are not available. There are many proposed treatments for schizophrenia, including megavitamins and herbs, but these do not replace the need for medication and may not be beneficial for all clients. There are many other treatments for schizophrenia that can increase the effectiveness of antipsychotic medication, including skill training and cognitive–behavioral therapy, but these do not replace the need for medication either. Although a small number of people with schizophrenia may do well without medication, for most people with this disorder, there are no effective alternatives.

Effectiveness of treatment is an important consideration. If you have a terrible disease, it may be worth taking medication even if it is very risky, if it is likely to work. The treatment for hepatitis C requires taking a medication for months that causes significant risk and side effects. Recent research suggests that some strains of hepatitis C are much more responsive to this treatment than other strains. A patient with one of the more responsive strains may decide that the risk of the treatment is worth it, whereas a patient with a less responsive strain may decide differently. Similarly, this is an important consideration for the treatment of mental illness. Some people with schizophrenia have a very significant, positive response to medication. They are able to return to a life that was impossible without medication. Tolerating risk and side effects may be well worth it. On the other hand, 30% or so of people with schizophrenia get little to no positive effect from antipsychotic medication. If a medication is not effective or is less effective, than it makes sense to tolerate less risk and side effects.

Finally, the degree that can be tolerated is different for each person. Some of us are big risk takers, and others not. Some sky dive off of planes, and others have trouble riding in a commercial airline. People individually weigh the risk of taking a medication against the risk of not taking that medication. The client, the therapist, the prescriber, the rest of the client's treatment team, and the other people in the client's support team will all weigh the pros and cons, risks and benefits of the medication, and make their own decisions of whether the risk is worth it.

Side Effects

Just as all medications have some degree of risk, all medications have at least the potential for side effects. All medications work in systems and in places that are outside their intended site of action. This means that every medication is doing something somewhere other than its intended purpose. These other actions in other places cause the potential for side effects. Side effects can be a huge problem or a small one, depending not only on the effect but also on its impact on the person's life. For example, a client whose main enjoyment is playing competitive basketball would be significantly bothered by a degree of motor discoordination that might be very minor for someone else. Staff often think that a 20- or 30-pound weight gain for a client is "moderate," but they may have real problems tolerating even a smaller weight gain in themselves. A colleague has gained 100 pounds as a consequence of her medication. As she puts it, she has the choice of being a "skinny crazy person or a fat sane person." She is well aware of the seriousness of this side effect, but chooses to take the medication anyway.

As with risk, which side effect is considered "worth it" depends on a complicated weighing of side effects and benefits. Therapists, prescribers, clients, and family members all have their own views of this weighing. What is too much of a side effect for a client may seem minor side effect to the therapist.

Sometimes there is concern that too much discussion about medication side effects will get clients to focus on side effects and even report side effects that are not real. Although this can happen, the alternative seems much more common: Side effects that have been discussed tend to be less alarming than those that are completely unexpected. If a side effect has been mentioned as possible—especially if it is something that tends to be temporary—the client is better able to incorporate it into the treatment. This does not mean that an endless list of side effects is useful, but a calm listing of the most common side effects and a discussion of the most serious side effects can help reinforce the sense of collaboration and increase the client's comfort that he or she is involved in the discussion. Those few clients who react to any discussion of side effects by immediately developing those side effects are the same people who will tend to be sensitive to side effects even if they are not discussed.

Dependency

Many clients are concerned about becoming dependent on the medications. This is not just an issue about the addictive potential of the medication, but more often an acknowledgment that taking a medication inevitably makes one dependent on someone else prescribing it and making it available. It is one more way that the client is not completely in charge of his or her own life. Anyone who takes a prescription medication goes through the process of contacting the prescriber to get it renewed, ponders thoughts of what happens if he or she runs out, perhaps worries that the factory will make the wrong stuff, or wonders what would happen if the medication were no longer available. Depending on the client, such concerns about becoming dependent—on either the medication or the system that makes the medication available—can become a significant issue.

Control

The issue of control is closely connected to that of dependency but with a difference. *Dependency* refers to concerns about relying on the medication and what would happen if it were no longer available. *Control* refers to how other people could control the client through the client's medication. There are two aspects to consider here. Many clients have lost much of the control over their own lives. People with serious mental illness, especially if they are also impoverished, are often told where they have to live, how they have to spend time during the day, and who gets to control the limited money that they have. The one area that they can control is what they ingest. Control also refers to someone else, be it therapist, prescriber, or family member, trying to control this one last area of the client's life. Other people are now attempting to control what the client takes into his or her body. Even if the client agrees with the need for medication and wants to continue taking it, unwanted issues of control enter. If a client decides that he or she needs a medication, does that mean he or she has to do what the therapist says, or cannot fire the prescriber, or cannot miss appointments, without a significant risk that the medication will be taken away?

A client hates coming in for appointments and goes many months without keeping an appointment at the mental health clinic. He agrees on the need for his antipsychotic medication and is legitimately concerned that he will become ill if he goes without it. At some point, be it 6 months or 12 months or 18 months, he is told that coming in to see the prescriber is required for the medication to be continued. Although this is good clinical practice, it is also an application of control over the client's life.

Cost

Many psychiatric medications are extremely expensive, and it may be well beyond the ability of most clients to pay for them. Very few clients without insurance will be able to pay $400 or more a month for medications. Most clients are on some kind of government-paid health insurance, Medicaid or equivalent. Some clients have private insurance or HMO coverage. In virtually all cases there is some co-pay of $1.00–$3.00, or more, per prescription. For clients with very limited incomes, this amount can add up to be a significant percentage of their disposable income, especially if they are on several different medications. When a client has to choose between cigarettes or medication, medication will often lose out. Even the relatively small co-pays required can be a significant cost for a client who would like to take medication.

Embarrassment

There is clearly a stigma about having a mental illness and about taking a psychiatric medication. However, there is a hierarchy of stigma, rendering some medications more acceptable than others. Although all medications have some attached stigma, it is now more acceptable, at least in some social groups, to take an antidepressant such as Prozac or an antianxiety medication such as Ativan. There is much more stigma attached to antipsychotic medications. Therapists and prescribers are well aware of this hierarchy. How many clinicians would casually mention to a friend or colleague that they are taking Prozac or an occasional sleeping pill? In contrast, how many would *not* be willing to casually mention that they are taking Haldol or Risperdal or another antipsychotic medication? For good or bad, taking a psychiatric medication labels the person, to him- or herself and to other people, as having a mental illness. We could say that there should not be such a stigma and the resulting embarrassment, but the reality is that these feelings are real and do exist.

Reminder of Illness and Loss

For some clients, every pill is a reminder of having an illness. The medication is also a reminder (again, more so for some people than for others) of the losses and struggles caused by the illness. Still, for some, every pill can be a way of taking back control, of doing something to fight the illness and coping more effectively. For others, however, every pill can be the constant reminder of how difficult their life has been and underscore their sad ponderings of what it might have been like if the illness had not occurred. This constant reminder of loss is extremely difficult for many people to face daily. From day to day a person may be able to forget about his or her losses and what life might have been like, but the medication can be the daily reminder that keeps these feelings in the foreground. Clients will say that they just cannot bear the medication because they cannot stand having that constant reminder. One of the therapist's task is to help the client convert these feelings of loss into constructive activity, to help them move from grieving to the conviction that they are now doing something to make things better. However, be aware that achieving this conversion is much harder for some clients than for others.

Disbelief That Medication Is Needed

When all is said and done—after all discussion of the problem and the solution—some clients just do not agree with the therapist and prescriber on the nature of the problem, and they do not believe that the medication is a good solution. This can be a constant belief, or can wax and wane with a certain amount of ongoing ambivalence. One day a client can believe that the medication is terrific and has allowed him or her to live life, and a day later come in saying that the medication is not needed, that he or she can do without it, or that the initial problem was not nearly as bad as everyone thought. Coming to an agreement about the problem and the solution is a process that occurs over time. If therapists want clients to listen to their point of view, they have to listen, seriously and respectfully, to clients' points of view. What is each client saying, beyond the surface statement that medication is not needed? With what internal struggles is the client grappling? And how can therapists use their therapeutic skills *not* to convince clients to take medication but rather to understand the conflicts that make the decision so difficult.

How to Approach the Ambivalent Client about Medication

Ambivalence around medication is the rule, not the exception. Even those of us who are absolutely committed to taking medication have some mixed thoughts and feelings—some ambivalence. The issue is the degree of ambivalence and whether it interferes with taking the medication consistently enough for it to be effective.

To begin addressing this ambivalence, focus on what the client wants the medication to do. Does the client have goals for the medication? Concerns about the medication? How would the client know if the medication was helping or not helping? Help the client come up with a specific list of what "doing better" and "doing worse" would mean. Is there a way that the client can track the effect of the medication over time? What specific behaviors would someone else observe, good or bad?

Help the client monitor medication by following target symptoms (those specific behaviors that the client or others could observe). These are often not symptoms of illness but rather behaviors that suggest that the clients is doing well or not so well. For example, ability to sleep through the night, leaving an apartment for errands or an outing, taking a shower regularly, and going to a volunteer job are all behaviors that the client can note. Being afraid of the voices, believing that other people can read his or her mind, and feeling hopeless are all internal states that the client can track. This list will be different for each person. It almost always includes behaviors that are not just typical symptoms of illness. A client may decide overall that he is doing "much better" but still exhibit specific target behaviors (e.g., the client has stopped going to his volunteer job, is yelling at people in his apartment building, is afraid of people that look at him when he is out of his apartment). Without a clear list of target symptoms, the conversation between client and clinician can dissolve into "I feel better/you look worse." Target symptoms allow client and clinician to focus on more specific issues that may allow for more agreement. For example, a client can state that she is doing better overall, while acknowledging that she is no longer doing those specific activities that she used to enjoy and that she had connected to her own recovery. This discrepancy between specific behaviors and overall subjective feeling is an important topic of discussion with which both client and clinician can grapple.

Encourage the client to become informed about his or her own medication. Information is generally a good thing. Clients cannot be true collaborators and participants if they do not have accurate information.

Clients should be encouraged to know:

- what medication they are taking.
- what each medication is supposed to do.
- what they would like the medication to do.
- what they want the medication *not* to do.

- what side effects or risks the prescriber is most concerned about.
- any other reasons that add to the client's reluctance to take medication.
- who in the client's life wants him or her to take medication.
- why other people want the client to take medication.
- how the medication help the client accomplish his or her life goals.
- how the client can assess how well the medication is doing this.

Working with a Client's Motivation to Change

Therapists often complain that a client is not motivated. Often, if a client *were* motivated, he or she would have much less need for the therapist! *Motivational interviewing* refers to an approach that helps the client overcome his or her ambivalence and move toward making real changes in his or her life. It does *not* refer to merely convincing or cajoling the client to do what the therapist has already decided is the right thing to do. Although motivational interviewing was developed for work with clients who have primary substance abuse issues, it is equally applicable to a broad range of problem areas.

The traditional view is that motivation is a trait; a client is either motivated or unmotivated. Momentary reflection cautions us that this view is way too simple. Clients are motivated to do some things and not others. Thus motivation, per se, comes and goes. One client may appear very motivated but not make any real change, while another client, or a different situation for the first client, may produce real change even without much apparent motivation. The reality is that motivation is a *state*; it is something that changes, that waxes and wanes in strength and can be influenced by friends, family, the situation, and the therapist. The therapist's job is not to take "poor motivation" as a given but to think about how motivation to make real changes can be enhanced.

People are not motivated to take medication for many reasons. As already discussed, they may not believe that the medication is needed, they may disagree on the nature of the problem, or they may believe that they can solve the problem in some other way. Clinicians often label this response as indicating "poor insight," but this tag does not provide an effective change strategy. Thinking about strategies that enhance motivation is another approach to helping a client think through the issues of taking medication. This approach assumes that the decision to take medication is like other life decisions: People can agree to do something and even want to do something, but still not do it. They may be ambivalent or feel overwhelmed or believe that the change is beyond them. They may want to make the changes but not have sufficient motivation to actually do so.

A therapist can use specific steps to structure the process of enhancing a client's motivation to change. Not everyone will go through these steps in the same way, of course. This approach and these steps apply to all kinds of change, not just those related to medication. This approach will be useful in motivating a client to take medication only if the medication is connected to goals. As stated many times in this book, medication is a tool. If a client sees medication as a useful tool to accomplish something that is important to him or her, then he or she is much more likely to use it. This strategy is most effective for those clients who agree that medication is important and helpful but still do not take the medication consistently. They agree but are unmotivated. How can motivation be enhanced?

It is useful to guide a client through five steps to enhance his or her motivation to make a life change. These are:

- Precontemplation
- Contemplation
- Preparation
- Action
- Maintenance

Precontemplation

Precontemplation is an invitation to the client to think about what life might be like if...the voices got better...he did not get into fights and get fired and evicted...she had an apartment that she liked. Planning or being realistic is not required. It is only the process of getting the person to imagine what life could be like. It is not the therapist telling the client what life could be like; rather, the therapist structures the conversation so that the client has the "space" to think about things a bit more directly than he or she might on his or her own. The therapist is neither passive nor directive but encourages an exploration of possibilities. Part of this precontemplation step involves an invitation to think about what things might be like if the client were taking medication more consistently. How has life gone when the client was taking medication regularly, and how was life going during periods when he or she was not taking medications? Was there a difference, whether or not the client thought it was directly connected to the medication?

Contemplation

In the contemplation step, the focus is on encouraging the client to think more specifically and concretely about change. What change would be most important? How would the change have to begin? What would be most difficult about making this change? Again, the therapist is not teaching or informing the client, but rather setting the stage with some structured questions to encourage the client to explore these issues and come up with his or her own answers. What would it be like if he or she really had a job? What would change? What would be better? What would be worse? What would have to happen for him or her to keep a job? How would he or she get up in the morning? How would he or she get to work? How would he or she get to work on days when he or she felt bad? What role might medication play in helping keep things under control? Would taking medication be required if he or she was really going to be stable enough to keep a job? What would be most difficult about taking medication, if this were a necessary step to working?

Preparation

Preparation is the process of inviting the client to plan how the change might actually happen. What would be the client's first step? What would have to be done to make it happen? Would preparation involve looking at the want ads in the paper, or making a list of businesses within walking distance, or learning to wake up in the morning so that he or she could get to a job on time? Preparation might involve getting some new clothes so that he or she could interview for a job more successfully. Preparation might include helping the client to think through what he or she would say to a potential employer if he or she went into a store to ask about a job. Preparation for taking medication more consistently might include thinking about how to connect the medication to some daily, routine activity, figuring out where he or she could keep the medication in order to remember to take it, or using a weekly pill box so that it would be easier to remember if he or she had taken the medication that day or not. Still another facet of preparation: What might the client say to a friend who disagrees with the value of medication? How might the client deal with a family member who has been pushing him or her to take medication?

Action

In the action step, the focus is on helping the client make real change. The first step in getting a job is not working full time. The first step is calling some of the numbers in the paper, or talking to nearby businesses about a part-time job, or calling the Department of Vocational Rehabilitation. Action involves helping the client break down the larger process of something as complex as getting a job into small steps, each of which is doable and not overwhelming. At times it is very useful to encourage the client to decide when this first action step will be taken. "When will you call those phone numbers from the want ads? Can you make a first call today? How about one phone call today and one tomorrow?" Encouraging small but concrete steps is often the best way to help the client make real changes. An initial action step involving medication might be a client's commitment to taking medication every day for 3 weeks and then evaluating if there has been any change, good or bad. Or it might be the client talking to his or her prescriber about the side effects that make it difficult to take the medication.

Maintenance

The step of maintenance is what needs to happen to keep things going well. Maintenance may involve getting enough sleep, not getting overly tired, staying away from alcohol, leaving the apartment to socialize, or taking medication consistently. There is a list of things that the client knows, or can figure out, that will help the new behavior continue; there is also a list of things that will get in the way. Helping the client to come up with a specific list can be very helpful in making a recent change permanent. Many clients who get a good response from a medication initially say they will take the medication forever, that they have learned their lesson and now see the need to stay on it. These same clients often discontinue the medication 6 months or a year later because they are feeling so good that they believe the medication is no longer needed. Having clients write a letter to themselves, describing how they stopped taking medication in the past and that they should not let themselves be drawn into this trap in the future. It is not the therapist coming up with this or any other specific strategy, but helping clients come up with their own strategies that is most helpful.

This step-by-step process assumes that ambivalence is normal and expected. The way to encourage motivation to change in a client is to first encourage him or her to talk about what he or she wants to be different, and then explore what steps the client can take to bring about those differences. Medication can play a role in this process only to the extent that that client wants the change to happen, believes it can happen, and believes that medication will help it to happen.

A number of treatment strategies underlie the idea of changing motivation:

- *Express empathy.* Acceptance and active listening facilitate change. Understand the client's point of view. The client is unlikely to listen to the therapist or prescriber if he or she is not really listening to the client.
- *Develop discrepancy.* The energy to motivate change comes from the client's perception of the gap between present behavior and how the client thinks things could be. It is the client, rather than the therapist, who must present the argument for change. If the therapist actively points out the negative side of the ambivalence and repeats what the client has said about the reasons *not* to make the change or *not* to take medication, then the client does not need to keep defending this side of the argument.
- *Roll with resistance.* The therapist should avoid directly arguing for change or directly challenging resistance. Rather, the client is the primary resource for finding solutions to the problem that he or she has already identified. Resistance—the client's attempt to fight with the therapist or disagree with his or her ideas—should be taken as a signal to the therapist to respond differently.
- *Support the client's belief that change is possible.* It is easy to give up if the expected behavior seems too big to accomplish. Help the client think about concrete steps that will help move him or her toward goals. If the change is too big, it can easily feel too overwhelming.
- *Remember that reward is a better motivator of change than punishment.* It is important to focus on what the client has

been able to do, rather than on what he or she has done wrong. It is important to celebrate even small victories.

• *Stay connected.* The goal is to work with the client to help motivate his or her change. While the clinician can have an important role in helping to facilitate change, it is important to always remember it is the client's change, not the clinician's. The goal is to support the client's journey of recovery.

PART II

Medical Issues in Mental Health Treatment

CHAPTER SIX

Psychiatric Presentation of Medical Illness: An Introduction for Non-Medical Mental Health Professionals

Introduction

Every time a client comes into a therapist's office, an emergency room, or a hospital, there is a very real possibility that what seems to be a psychological problem is caused by some physical illness. The depressed client may have an underactive thyroid gland. The client with panic attacks may have a pheochromocytoma, a tumor that secretes epinephrine. And the client whose personality changes and increased irritability are thought to be caused by marital problems may actually have a brain tumor that is triggering the personality changes and exacerbating longstanding marital issues.

Overview of the Problem

How common is this problem? Very... and not very. Most clients do not have a medical disease masquerading as an emotional problem. In fact, one of the problems is that most really serious medical illnesses are rare enough that we all get sloppy and stop looking for them. Most of the time our medical workups are unnecessary—but *most* of the time is not the same as *all* of the time. It is not necessary to live in abject terror of over-looking medical illnesses in clients who come to you with symptoms of depression or anxiety. On the other hand, medical causes of psychiatric symptoms should always be considered. As a mental health professional, you need to know enough about these medical illnesses to make some basic determination about whether a further medical assessment is necessary and how to focus that assessment so as to make it as productive as possible. The following sampling of research underscores the need for careful discernment of possible underlying medical conditions.

Johnson (1968) performed detailed physical exams on 250 patients admitted to an inpatient psychiatric unit; 12% of these patients were admitted to the psychiatric unit for problems that seemed to be caused by physical illness.

- 80% of these had been missed by the physician before admission.
- 6.6% were initially missed even after the admission workup.
- 60% had abnormal physical findings.

Hall (1978) performed a detailed assessment on 658 consecutive psychiatric outpatients.

- 9.1% had a significant medical illness.

Slater (1965) studied 85 patients (32 men, 53 women) diagnosed as having "hysteria."

- Patients were followed 7–11 years.
- More than a third proved to have organic disease.

Sox et al. (1989) did a thorough medical evaluation on 509 clients in community mental health programs in California.

- 200 (39%) had at least one active, important, physical disease.
- Staff at the mental health program was aware of only 47% of these.

- Research program discovered previously undiagnosed important diseases in 63 of these clients.
- 14% had a medical illness that was causing or exacerbating their mental illness.

Bartsch et al. (1990) performed a comprehensive evaluation of 175 clients from two Colorado community mental health centers. A previously undiagnosed physical health problem was found in 20% of the clients.

- 16% had conditions that could cause or exacerbate their mental disorder.
- 19 clients had a metabolic abnormality (e.g., elevated calcium).
- 7 clients had a neurological disorder (e.g., memory loss, post-concussion syndrome).
- 7 clients had an adverse medication effect.
- 4 clients had some other disorder or disease, including cancer.

Koran et al. (2002) screened 289 clients consecutively admitted to a public psychiatric hospital. Of these, 29% were found to have an active and important medical problem. Twenty percent of these had not previously been diagnosed, and medical problems may have caused or directly exacerbated the psychiatric problems in 6% of the admissions.

Reeves et al. (2000) studied 64 patients with unrecognized medical emergencies who were inappropriately admitted to a psychiatric unit after having been assessed in a medical emergency department. The medical diagnosis most often missed was severe drug or alcohol intoxication, withdrawal, delirium tremens (DTs) or prescription medication overdose. Common problems included inadequate physical examination, failure to obtain appropriate laboratory tests, and failure to obtain an adequate history.

Conservative estimates suggest that 10% of persons initially seen in outpatient settings for psychological symptoms have an organic disease causing the symptoms. This figure is higher in the elderly, in persons with certain psychosomatic disorders, and much higher in inpatient settings.

Even internists and neurologists working in academic centers and well aware of the possibility of organic illness miss medical illnesses with disturbing frequency. There is no set of tests that can definitively rule out everything. Some illnesses are hard to diagnose, especially at the beginning. Others are so rare that they are overlooked; hence the specific tests that would allow the diagnosis are not considered. Still other times the illnesses present atypically; the client's symptoms seem different from those described in the medical textbooks, so the medical illness is missed.

The most common problem, however, is that we do not think about the possibility of medical illness and therefore we do not specifically look for it. *If you do not look for it, you will not find it.* The goal of this chapter is not to get you to the point of being able to diagnose every possible disease. Rather, it is to give you a starting point—to know when to be particularly suspicious (or worried), to know something about the most common illnesses, and to learn enough to communicate with physicians and ensure that your clients receive the best possible evaluation.

There are at least three problems with presenting this kind of brief review for nonmedical mental health professionals:

1.   There are a huge number of possible illnesses of which to be aware. We are not going to try to list all possible illnesses or to give complete descriptions but, rather, to give you sketches of some of the common illnesses that you are most likely to see in your practice.

2.   It is almost impossible to talk about medical illnesses without lapsing into medical jargon. This chapter is partly about medical illnesses and partly about learning a new language that

will hopefully help you when you need to communicate with medical members of your treatment team or community health care providers.

3. A subtler and more serious problem is that nonmedical mental health providers organize the world according to psychological or psychiatric symptoms. The question is, what medical illnesses can cause depression, anxiety, etc.? The problem is that the depression caused by a brain tumor may be identical to the depression caused by marital discord or by an endogenous depression. What is likely to be different is the client's history and the associated signs and symptoms apart from the depression. Unfortunately, listing illnesses according to which ones can cause depression or which ones can cause anxiety does not produce a coherent organization. Many illnesses can cause many different psychological symptoms. More importantly, such a listing would not help you understand what other questions you could ask to help separate physical from psychiatric illnesses.

Physicians and nurses organize the world much differently. The easiest way to remember all of the separate facts and to see patterns is to organize illnesses according to physiological systems. Throughout this chapter we talk about endocrine, neurological, and cardiopulmonary systems. For someone who has been through medical or nursing school, using these major systems becomes the obvious way to organize things, but it is not always so obvious to the rest of the world. The problem with categorizing according to psychiatric symptoms will become obvious as you go through this chapter. A huge number of illnesses can present as depression, and the vast majority of these illnesses can also present as anxiety or delirium. It does not do much good to think about all the illnesses that can present as depression unless you begin to think about the other associated symptoms that those illnesses also have—and the best way to organize these associated symptoms is to understand which organ systems the illness affects.

Having said that, in this presentation we organize illnesses by their psychological effects and, at the same time, introduce the way physicians and nurses would organize their thinking about those illnesses.

General Approach to Considering Possible Medical Conditions

Always Consider the Possibility of Organic Disease

If you do not look for it, you will not find it.

1. *Be suspicious of "medical clearance."* Unfortunately, physicians tend to dismiss psychiatric clients for several reasons: (a) There may be a tendency to assume that all psychiatric patients are just "nuts" and do not have a "real illness"; (b) physicians are often uncomfortable around patients who are obviously depressed or act bizarrely, or whom they fear might act bizarrely; (c) at times these patients behave in ways that make evaluation more difficult, either by being unwilling to give a full history, unable to give an accurate description of symptoms, or too frightened to allow a full physical examination.

2. *People with mental illness get sick too.* The fact that someone is experiencing active psychiatric symptoms does not mean that he or she does not also have a serious medical illness. Therapists should always be aware that a medical illness might, in fact, be the cause of the psychiatric symptoms. But even in clients who clearly have schizophrenia or some other diagnosable mental illness and who have had an excellent medical workup in the past, it is important to consider whether their current complaints or recent changes in behavior could be related to a medical illness. As noted, psychotic clients are more difficult to evaluate, and if they do happen to have a serious medical illness, it is more likely to get missed.

Studies have demonstrated that disliked patients are more likely to have an undiagnosed organic brain syndrome than more likable patients; sadly, disliked patients often get the most cursory and incomplete physical evaluation. Patients who are most different from their physicians are probably more likely to have a medical illness missed, and this is especially true of psychiatric patients.

3. *Be alert for presentations that make medical illness more likely*–but do not stop considering medical illness just because these are not present:

☐ A client over 40 with no previous psychiatric history
☐ No history of similar symptoms
☐ Coexistence of chronic disease
☐ A history of head injury
☐ A client who gets worse when given antipsychotic or anxiolytic medications

4. *Look for symptoms that make medical illness more likely:*

☐ A change in headache pattern
☐ Visual disturbances (e.g., double vision or partial visual loss)
☐ Speech deficits, either dysarthrias (problems with the mechanical production of speech sounds) or aphasias (difficulty with word comprehension or word usage)
☐ Abnormal autonomic signs (e.g., blood pressure, pulse, temperature)
☐ Disorientation or memory impairment
☐ Fluctuating or impaired level of consciousness
☐ Abnormal body movements
☐ Frequent urination, increased thirst (possible symptoms of diabetes)
☐ significant weight change, gain or loss

5. *Do not assume that a certain symptom must be of psychological origin.* For example, it used to be thought that male impotence was almost always a psychological problem. A recent study of 105 impotent men reported that 75% had impotency based either on a medical illness (such as diabetes

mellitus), or on drug use that was likely to cause impotence. Of 34 men with hormonal problems who accepted medical treatment, 33 had a return of sexual function; 14 of these men had previously undergone psychotherapy for this same problem.

Be Holistic

A psychiatric assessment should include the whole person, including the medical history and physiology of that person. This information is needed to rule out a medical illness but also so that you can understand the person's current feelings and functioning within the context of what has happened to the person in the past and what is happening now. Medical and psychological issues cannot be divorced from one another. Physical symptoms—be it pain, tiredness, shortness of breath, or anything else—will impact a person's psychological and social functioning, just as a person's psychology and social supports can have a large influence on the course and treatment of medical illness. Being holistic means considering all aspects of the client: medical, psychological, and social. It is not the psychotherapist's responsibility to conduct a physical exam or prescribe medical treatment. It *is* the psychotherapist's responsibility to be aware of these issues and, when appropriate, communicate with the treating physicians to ensure that all aspects of the client are being addressed in an integrated treatment approach. Psychotherapists may also have information that would be very useful to the treating physician. For example, complaints of growing fatigue out of keeping with a client's normal psychology and not connected to a depression could be the earliest sign of a medical illness. Subtle changes in a client's ability to function may be more apparent to the therapist than to anyone else. A client's fears, especially if they are new or different, can be a sign that something in the person's body is not working quite right and can be explored with attention to physical as well as psychological causes. Although therapists are not responsible for conducting a physical exam, they should have a general sense of a client's medical history and may even find it useful to review medical reports of significant events.

Much of the information that you need to suspect a medical illness is readily available as part of a psychiatric assessment. It is important to know how to organize this information so that it is useful and to fill in gaps in your information so that important areas are not missed. (Note that a comprehensive psychiatric evaluation would include additional areas such as personal developmental history and current social support system, in addition to the assessment areas discussed below.) The domains noted below identify important areas that should be included within a comprehensive history and assessment. Ideally, specific parts of this information will be gathered by designated members of the treatment team as part of a multi-disciplinary history and assessment process. Unfortunately, not every client or every treatment setting has such a comprehensive multidisciplinary team available. Again, our goal is not to suggest that a therapist should become an expert in medical illness or, in essence, conduct a medical exam. It is to suggest that a therapist should be concerned about the presence of unsuspected medical disorders and should be aware of the interaction of medical and psychological problems when they coexist.

Symptoms

- Start with a clear description of all of the client's symptoms: How did they begin? How long has he or she had them? How have the symptoms progressed?
- Include a careful review of other "extraneous" symptoms the client may have, starting at the top with questions about headache and dizziness and ending at the bottom with questions about leg sores and trouble walking. This review of systems is an extremely important part of a medical assessment.

History

- Include history of similar problems in the past.
- Take a history of past medical problems, including all medical hospitalizations and surgeries.
- Take a family history, both medical and psychiatric.

Current Medical Status

- Ask about all current medical illnesses.
- Ask about all current medications (include specific questions about vitamins, herbal supplements, birth control, over-the-counter medicines).
- Ask about any head injury, coma, periods of unconsciousness, seizures.
- Obtain name of person's physician, date of last contact, and purpose of last contact.

Current Habits

- Ask about drug use, starting with questions about tobacco, caffeine, and alcohol and proceeding on to questions about other drugs.
- Ask about exercise activity patterns and sleep patterns.

Observation

The assessment starts when you first meet the client, not when you first sit down to begin talking in your office.

- *General appearance:* How does the person look? How is he or she dressed? Does he or she appear ill? Then go to more specific observations.
- *Skin:* Is it very dry or abnormally colored? Extremely pale skin or lips may suggest anemia; a yellow skin may indicate jaundice and liver disease; dry skin and hair may be a sign of hypothyroidism.
- *Eyes:* Are they focused? Are the pupils equal? Are they aligned with each other? Differences in pupil size may

indicate brain masses such as tumors. Wildly dilated pupils may indicate a variety of drugs, including hallucinogens, stimulants, and anticholinergics. Constricted pupils may indicate opiates. Bulging eyes can be a sign of hyperthyroidism.

- *Body movement*: Rule out weakness, clumsiness, ataxia, facial asymmetry, asymmetry of movements, choreiform movements ("worm-like" or other involuntary movements, usually occurring less than two times/second), tremors; observe for other neurological abnormalities such as motor stereotypy (repetitive stereotyped movements).
- *Gait disturbance*: Rule out a very common finding in a wide range of medical conditions. Dubin (1983) studied 1,140 patients cleared medically on a psychiatric service.
  - ✓ 38 subsequently were found to have a medical illness.
  - ✓ 14 of the 38 had either gait disturbance, weight loss, hypertension, abnormal vital signs, or significant medical history.

Mental Status Examination

Consider the following areas/factors when evaluating mental status:

- Appearance
- Degree of cooperation
- Presence of perceptual distortions (hallucinations and illusions)
- Mood (both appropriateness and quality)
- Speech (both quality and content)
- Motor activity
- General cognitive abilities
  - ✓ attention
  - ✓ memory
  - ✓ judgment
  - ✓ fund of knowledge

- Also consider evidence of specific neurological deficits (each of these can occur with varying degrees of severity):
  - ✓ *Aphasias* (difficulties with speech) can be broken down into
    - Word finding difficulties (nominal aphasias)
    - Difficulty understanding speech (receptive aphasias)
    - Difficulty producing speech (expressive aphasia)
  - ✓ *agnosias* (difficulties recognizing complex shapes)
  - ✓ *apraxias* (difficulties executing proper manipulation of objects)
  - ✓ *perseveration* (inability to switch tasks or mental sets)

Physical Exam

A full physical examination is generally conducted only by a physician or physician's assistants or advance practice nurses. Some parts of a medical assessment may be done by nurses or even by nonmedical staff if they are appropriately trained and the policies of the agencies allow.

- Blood pressure, preferably both lying down and standing (or you can ask a client about any recent blood pressure checks, or ask him or her to take a blood pressure test at one of the blood pressure machines that seem to be in every bank and drugstore and an increasing number of mental health centers)
- Pulse, for evaluation of rate and arrhythmias (irregularities of heart rhythm)
- Check eyes to see if they move equally and fully in all directions, equal and reactive pupils, and eliminate nystagmus (small "jerky" movements of eyes when client looks up or to the side)
- Assessment of the condition of the client's skin, looking for such things as dryness, dehydration, nutritional status, rashes, edema (swelling, typically of legs and feet),

petechiae (small bruises that can look like a rash and suggest abnormal bleeding)

A useful screen for picking up physical disease in psychiatric clients includes (adapted from Sox et al., 1989):

- Laboratory tests: TSH (thyroid test), CBC (complete blood count), SGOT (liver function test), fasting glucose (or random glucose if fasting not possible; screen for diabetes), serum albumin, serum calcium, vitamin B12, and urinalysis
- History of epilepsy, emphysema, asthma, diabetes, thyroid disease, high blood pressure, blood or pus in the urine
- HIV positive or history of high-risk behavior for HIV
- Symptoms of chest pain while at rest, headaches associated with vomiting, or loss of control of urine or stool
- Physical findings of high blood pressure

Develop a Differential Diagnosis

As a way of organizing your information about the client and focusing your attention, develop a system that systematically considers possible medical illnesses. Consider all of the medical illness that could fit the set of symptoms. What further information would help distinguish between these various possibilities?

The goal is not to come up with a specific diagnosis but to organize the data that have been collected about the client so that the treatment team can decide what to do next, how at risk the client might be, and when and how and what to say to the consulting physician if the team decides further medical assessment is necessary.

The basic mental health assessment must, of course, be supplemented with appropriate medical consultation, which will include a complete physical examination and appropriate laboratory tests, but this physical component should be focused by the differential diagnosis. *Both you and the doctor are more likely to find a medical problem if you are looking for something specific than if you are groping randomly.* For example:

- with mental status changes occurring over days to weeks, together with alcoholism or chronic headache, consider subdural hematoma (slow bleed inside the skull under the dura membrane that covers the brain).
- with depression along with weight gain, ask about cold intolerance and dry skin and consider hypothyroidism.

Laboratory and other diagnostic tests should be used to pursue specific parts of the differential diagnosis list. Diagnostic tests are much more likely to give useful results when the treatment team and the consulting physician are clear what question is being asked and what specific test is needed to answer that specific question. For example:

- EEG detects abnormal brain function.
- CAT and MRI scans detects abnormal anatomy.

If you are asking for a drug screen to find out if the client has recently used an illicit drug, find out if your laboratory can measure the drug or drugs that you expect this person might be using, and whether blood or urine tests would be better, depending on the particular drug and time since ingestion. Most labs can test for the presence of cocaine, but LSD is used in much smaller amounts and may not be detectable even if recently used. Common screens for benzodiazepines often do not detect clonazepam, a very commonly used benzodiazepine. These kinds of question can usually be answered by talking with medical members of your treatment team or by making a call to the chemistry lab of the local hospital. However, such conversations require that you step out of your typical nonmedical role and interact with a strange and often complex medical system.

Work with, and Actively Involve, the Consulting Physician

It may be preferable for medical members of the psychiatric treatment team to interface with medical health care providers. The nursing member of the psychiatric treatment team may be better equipped than the nonmedical therapist to talk with a community physician or to facilitate and coordinate treatment needs and diagnostic assessments. Often, however, depending on the skills and inclination of both therapist and physician, a direct communication between the primary treating physician and the therapist who knows the client best may be a very useful and efficient way to integrate the client's medical and mental health care. The therapist may have information useful to the physician that no one else on the treatment team knows, and may be able to explain issues to the client more effectively than anyone else.

Consultation between a therapist and physician will mean different things to different doctors and in different clinical situations. If asking for a medical assessment or consultation, it is very useful to make the request as clear as possible. What observations by the therapist or complaints from the client prompted the request for medical assessment? What kind of answer do you want back from the doctor? Are you hoping for a diagnosis so you know if there is a medical problem, a prognosis so you know how bad that problem could become, or information about the client's medical treatment? What are you most worried about? What information do you already have about the client? You might think that your job is only to get the client to see the doctor, and the rest is up to the doctor. This is true—and not true. The doctor will typically spend less than 15 minutes with the patient to collect a history, do the physical, order the tests, and write a note in the chart.

If the client is less than articulate, important information is likely to get lost. This is a particular problem with older clients, those who are hard of hearing or who have other communication problems, or those who are less organized or less clear in their thinking. It is also a problem when the symptoms you want evaluated are vague, or your concerns leading to the referral do not relate to a particular medical symptom. Your job must include organizing the information that your team has collected and transmitting it to the doctor in such a way as to do your client the most good.

Telling the client to see his local doctor or phoning the local internist with a request to "please do a physical exam on this client" is much less likely to lead to a useful and informative consultation result than a more specific request: "This client has a depression that seems very atypical. Could you please see if there could be a medical illness involved?" Or even better yet: "This patient is complaining of depression with decreased energy level, but he is also complaining of increased weight, cold intolerance, decreased libido, and extremely dry skin. He was treated for hyperthyroidism 15 years ago. Could you see if thyroid problems or any other medical problems might be increasing his depression?"

When possible, it is generally wise to get input from the medical members of the treatment team in formulating the question that will be asked of the consulting physician. Most of the time the treatment team will not be able to frame a consult request with as much detail as this last example—but in all cases, the more detail, the better. Often, the referral to the physician is based on a pattern that suggests a higher probability of medical illness, rather than any particular symptom suggesting a particular illness. For example, any client who initially develops psychiatric symptoms over the age of 40 should have a medical workup. If this is the reason the team is referring the client, then the physician needs to have that information.

Finally, as noted previously, there are differences of communication styles between mental health professionals and physicians. The social worker or psychologist is likely to want to give the physician a complete description of the client and the problem in a phone discussion that may go on for many minutes. The physician is likely to be in the middle of office hours, with a clinic full of patients waiting to be seen. A brief, succinct, and very focused description and problem statement with a focused consultation request is likely to be better received by a physician than the more complete communication often expected between mental health therapists.

Finally, a brief note about common errors that lead to missed diagnosis:

- Mistaking symptoms for their causes: a person may be tired and short of breath because he has an underlying medical illness, and not just because he stays in his apartment and gets no exercise.
- Listening without fully considering all possibilities: it may be assumed that a person's rapid weight loss is connected to their increased psychosis and poor self-care, rather than considering medical problems that can also lead to weight loss
- Equating psychosis with schizophrenia: confusion of delirium can easily be mistaken for psychosis. Some medical illness and some medications can cause a cause psychotic symptoms.
- Relying on a single information source: a person may minimize or even dismiss pain, weight loss, or other functional impairments that have been very obvious to those around him or her.

Psychosis: Clients who Appear Out of Touch with Reality

Consider Organic Disease

If you do not look for it, you will not find it. As noted in the previous section on general approaches, be suspicious of "medical clearance."

1. Symptoms that suggest the possibility of organic disease include:
   ☐ hallucinations that are visual and vivid in color and that change rapidly.
   ☐ olfactory (smell) hallucinations.
   ☐ illusions: misinterpretations of stimuli.
   ☐ large recent weight changes.

2. A brief, minimal neurological exam can be easily and rapidly done, even on very agitated clients (this exam may be conducted by a psychiatrist, nurse, or other qualified member of the treatment team).
   • Observe gait and body movement to rule out weakness, paralysis, ataxia, and other gait disturbances and choreoathetoid movements (slower, "writhing" movements).
   • Check eyes:
     ✓ Make sure pupils are equal and reactive to light.
     ✓ Check to see if eyes move fully in all directions.
     ✓ Check for vertical and horizontal nystagmus (rapid, jerky movements of the eyes, can be either up and down [vertical] or back and forth [horizontal]). It is most easily seen if the client is asked to look up or over to the side as far as possible. Nystagmus is frequently present with drug intoxications, and vertical nystagmus is never a normal finding in functional psychosis.
   • Observe face for asymmetries.
   • Observe speech for slurring, aphasias, word-finding difficulties, and perseveration.
   The above observations are possible on a completely uncooperative client. Summers et al. have outlined a very rapid physical exam for screening purposes (see Bibliography).

3. Consider medical emergencies that can present as psychiatric illness:
   • *Hypoglycemia* (low blood sugar): Symptoms can be variable and include delirium or coma. Less serious

symptoms include palpitations, sweating, anxiety, tremor, vomiting. If in doubt, give candy or orange juice sweetened with sugar. In an emergency room, give 50 cc of 50% dextrose for both treatment and diagnosis.

- *Diabetic ketosis or nonketotic hyperosmolarity* (blood sugar so high that it upsets body chemistry): Delirium with history of diabetes, increased breathing, sweet smell of acetone on breath (can be mistaken for smell of alcohol), dehydration, decreased blood pressure.
- *Wernicke–Korsakoff syndrome:* Acute thiamine (vitamin B6) deficiency so severe that it can cause rapid brain damage. Usually found in people with alcoholism. Symptoms include nystagmus (rapid, small jerking movements of eyes), evidence of peripheral neuropathy, ocular palsies (inability to move both eyes together in all directions), and cerebellar ataxia (person moves as if drunk). If in any doubt, give thiamine 100 mg IM. This is not diagnostic but will prevent any further brain damage.
- *DTs* (delirium tremens): Drug withdrawal from alcohol or other sedative hypnotics; frequently missed and can be medically very serious. Symptoms include elevated autonomic signs, agitation, visual and tactile hallucinations: Onset is usually 3–4 days after reduction or discontinuation of alcohol.
- *Hypoxia* (low blood oxygen): From pneumonia, heart attack, COPD (chronic obstructive pulmonary disease), arrhythmias (abnormal heart rhythm).
- *Meningitis* (infection of the covering of the brain): Be alert for stiff neck and fever.
- *Subarachnoid hemorrhage* (rapid arterial bleeding into the brain): Stiff neck, fluctuating consciousness, and headache. A spinal tap for diagnosis needs to be done immediately.

- *Subdural hematoma* (bleeding from veins under the outside covering of the brain, which compresses the brain over hours to weeks or even longer): Symptoms are variable but frequently (not always) there is a history of head trauma.
- *Anticholinergic (atropine) poisoning:* From overdose of tricyclics or over-the-counter drugs or from organophosphate insecticides. Classic symptoms include:
  - ✓ Flushing ("red as a beet")
  - ✓ Dry mouth ("dry as a bone")
  - ✓ Dilated pupils ("blind as a bat")
  - ✓ Delirious ("mad as a hatter")
  - ✓ Increased pulse and sometimes elevated blood pressure
  - ✓ Most fatalities are from cardiac arrhythmias, although seizures are not uncommon.

Differentiate Psychosis from Delirium

Psychosis refers to an impairment in reality testing because of hallucinations, delusions, or grossly disorganized thinking. Psychosis can be caused by organic diseases, for which we know the cause, or by a variety of mental illnesses ranging from a brief reactive psychosis to schizophrenia, major depression, and bipolar disorder.

Delirium refers to an acute organic brain syndrome causing a global cognitive impairment, with disorientation, memory impairment, and disturbance of consciousness. Illnesses causing deliriums are often life threatening, and a delirium should be considered a medical emergency. Symptoms of delirium include:

- disorientation or memory impairment.
- fluctuating or impaired level of consciousness, decreased awareness of environment.
- labile affect.
- impaired judgment or insight.

- abnormal autonomic signs (changes in blood pressure, pulse, temperature, abnormal sweating, flushing).

Medical Illnesses That May Presents as Psychosis

Progressive Neurological Diseases

- *Multiple sclerosis*: No typical signs or symptoms. The disease may begin very suddenly and affect any part of the neurological system. Early in its course, diagnosis may be extremely difficult.
- *Huntington's chorea*: Hereditary illness that includes movement disorder but can present with psychosis initially.
- *Alzheimer's disease and Pick's disease*: Progressive diseases that cause dementia, but can initially present in a wide variety of ways. Alzheimer's causes diffuse dementia, with prominent memory impairment; while Pick's primarily causes early personality changes, loss of judgment and socially inappropriate behavior, without significant memory problems.

Central Nervous System Infections

- *Encephalitis* (viral infection of the brain): Usually presents with fever and seizures, but various mental symptoms, including confusion, lethargy, catatonia, or psychosis, may present before any clear-cut neurological symptoms. The person usually shows a fluctuating mental status. Most cases of viral encephalitis clear without any lasting problems, but some viruses are more damaging than others, and some people can be left with permanent neurological problems.
- *Neurosyphilis* (syphilis of the central nervous system).
- *HIV infections*: HIV encephalopathy commonly includes apathy, decreased spontaneity, and depression and may present before any other signs of AIDS are present. AIDS can also present first as delirium with paranoia and other prominent psychotic features.

Space-Occupying Lesions within the Skull

- Brain tumors
- Bleeding within the skull
- Brain abscess

Metabolic Disorders

- Accumulation of *toxins* from severe liver or kidney disease
- Disturbances in *electrolytes* (either too low a serum level of sodium or too high a serum level of calcium)
- Acute intermittent *porphyria* (disease of porphyrin metabolism): Very rare, but may present as classical psychosis. Often includes abdominal pain or other gastrointestinal symptoms such as vomiting.
- *Wilson's disease*: Abnormality of copper metabolism that causes damage to brain and liver if untreated.
- *Systemic lupus erythematosis* (autoimmune disease): Usually a slowly progressive illness with joint and muscle pain, but it can present very suddenly. The nervous system is commonly involved, and the disease can present with depression, dyscontrol syndromes (unexpected impulsive or aggressive behavior), or psychosis.

Endocrine Disorders

- *Myxedema* (underactive thyroid gland; hypothyroidism)
- *Cushing's syndrome* (too much cortisol caused by overactive adrenal gland or overactive pituitary gland)
- *Hypoglycemia*, either from insulin-secreting tumor or administration of insulin

Deficiency States

- *Thiamine deficiency*: Wernicke–Korsakoff's amnestic syndrome

- *Pellegra* (nicotinic acid deficiency) and other B-complex deficiencies
- *Zinc deficiency*

Temporal Lobe Epilepsy (or partial complex seizure disorder)

- can begin at any age
- can be secondary to head injury or meningitis
- often the cause is unknown

Drugs

- Prescription
  - ✓ L-dopa
  - ✓ Amphetamines
- Illicit drugs
  - ✓ Cocaine, crack, methamphetamines, stimulants
  - ✓ Hallucinogens

Not All Psychosis is Schizophrenia

Consider other mental illness in addition to schizophrenia. Do not over diagnose. Without a history, it is impossible to distinguish an acute psychotic episode that will rapidly resolve from an exacerbation of schizophrenic illness that will continue to be an ongoing problem.

Anxiety

Think about the Phenomenology of Anxiety

1. *Psychological manifestations:* Inner feelings of terror, tension, apprehension, dread, derealization, depersonalizations; fear of impending insanity
2. *Intellectual disturbances:* Decreased concentration, disorganized thinking, sensory flooding

3. *Somatic manifestations:* Autonomic or visceral symptoms, including palpitations, chest pain, tachycardia, fatigue, weakness, perspiration, flushing, numbness, tingling of extremities, vertigo, shortness of breath, headache, blurred vision, tinnitus, diarrhea, tremor, fainting

Differential Diagnosis of Anxiety

Primary Anxiety Disorders

- Panic disorder with or without agoraphobia
- Social phobia and other simple phobias
- Obsessive–compulsive disorder
- Posttraumatic stress disorder
- Generalized anxiety disorder
- Adjustment disorder with anxious mood
- Depression may be a secondary feature

Other Mental Illness That Can Present as Anxiety

- Psychosis
- Agitated depression
- Bipolar disorder (depressed phase)

Hyperventilation Syndrome

- an acute anxiety attack that begins with shortness of breath
- can include chest pain, nausea, tingling, or dizziness
- always associated with rapid breathing and pulse

Medical Illness Presenting with Anxiety

Strongly suspect medical cause for anxiety in clients younger than 18 or older than 35 who suddenly develop anxiety that disrupts their normal activity and who have an otherwise negative psychiatric history (Hall, 1980).

Anxiety Secondary to Organic Brain Syndromes

- Apt to have a labile mood.
- Confusion that may be confused with psychosis.
- Mental status exam should demonstrate cognitive deficits, especially memory deficits.
  - ✓ Delirium
  - ✓ Dementia

Other Neurological Illnesses

- 25% of medical causes of anxiety symptoms are other neurological illnesses.
- *Cerebral vascular insufficiency:* Transient ischemi attacks lasting from 10 to 15 seconds up to an hour (brief blocks in the arteries to the brain causing temporary loss of brain blood supply)
- *Anxiety states* and *personality change* following head injury
- *Infections of the central nervous system*
  - ✓ Meningitis: Fever, stiff neck, and delirium
  - ✓ Neurosyphilis: May present as almost anything
- *Degenerative disorders*
  - ✓ Alzheimer's dementia
  - ✓ Multiple sclerosis: May be marked early on by vague and changing medical complaints
  - ✓ Huntington's chorea: May present early on as anxiety or other functional disorder before the movement disorder is evident; always has a positive family history
- *Toxic disorders*
  - ✓ Lead intoxication: From old paint or ingesting lead objects
  - ✓ Mercury intoxication: From contaminated fish
  - ✓ Manganese intoxication: From industrial exposure
  - ✓ Organophosphate insecticides (similar to nerve gas): From chemical or insecticide exposure
- *Partial complex seizures*
  - ✓ can begin at any age

✓ often do not have any motor component, and therefore may not seem to be a seizure

✓ can present with confusion, hallucinations, or odd behavior.

✓ at times are accompanied by autonomisms, repetitive meaningless activity such as picking at clothes

Endocrine Disorders

- Twenty-five percent of medical causes of anxiety symptoms are endocrine disorders.

- *Hyperthyroidism* (increased thyroid hormone): Commonly presents as anxiety, but may present as depression and is one of the most common endocrine abnormalities. Most common in 20- to 40-year-old women. The anxiety of hyperthyroidism may present with manic-like euphoria or agitation, along with weight loss, heat intolerance, rapid pulse, fine-intention tremor, and often exophthalmoses (bulging of the eyes caused by abnormal deposition of fat behind the eyeball).

- *Adrenal hyperfunction or Cushing's syndrome*: Has a variety of causes, including tumors of the pituitary or adrenal glands or steroids given to treat other illnesses. There is often a change in fat distribution, with dorsal (back) hump, round face, thin arms and legs, hirsutism (abnormal hairiness), acne, decreased menstruation in women and impotency in men.

- *Hypoglycemia* (decreased blood glucose): Usually associated with a history of diabetes and insulin or other hypoglycemic medications; rarely due to an insulin-secreting tumor. Hypoglycemia as a response to dietary carbohydrate challenge is probably overdiagnosed, and associated symptoms may not always be due to changes in blood glucose.

- *Hypoparathyroidism* (decreased parathyroid hormone): Almost always associated with a history of thyroid surgery; it often presents with overwhelming anxiety, either with or without personality change.

- *Menopausal and premenstrual syndromes*:
- change in anxiety, irritability, or mood that regularly occurs right before the beginning of a woman's menses, or similar changes associated with the onset of menopause

Cardiopulmonary Disorders

- Often present with shortness of breath, rapid breathing, complaints of chest pain, chest pain that is worse with exertion.
- Types of disorders:
  - ✓ Angina
  - ✓ Pulmonary embolus
  - ✓ Arrhythmias (irregularities of heart beat)
  - ✓ Chronic obstructive pulmonary disease (COPD)
  - ✓ Mitral valve prolapse (generally harmless)

Medications as a Cause of Anxiety

Take a careful and detailed history:

- ask about all drugs that a client is taking, licit and illicit, prescribed and over the counter. All of the medication mentioned below can cause symptoms of anxiety.
- ask about all illnesses that a client has had.
- clients with asthma take combinations of sympathomimetics and xanthines (aminophylline, theophylline).
- clients with allergies may take ephedrine.
- clients with diabetes may be hypoglycemic from their insulin.
- thyroid preparations may be prescribed for thyroid illness, following thyroid surgery (from years ago), or even for weight loss.

Nonpsychotropic Medications

- Sympathomimetics (often found in nonprescription cold and allergy medications): epinephrine, norephinephrine, isoproteronol, levodopa, dopamine hydrochloride, dobuta-mine, terbutaline sulfate, ephedrine, pseudo-ephedrine

- Xanthine derivatives (asthma medications, coffee, colas, over-the-counter pain remedies): aminophylline, theophyl-line, caffeine
- Anti-inflammatory agents: indomethacin
- Thyroid preparations
- Insulin (via hypoglycemic reaction)
- Corticosteroids
- Others: nicotine, ginseng root, monosodium glutamate
- Drug withdrawal: caffeine, nicotine

Psychotropic Medications

- Antidepressants (including MAO-inhibitors), drugs for treat-ment of attention-deficit disorders (on rare occasions cause anxiety-type syndromes)
- Tranquilizing drugs: benzodiazepines (paradoxical response most common in children and in elderly), antipsychotics (akathisia may present as anxiety)
- Anticholinergic medications can cause a delirium which, in early stages, may easily be confused with anxiety: sco-polamine and sedating antihistamines (found in over-the-counter sleep preparations) antiparkinsonian agents, tricyclic antidepressants, antipsychotics

Drugs—Licit and Illicit

- Caffeine—intoxication or withdrawal
- Nicotine—withdrawal even more than acute intoxication
- Stimulants—cocaine, amphetamines, etc.
- Alcohol or alcohol withdrawal

Drug Withdrawal Is a Common Cause of Anxiety-Type Syndromes

A large number of drugs can cause withdrawal states with symptoms of anxiety or even agitation. All sedative hypnotics, tricyclic antidepressants, and anticholinergics can cause withdrawal.

Depression

Differential Diagnosis: Psychiatric Illness

- Primary affective disorders
  - ✓ Major depression, either single episode or recurrent bipolar disorder
  - ✓ Dysthymia
  - ✓ Adjustment disorder with depressed mood
  - ✓ Bereavement
- Depression secondary to other functional disorders

Medical Illnesses That Can Present as Depression

- *Postviral depressive syndromes*: Especially influenza, infectious mononucleosis, viral hepatitis, viral pneumonia, and viral encephalitis
- *Cancer*
  - ✓ Cancer of the pancreas
  - ✓ Lung cancer, especially oat-cell carcinoma
  - ✓ Brain tumors, either primary tumors or metastastic
- *Cardiopulmonary disease with hypoxia* (decreased oxygen in the blood): Acute hypoxia often leads to symptoms resembling anxiety or panic. Chronic hypoxia may present with lassitude, apathy, psychomotor retardation, and other symptoms confused with depression.
- *Sleep apnea*: Should be suspected in a client with sleep disturbance and daytime somnolence.
- *Endocrine disease*
  - ✓ Hypothyroidism (underactive thyroid): Causes a general slowing of all body functions. Client complains of fatigue, weight gain, constipation, and, when asked, will describe cold intolerance, dry skin and hair, and hoarseness or deepening of the voice. Often very insidious but easily diagnosed and treated once suspected.

✓ Hyperthyroidism or thyrotoxicosis (overactive thyroid): Usually associated with anxiety but may present as depression, especially in the elderly, who may have few classical signs of thyroid disease.

✓ Adrenal hypofunction (Addison's disease): Often presents with weakness and fatigue, along with low blood pressure and hyponatremia (low serum sodium) and hyperkalemia (increased serum potassium).

✓ Adrenal hyperfunction (Cushing's disease): Either from steroid medication, pituitary, adrenal, or other ACTH-secreting tumors. Various affective disturbances, either depression or mania, are common. Syndrome is marked by truncal obesity, hypertension, puffy face, and hirsutism.

✓ Hyperparathyroidism: Usually from small tumors of the parathyroid glands. Early symptoms develop insidiously and can include lassitude, anorexia, weakness, constipation, and depressed mood. The classic symptoms of bone pain and renal colic often develop only years later.

✓ Postpartum, postmenopausal, and premenstrual syndromes

• *Collagen–vascular diseases*: A strange set of different diseases where in the person essentially becomes allergic to parts of his or her own body; can affect all parts of the body and can, at times, cause death. Systemic lupus erythematosus (SLE) is most often seen in women 13–40 years old. It often presents initially with nonspecific symptoms such as fatigue, malaise, anorexia, and weight loss, all of which can lead to the diagnosis of functional depression.

• *Central nervous system disease*

✓ Multiple sclerosis

✓ Brain tumors and other intracranial masses (masses inside of the skull) such as subdural hematomas (bleeding under the dural sack that surrounds the brain): Masses, especially in the frontal and temporal areas, can grow for years and cause psychiatric symptoms before any focal neurological abnormality is apparent.

✓ Complex partial seizures: Ictal-repetitive behaviors during the seizure, interictal-personality changes between seizures, increased lability of emotions, quick to anger, increased preoccupation with religion, hypergraphia (increased writing).

✓ Strokes, especially effecting left side of brain (right side of body).

Medications That May Cause Depression

Katerndahl (1981) found that 43% of patients diagnosed as depressed in a family practice clinic were taking medications that could cause depression.

- *Interferon* (for treatment of hepatitis C infections)
- *Antihypertensive medications* (used to control high blood pressure): Reserpine and alpha-methyldopa are probably the worst, but propranolol has been implicated, and all antihypertensives are suspect.
- *Digitalis preparations*, along with a variety of other cardiac medications
- *Cimetidine* (used for gastric ulcer disease)
- *Indomethacin* and other nonsteroidal anti-inflammatory medications (NSAIDS)
- *Disulfuram* (Antabuse): Usually described by clients as more a sense of fatigue than true depression.
- *Antipsychotic medications*: Can cause akinesia or inhibition of spontaneity that can both feel and look like a true depression. Even though this can still occur with the newer atypical antipsychotic medications, it is much less common than with the older antipsychotic medications.

- *Anxiolytics*: All sedative hypnotics, from the barbiturates to the benzodiazepines, have been implicated in causing depression and making it worse in susceptible individuals.
- *Steroids*, including prednisone and cortisone

Drugs of Abuse That May Cause Depression

- *Alcohol*: Very commonly a cause of depression, as well as a reaction to depression.
- *Stimulant withdrawal*: Depression is not a problem during the period of active use, but follows withdrawal from the drug. This depression associated with the post-stimulant-abuse period can last several months or longer.

CHAPTER SEVEN

Working with Primary Care Physicians

For clients whose main problem is anxiety or depression, a primary care physician often plays a critically important role in their overall mental health treatment. Primary care physicians often prescribe psychiatric medication, especially for clients whose primary problem is anxiety or depression. Many medical illnesses can cause what appears to be a psychiatric illness or make a preexisting psychiatric problem worse. For example, thyroid problems can cause or exacerbate anxiety, mania, or depression. Certain cancers can initially present as depression. A number of medical disorders can cause a person to become psychotic. Medical illness is much more common in clients with serious mental illness than in the general population. People with serious mental illness have a shorter life expectancy than the general population and have an increased risk of dying from cancer, heart disease, and virtually everything else. Diabetes and metabolic syndrome, in particular, are growing problems in all parts of the population, but especially among people with mental illness.

Just as serious psychiatric disorder is associated with an increased risk of having a serious medical illness, psychiatric disorder can also complicate the treatment of medical illnesses. Diabetes is difficult for anyone to manage well. If a person also has a significant depression, bipolar disorder, or schizophrenia, it can make this management much more difficult. The therapist often has information about the client's behavior or complaints of physical problems that can assist the medical assessment. The therapist is also in a position to reinforce the importance of following through with medical treatment, and can help the client to better cope with the stress and problems caused by medical illness. If the client has a psychiatric treatment team that includes a nurse (LPN or RN), then these functions may be best fulfilled by the nurse rather than the therapist. However, many mental health programs have relatively few, if any, nurses. In such instances, it is important for the therapist's role to include working with primary care providers. This chapter addresses issues surrounding the therapist's role in working with primary health care providers and assumes that no psychiatric nurse is available to serve these functions.

Collaboration between the primary care physician, the therapist, and the psychiatrist can make treatment for both the psychiatric problem and the medical problem much more effective. Unfortunately, although both mental health clinicians and primary care physicians would acknowledge the importance of such collaboration, it rarely happens.

Social Barriers to Collaboration

Primary care physicians and nonmedical mental health clinicians live in different worlds. They rarely know each other well, rarely have occasions to informally "chat" with each other or have other informal contacts, and are often awkward with each other. Primary care physicians rarely call mental health therapists, and therapists rarely call primary care physicians. Each knows they should be in contact with the other, but in reality this contact rarely occurs. There is an emotional hurdle that must be overcome for either therapist or physician to call the other. This is very different from the energy required for a therapist to call another therapist, or for a physician to call another physician.

There are many reasons for this gulf. If the therapist attempts to call a physician, he or she is immediately fed through a phone tree of decision points that are designed to provide rapid access for other physicians and various levels of screening for a call from a patient. The therapist calls the physician's office and is asked if he or she is a patient or a doctor. Neither answer seems to fit. The call is forwarded from the receptionist to the nurse, put on hold, and finally reaches a physician who is scheduled to see a new patient every 12 minutes and is now returning the call while three other patients are waiting. The therapist immediately picks up the need for speed and realizes the impossibility of a useful conversation, and the reason for the phone call becomes unclear and confused.

If the physician attempts to call the therapist, he or she is often calling into a clinic, and has only a vague idea about the nature of the clinic or the name of the specific treatment program. Often the phone is answered by someone from "Yahara House" or "Gateway Recovery" or some other clearly nonmedical name, and the physician may not even be sure if he or she is calling the correct place. The physician is told that the therapist is in session and will return the call, but there is rarely an immediate response or anyone to whom the physician can talk right away. By the time the call is returned, hours or even days later, the physician does not have the patient's chart readily available, making it hard to remember specific information or to write a note that would document the phone contact. When the call is returned, the physician is again responding in a few minutes taken between patient visits. On both sides, the call is to a clinic or organizational structure that seems alien and unclear.

Even the salutations used can cause awkwardness. When one physician calls another whom he or she does not know well, the introduction is typically framed by, "Hello, I am Dr. X calling about our mutual patient." The conversation then becomes much more informal, and physicians rarely continue to address each other as "Doctor" unless there is significant age or status difference between them that seems important to acknowledge. When a master's-credentialed social worker calls a physician, the initial greeting does not have the same accepted structure. The greeting "Hello, I am John Smith's therapist" does not immediately set the context for the shared responsibility and working relationship as would the call from another physician. It also continues to be unclear whether the therapist is supposed to continue to address the physician as "Doctor," acknowledging the status difference between them, or should take the risk of addressing the physician by first name. Should the physician respond formally by addressing the therapist as "Mr." or "Ms.," it is obvious that the therapist should continue to be formal in return. If, as is more common, the physician refers to the therapist by first name, the therapist has to choose between asserting status equality by use of first name back, or accepting the status difference between them by continuing to the use of "Doctor." Often both sides of this interchange will attempt to avoid the problem by not addressing the other by name. Although this strategy avoids the need to make a decision, it does not change the underlying power dynamics of what is taking place.

The issue of title is equally problematic if the therapist has a PhD or another doctoral level degree and uses the term "doctor" professionally. To some physicians, a "doctor" of psychology or social work is not a "real doctor," and they may bridle at the use of the term "doctor" to address someone who is not a physician. The psychologist or social worker who has legitimately earned the title of "doctor" may react strongly to any sense of condescension on the part of a consulting physician.

This issue of status and power and the use of honorific titles is so imposed by social roles and expectation that it is difficult for individuals to overcome them. The senior author of this book, Ron Diamond, regularly invites nonmedical clinicians with whom he works to call him by first name. Although many staff respond to this invitation, many others continue to call him "Doctor" or avoid calling him anything as a way of sidestepping the problem. On the other hand, some therapists, including the social worker coauthor of this book, Patricia Scheifler, choose to consistently refer to psychiatrist colleagues as "Doctor." Each psychiatrist responds in his or her own way. At the same time, senior, nonmedical therapists may have their own negative reaction if expected to refer to a physician of equal age and seniority by the term "Doctor." These issues become emotional barriers to easy communication and collaboration and are likely to influence the therapist's work with primary care physicians.

The question can be raised about why this discussion is directed to the therapist and not to the physician. In part, we address therapists because this book is much more likely to be read by therapists than by physicians. In part, it is because we believe that therapists are more likely to be flexible about communication styles than are primary care physicians. Ideally, each of the clinicians working with a client should take responsibility for communicating with the other clinicians working with the shared client. In reality, the therapist is much more likely to initiate such contact. When we teach physicians, we do stress what they need to do to communicate with therapists and what barriers may get in the way of such communication. This chapter is one half of what must be a two-way street.

How Different Professionals Judge and Demonstrate Competence

The potential disconnection between physicians and therapists is accentuated by our different training, the different ways that we assess professional competence, and the different structure to our jobs. For example, a physician may believe that a therapist is not competent, and the therapist in turn may question the competence of the physician. All of us have ways of judging the competence of the people with whom we work. Part of this judgment is based on personality style or preference, and part is influenced by what we know of the other person's experience, credentials, and recommendations from our colleagues. Those of us who are professionals are also trained or socialized to look for particular qualities that indicate competence within our own professional group.

How Therapists Demonstrate Competence

Many therapists demonstrate competence by demonstrating how well they know all aspects of their clients. Communication between therapists may take a significant amount of time, certainly 10 or 20 minutes, especially if a complicated, difficult decision needs to be made or if treatment needs to be coordinated. Communication around a complex problem often occurs in a meeting where time is specifically set aside to allow for a full discussion of the situation. Competence is judged by the richness with which the therapist knows the nuances of the client's life. The following summary is an example of a therapist's perspective of what constitutes a competent report.

Therapist's note:
John, now 32, has been married three times, but has had lifelong trouble with commitment. He has wandered through different relationships, different jobs, and different areas of the country. This pattern stemmed, probably, from the moves he experienced as a child, when his father was in the army and they moved frequently, never staying in the same place for more than 2 years. His father was the disciplinarian in the family, the classic sergeant, whereas his mother was sweet but a bit ineffectual. He grew up

primarily in the South, and living in the North has been a difficult adjustment for him. He thinks about moving back south, but realizes this is just one more move. He has been married to his third wife for 5 years, but he has also been having an affair that he does not think his wife knows about. He and his wife are fighting, and he gets depressed whenever he is home. She is actually very competent, but he treats her in some of the same critical ways as his father treated his mother. He realizes this but has trouble changing this pattern. He is also having a lot of trouble with his boss, who has, in reality, been very supportive of him until recently, when he started missing a lot of work. He would like to break this pattern of constantly moving around the country and moving from one relationship to another, but he is having a lot of difficulty.

He is now feeling depressed, has not wanted to eat, sleeps all the time, and sees his future as bleak. He is not drinking excessively and he is not really suicidal, but he seems very stuck in his depression and is considering alternatives for himself. He has been depressed on and off most of his life, but has never tried any prescribed medication for this. He is worried about what his wife and his parents will say if they find out he is taking medication. His father will attack him for being weak, his mother will be silent, and he is not sure about his wife but he expects that she will be supportive. He wants to give medications a try.

How Physicians Demonstrate Competence

Physicians, on the other hand, have been trained to judge competence by the ability to communicate, clearly and succinctly, all of the core elements needed to make a specific decision. Communication about clients typically occurs in the few minutes between client appointments, and time is at a premium. Extraneous information, not needed for the immediate decision, is perceived as a demonstration of disorganized thinking and lack of clarity. Ideally, all relevant information between physicians occurs in a single breath.

Physician's note:
John is a 32-year-old medically healthy man who has had episodes of recurrent depression his entire life. He has tried psychotherapy but has never had an antidepressant med trial. He has no personal or family history of mania, drinks very minimally, has suicidal ideation but no plan or intent, is currently anhedonic, hypersomnic, with poor appetite, poor concentration, and poor motivation. I think that a trial of antidepressant medication is indicated.

Impact of Communication Differences on Relationships

In a communication between therapist and physician, the therapist may think that the physician's succinct response suggests that he or she is cold, aloof, does not know the client very well, and does not even seem very interested in him or her. The physician is likely to believe that the therapist's much longer response indicates someone who is disorganized, cannot get to the point, and has trouble focusing on the question at hand. Each will come away with the sense that the other professional is not really competent, at least as judged within his or her own discipline. These cultural differences between disciplines make communication difficult and exacerbate differences that may really exist or that may only appear to exist.

These potential disagreements and differences between staff therapist and primary care physician can complicate the relationship between staff and client. If the therapist openly criticizes the physician to the client or even supports the client's own criticism of the physician, collusion can rapidly develop between different parts of the treatment team. This collusion can interfere with the relationship between client and physician, can make sharing of information between therapist and prescriber primary care physician even more difficult, and will certainly decrease collaborative decision making. On the other hand, if the therapist has the wisdom not to engage in such "splitting"—that is, if the client voices criticism of the physician that the therapist shares but is unwilling to voice—then the client may sense a lack of support and the relationship between client and therapist may suffer.

Different Areas of Interest

Both physician and therapist may think that they *should* be interested and involved in each other's area of practice, but one or both may have a sense of incompetence in the other's area or believe that they have little to add to what the other is doing. If a physician starts describing the problems that a mutual client is having with keeping his hemoglobin A1C within reasonable limits, or the concern about the client's rising creatinine clearance, the therapist may be uninvolved and unmotivated or, too incompetent to become involved. In reality, the hemoglobin A1C refers to the client's management of his or her diabetes, and the therapist can have a direct and important role in helping the client cope with the lifestyle management changes required to manage diabetes. The rising creatinine clearance refers to kidney function and may indicate a client who is facing either renal dialysis or a kidney transplant—medical interventions that have very significant psychological impact. If the physician does not help with this translation from medical to life concerns, and if the therapist does not inquire about the life meaning of these issues, important areas of collaboration can be missed.

The physician, too, may disregard or discount jargon and concerns that seem outside of the practice of medicine. A client's growing irritability, depression, marital discord, or sleep problems can all have medical causes or can influence how willing the client is to participate in medical treatment. Most people who kill themselves have seen their primary care physician in the month before their suicide, and in most cases the physician has not directly asked about suicidal ideation or plan.

Solutions and Suggestions for the Therapist

• *Become informed.* Make sure that you know the name of your client's physician, that you have signed release-of-information forms that have been sent to the physician's office, and that you understand the client's medical concerns. Be clear about what you know about the client's medical condition, and what you do not know. The client's medical illness and medical concerns are an important part of your holistic concern for the client.

• *Acknowledge that communication and collaboration with a client's primary care physician is both important and difficult.* There is good reason why contacting the primary care physician is more often thought of than actually done. Acknowledging the difficulty is often the first step in overcoming those difficulties.

• *Be clear about the purpose of the communication.* What do you most want the physician to know, or to what questions do you most want answers? Is this a call to introduce yourself and make sure that the physician knows you are available and how to contact you? Is this to inform the physician that the client is more incapacitated by pain but is unlikely to say this at the next medical visit? Is it to ask whether the client's chronic depression could have a medical cause, and whether there is any further medical workup that would focus on symptoms of chronic fatigue, poor sleep, and decreased concentration for a client who is obese and a chronic smoker? Has recent lab work revealed abnormal values that could be important and might suggest a need for further medical evaluation?

• *Focus on what decision or action you want the physician to take.* Is it to pursue a medical workup, or jointly encourage an exercise or activity program, or inform you of future appointments? Successful communications with physicians should, for the most part, be action oriented and focused on a specific plan or decision.

• *Be as specific as possible about the information you want to convey.* If the client complains of pain, do your best to figure out where the pain is, how often, when it occurs, and if it is associated with meals or with activity. If the client is going to see the doctor about dizziness, what can the therapist add about when it occurs, in what context, with what apparent severity. The more specific, the better. It is not helpful to ask for a "medical clearance." It is a bit better to ask if there are any medical problems that could be causing or worsening a client's depression. It is still better to note that the client feels tired much of the day, is cold all of the time, and complains of gaining weight.

Providing useful information is actually a complicated task. What may seem important to the therapist may not be considered relevant for the physician. The need to be succinct and focused has already been stressed. The issue is not to provide the information from the therapist's perspective, but rather to figure out what kind of information the physician needs to do a medical assessment. The therapist may not know all of the specific questions a physician might want to know, but the more medically focused the information, the better. One approach is to give more information about anything related to the specific symptom of concern, and relatively less information about the client's social or psychological background, unless it seems to directly affect the specific medical issue at hand.

• *Let the physician know how the therapist can improve the medical care of their shared client.* Often, physicians have little real sense of what a therapist does. Therapists can work on strategies to help clients eat healthier, exercise regularly, take medications regularly, and keep appointments more reliably. Once a physician understands how the therapist can help, he or she is much more likely to be open to the collaboration. For example:

> A client with both schizophrenia and a neurological condition required a medication that had to be administered in the physician's office, had to be prepared hours before the appointment, and had to be thrown away if the client did not show up for the appointment. After the physician had to throw out a number of vials of this very expensive medication because the client repeatedly failed to show up for appointments, he threatened to fire the client despite the impact on her neurological disorder. The therapist contacted the neurologist and guaranteed that if the schedule for future appointments involved the therapist, there would be no further missed appointments. The therapist worked with the client to ensure that no appointments were made until the client was really ready, and then the therapist made arrangements to pick the client up and take her to the appointments. This strategy was successful in allowing the client to complete treatment with no further missed appointments and completely changed both the neurologist's and the primary care physician's attitude about involving the therapist.

• *Practice getting the communication down to 2 minutes.* Practice this condensed style of communication with a colleague or friend. Pretend you are calling a busy physician who is answering the phone between patients. Time how long it takes you to say what you want to say. Now practice it again until you have cut out everything but the essentials. If the physician wants additional details, he or she can ask, but the initial exchange should be a couple of sentences lasting a couple of minutes. This will be much harder to do than it seems.

• *Acknowledge at least to yourself the issues of status and power that exist in our larger society and that will be present in your interaction when you collaborate with physicians.* This acknowledgment does not require that you like or agree or disagree with these issues. You may find them particularly annoying or of little concern. In either case, insofar as they influence your attitude and put up a barrier to communicating with a physician, work to ensure that they do not interfere with your collaborating with a physician if that is what your client requires.

• *Make the call.* As already discussed, it often seems awkward for a therapist to call a primary care doctor, and it is equally awkward for the physician to call the therapist or psychiatrist. Nevertheless, the client needs the therapist and prescriber and primary care physician to be in communication with each other. The potential awkwardness of the situation is real, but the call should be made anyway. It should also be followed up until the needed information is communicated.

Psychiatrists and Nurses as Cultural Translators

Mental health clinics, medical clinics, and other organizations each have their own culture. Most of us do not even realize the culture of the organization in which we work, unless we come from a discipline or perspective that makes us see the world in those terms. Medical clinics, of course, have a medical culture that doctors and nurses understand and have learned as part of their education. Many mental health clinics, especially community mental health centers, have a social work culture. In such agencies, most of the staff are social workers, most of the senior administration are social workers, and the expectations of how teams should work and how supervision should be provided are also part of this culture. If you are a social worker within a social work culture agency, this discussion will not even make sense. It is so assumed that it is hard to even consider how else things could be done. But if you are a social worker within a medical clinic, or a physician within a social work culture agency, then this sense of *clinic culture* will be very apparent.

An easy example is to think about the socialization learned as part of professional training. Although schools vary, some social work and psychology graduate schools organize groups of students who stay together for a semester or a year. Supervision is often group supervision. There is training on working within a group, learning how to work within a team, learning how to collaborate over periods of time with colleagues with whom one can become interdependent. Medical school is very different. In the clinical years, medical students rotate to a new rotation every 4 or 6 weeks. As soon as a student begins to have a sense of competence on a rotation, he or she changes to a new rotation. Each rotation brings a new group of fellow students, new faculty, and new supervisors. Medical students learn early how to immediately jump into a new situation and appear competent, no matter how they might think or feel. They learn to work as individuals, since there are no fixed teams or collegial relationships.

In graduate school significant supervision time is allocated to processing the richness of clinical experience. The clinical rotations in medical school and later in residency focus on clinical rounds, where each patient is discussed for a few minutes, the most relevant information is rapidly brought to bear in a rapid rendition of physical findings and lab values, a decision is made and the group moves on to discussing the next patient.

Social work and psychology training tends to stress working within teams, having scheduled time within the group for supervision and planning, taking time to process what is happening, thinking about the richness of the clinical situation, and coming to a decision after significant discussion. To some extent, process may be stressed more than the final decision. Medical training stresses the value of being an individual, includes very little training on how to work with a team, stresses the use of colleagues as a way of coming to a decision and involving someone else's expertise rather than as a way of sharing process. Little time is allocated to process, and the focus is on making immediate decisions by pulling together as much information as possible, as rapidly as possible.

This overview is, of course, something of a stereotype. Not all social workers, or psychologists, or physicians fit this mold equally well. Psychiatrists are clinicians who have gone through medical school but have then gone on to work in multidisciplinary settings, often involving extensive contact with social workers, and often as integrated members of teams. Nurses also have medical training, but also have training that stresses more collegial support and work within teams. Psychiatrists and nurses, with training and experience that have elements of both medicine and social work, can help other therapists figure out how to cross the cultural divide. At times, they can advise therapists about how to approach a physician more effectively. Sometimes very specific training, even including role-playing, can be useful. At times, these cultural translators can bridge the gap directly, making the call to the physician. Some physicians are very difficult for a nonphysician to approach. In some cases, it might be much easier for a psychiatric nurse or a psychiatrist working with the therapist to get through to the primary care physician. But the bottom line is: *Make the call.*

PART III

Psychoeducation and Client Workbook

CHAPTER EIGHT

Beyond Medication: Integrating Medication and Psychoeducation

The goals of treatment are to help the client get closer to his or her life goals and improve his or her quality of life. It is important to always keep these goals in mind. Decreasing symptoms, avoiding rehospitalization, and maintaining stability may be important steps to achieving client goals, but it is the goals that are the eventual focus. Indeed, it is the shared goals between client, therapist, and prescriber that form the basis for collaboration.

As noted previously, medication is often extremely helpful, but medication alone is seldom sufficient for a person to achieve his or her life goals. Most people with severe mental illness require a holistic and integrated treatment approach. Such an approach usually includes medication, a focus on recovery, access to skill training, and other psychosocial treatments that are focused on the person's specific goals. Such an integrated approach can create a synergy that helps an individual achieve and sustain recovery. Fostering *synergy* and *integration* may sound complicated, but it is actually simple and straightforward. The treatment goal is to help individuals overcome barriers that interfere with their ability to achieve their own life goals. The barrier may be caused by symptoms such as hearing voices, by not knowing how to talk to people or get a job, by substance use, or by a chaotic lifestyle that precludes consistent lifestyle practices. Whereas medication can help the person cope better with some of these barriers, specific help with learning skills or changing life patterns is often also a very important part of success. When combined, medication and psychosocial treatments that focus on overcoming specific barriers can reduce symptom severity, decrease the chances of relapse, and help individuals reemerge from patienthood into personhood and achieve personal life goals.

Illness Management

A person who is activity engaged in managing his or her own illness is more likely to achieve personal life goals. *Illness management* refers to all of the different things that a person can do, including behaviors that the person can change, that will help him or her overcome problems caused by illness and move forward in his or her life. For many people it is already clear that effectively using medication, learning to better manage persistent symptoms, and practicing recovery lifestyle habits can help them get closer to what they want their life to be. For example, it is usually easier to achieve personal life goals when symptoms are less of a problem and the client can function better. Anything that the client can do to decrease the problems caused by symptoms, or to increase his or her ability to function better, is likely to support recovery. This does not mean that a person needs to get symptoms under control before working toward his or her life goals. In fact, having goals can often help decrease symptoms. However, a client's ability to manage his or her illness more effectively is often important.

Although many different psychosocial treatment and rehabilitation services can help facilitate functional and role recovery, this chapter, and the chapters that follow, focus primarily on psychoeducation to help people manage their illness and optimize symptomatic recovery.

What Is Psychoeducation?

Psychoeducation is a way of teaching knowledge and skills while facilitating choice and practice. Psychoeducation is an umbrella term that includes three subsets of interventions: (1) what is traditionally referred to as "psychiatric patient education," (2) skills training, and (3) illness management skill training, which is the application of the skill training specifically to illness management.

Patient education is that part of psychoeducation involved in teaching the person about his or her own illness and the range of treatment options for that illness. It involves educating the client and the client's support system about diagnosis, causes, symptoms, medication and other treatment. Educating clients about the stages of relapse, as well as how relapse begins and how it can be stopped, is an important part of this education.

Skills training involves learning, practicing, and applying new skills. It is not just hearing someone else talk about how to talk to a stranger or hold a conversation with a friend; it is also practicing those skills and making them real. All of us have some skills that we can do well, and others that give us more trouble. Skill training must be carefully individualized so that the focus is on those skill that are most important to meeting the client's own life goals.

Illness management skills training refers to teaching those skills that will help the client manage his or her own illness. This may involve learning to manage stress, cope better with symptoms, or learn relaxation techniques. It almost always involves learning to monitor symptoms and early signs of relapse, and learning recovery lifestyle habits that support a healthier life (Figure 8.1).

Psychoeducation is a structured approach that is different from the approach in which a therapist makes suggestions,

What is Psychoeducation?

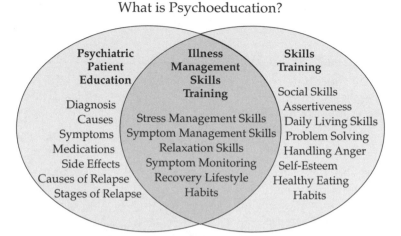

Figure 8.1. The three domains that comprise psychoeducation: psychiatric patient education, illness management skills training, and skills training.

recommendations, and admonishments. The chapters that follow are primarily focused on a few of the skill training topics that can play a critical role in symptom reduction. This approach is likely to work much better when used in combination with medication.

Although prescribers can provide psychoeducation, it is more typically part of the services provided by therapists, paraprofessionals, and peer support specialists. Therapists generally have more time than prescribers to invest in the long-term psychoeducation that is needed to help people understand and manage their illness more effectively. Psychoeducation is an important piece of recovery-oriented treatment, and it can help support a more collaborative relationship. It is designed to support, complement, and augment the work of the prescriber. The following information is geared for use in classroom psychoeducation, but it can also be modified to be used in individual sessions, as part of group therapy, and as self-study.

The following 18 steps can help make psychoeducation more effective.

1. *Arrange the learning environment for success.* Psychoeducation is best conducted more like a class than a traditional psychotherapy group. The main objectives of psychoeducation are to help clients learn and use knowledge and skills. Therapist–client interactions are more frequent and more essential than peer–peer interactions. Psychoeducation is usually arranged in classroom-style seating with a whiteboard or chalkboard. The instructor is usually at the head of the class. Everything about the physical setting of the session suggests a class rather than a "group in the round" (see Figure 8.2).

2. *Limit the number of participants per session.* The optimal number of participants may vary depending on the experience and skills of the therapist, acuity level of the participants, space available, regulations, and the topic or skills being taught. In some instances 6–10 participants is optimal. However, 12–15 participants may be manageable for experienced therapists and may also be necessary for financial viability.

3. *Set length of sessions based on the attention span of participants.* Usually 45-minute sessions are best in inpatient settings

Classroom-Style Teaching

1. Chalk/white board

2. Paper and pencils

3. Tables/notebooks

4. Extra room between chairs

5. Extra space between rows

6. Clock that all can see

7. Maximum 15 participants

Classroom Style

Figure 8.2. Components and layout of classroom-style psychoeducation.

and crisis stabilization units. Sessions of 60 minutes usually work well in rehabilitation, day treatment, partial hospitalization, and outpatient services. Sessions of 90 minutes are typically used only in outpatient services when participants are able to sustain attention and concentration. Sessions of 30 minutes are not typically recommended. By the time the participants are gathered and attendance is taken, little time remains for the task at hand.

4. *Structure the format.* A consistent structure and format helps make classes predictable and less threatening for participants. As noted in "Effective Educational Strategies" at the end of this chapter, classes can be divided into five main segments, and each segment includes a subset of strategies for effective education:

    a. Attendance and review
    b. Engagement of participants
    c. Repetition and renforcement
    d. Application and multimodal teaching
    e. Reengagement and recitation

5. *Provide didactic instruction.* Psychoeducation is primarily a teaching–learning experience with didactic instruction. It is a class with a teacher, a topic, a curriculum, and a lesson plan. The therapist is in the role of a teacher, and participants are in the role of students. The main objective is to teach information and skills through classroom educational methods. This format is very different from traditional group therapy, which rarely has an organized topic or curriculum and the format is one of discussion rather than classroom instruction.

6. *Take an incremental approach.* Break information and skills into small chunks, segments, steps, or subcomponents. Less is more. Avoid covering too much information in a single session. There is a concept called "errorless learning" that is discussed in general education and is of particular relevance in teaching people with mental illness. The idea is that you teach each small

segment of a topic and then only test or ask the person to answer a question when you are absolutely sure that he or she will be able to answer correctly. It seems that many people learn better with this technique, but people with schizophrenia and other major mental illnesses seem to find this approach particularly effective.

7. *Use multimodal teaching.* Consciously include all five learning pathways in your teaching. Leave no learner behind. A majority of participants who have cognitive impairments or literacy problems are capable of benefiting from psychoeducation when all five modalities are consistently employed (Figure 8.3). Different people will find one pathway more effective than another. Some of us are visual learners and learn best when we see something written or diagramed. Others of us are auditory learners and learn best when we hear information. And some of us are verbal learners, and learn best when we have a chance to repeat the material, say it out loud, and discuss it. All of us learn better when multiple modalities are combined and when the learning includes practice and actual use of the material.

a. See it: Visual learning pathway. Provide handouts, encourage participants to read along as information is read aloud, and write the main points on the board.

Five Parts of
Multimodal Teaching

Figure 8.3. The five elements of
multimodal teaching.

b. Hear it: Auditory learning pathway. Engage participants in reading aloud, summarizing the main points, and giving personal examples so all hear the information several times.

c. Say it: Verbal learning pathway. One person reads two or three sentences, another participant summarizes the main points, and a third participant gives an example. In addition, all participants recite the main points aloud to ensure that everyone has the opportunity to benefit from saying the main points.

d. Write it: Note-taking learning pathway. Prompt participants to take notes and to write down the main points that are written on the board.

e. Use it: Experiential learning pathway. Engage participants in role-play, demonstration, behavioral rehearsal, and goal setting for application of knowledge and skills in their personal lives. Simply learning information without utilizing it does not typically create change in people's lives.

8. *Provide coaching to increase knowledge and improve skills.* Cue, clue, prompt, and shape behavior during discussion and experiential learning to gradually improve knowledge and skill level.

9. *Give positive feedback.* Provide frequent, genuine, positive feedback for attendance, attention, and participation. Reinforce correct answers, improved skills, application of knowledge and skills to personal life experiences, and other indications of progress and effort.

10. *Give constructive corrective feedback.* Provide immediate, therapeutic prompting for inattentive behavior, cues to shape skill performance, and feedback for irrelevant and digressive input.

11. *Frequently repeat main points and key skills.* Overlearning is one of the educational strategies that can help people

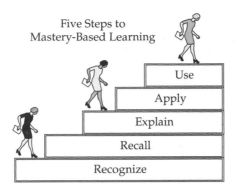

Figure 8.4. The five steps that contribute to individualized and mastery-based learning.

move from retention recall and explanation to application and utilization of knowledge and skills.

12. *Measure skill level and train to* ≥ *80% mastery.* Assess, score, document, and improve skill level over time to achieve competency, encourage application, facilitate utilization, and demonstrate progress. Participants are more likely to use and retain skills that have been mastered.

13. *Include problem solving to anticipate utilization obstacles.* Discuss and identify potential obstacles to utilization of knowledge and skills. Use problem solving to help participants resolve problems and overcome anticipated obstacles.

14. *Facilitate and reinforce generalization.* Encourage, plan, establish goals, discuss, and provide positive feedback for using and practicing acquired skills at home and in the community. Knowledge alone is insufficient. Practice of skills in class is only preparatory. The ultimate objective is to use knowledge and skills in everyday life.

15. *Encourage participants to practice instead of try.* New habits are a matter of deliberate choice, mindfulness, repetition, and practice. While working with people toward behavioral

Optimal outcomes can be
achieved when the client:

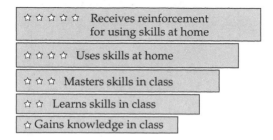

Figure 8.5. A progressive method for optimizing
client outcomes.

changes, it is usually a good idea to listen for and avoid the "I'll
try to do better" trap. An often repeated expression "Try is a lie"
suggests that most of the time, people say *try* when they are not
really ready to make a change. Sometimes people say "I'll try"
when they think they *should* make a particular change. Clients
may say *try* when the therapist or prescriber encourages a
specific change. If a client's stated goal is to try, then simply
having tried is sufficient, as in "I tried to eat healthy." "I tried,"
tends to be an out and a hedge against self-recrimination and
anticipated criticism for not reaching the goal. *Practice* suggests
repetition and gradual improvement over time. This difference
underscores the importance of client choice. It is usually a good
idea to encourage clients to set concrete practice goals based on
their own personal choices and preferences and to *practice* instead of try.

16. *Incorporate motivational interviewing and cognitive-
behavioral techniques.* Although a detailed description of these
two techniques is beyond the scope of this chapter, both can
make valuable contributions to psychoeducation when woven
in with knowledge acquisition and skill building. Some of the
techniques are built into the chapters that follow.

17. *Provide self-monitoring tools.* Counting and keeping track of behavioral changes can help people remain mindful of achieving practice goals, reinforce change, and monitor progress. Monitoring tools can play an important role in creating new habits. Marking a calendar is a relatively easy self-monitoring tool that can be quite helpful. "Symptom Tracker," a monitoring tool for symptoms and recovery lifestyle habits, is available online at www.recovery.bz.

18. *Use adult-to-adult interactions.* These psychoeducation strategies are designed to leave no learner behind by emphasizing strategies that help compensate for the impairments and limitations caused by the illness. The focus is on adult learning. Respect is a critical component of effective psychoeducation. It is important to use an adult tone of voice and avoid any sense or hint of talking down to participants.

Table 8.1. Effective Educational Strategies

Skills & Techniques for Teaching People Who are Recovering from Severe & Persistent Mental Illness

		Effective Educational Strategies	Yes	No	NA
Attendance & Review	1.	Start session on time.			
	2.	Prompt people to go to class in a directive (Give Clear Directives), non-critical, therapeutic manner (Avoid Adversarial Interactions).			
	3.	Check attendance.			
	4.	Locate people who are present but unaccounted for in class.			
	5.	Provide each person with a handout.			
	6.	Involve people in a short review of at least one main learning point from last lesson.			
Engage Participants	7.	Engage people in reading aloud.			
	8.	Direct majority of questions to individuals by name (say name then ask question).			
	9.	Help participants pronounce, define, and understand complex words, phrases, and concepts as needed.			
	10.	Facilitate summarization of each small section of information after it is read aloud by a participant.			
	11.	Ask questions about main points to assess and increase comprehension.			
	12.	Maintain a balance of input. Involve each person about the same number of times.			

Repetition & Reinforcement	13.	Identify, write on board, discuss, & repeat the main learning point(s) of the lesson.				
	14.	Encourage participants to write down the main learning point(s) of the lesson.				
	15.	Utilize recitation of main learning points.				
	16.	Provide positive feedback for relevant input, responses, questions, & comments.				
	17.	Handle irrelevant, digressive, incoherent, disorganized, tangential, manic, and egocentric remarks in a non-critical, therapeutic manner.				
Application & Multimodal	18.	Give concrete, real life examples that are relevant to lives of participants.				
	19.	Encourage participants to identify personal examples of main learning points.				
	20.	Circulate and check written work throughout the session.				
	21.	Apply all 5 teaching modalities (see it, hear it, say it, write it, use it).				

Table 8.1. (continued)

Effective Educational Strategies		Yes	No	NA
Reengagement & End with Recitation	22. Use adult-to-adult tone of voice & interactions (avoid talking "down" to participants).			
	23. Provide immediate prompting for inattentive behavior (sleeping, slouching, head down on table, reading a magazine, responding to hallucinations, looking out the window, writing other things, etc.).			
	24. If anyone leaves group, express the expectation that s/he will return shortly.			
	25. Locate individuals who leave group and fail to return shortly.			
	26. Complete 2–3 workbook pages within time allotted.			
	27. End with recitation of main learning points.			
	28. End group on time.			
	TOTAL SCORE			
	PERCENT			

Instructor: **Date:**

Class/Topic: **Reviewer:**

Scoring Formula: Total Yes ÷ (Total Yes + Total No) = % Yes   100% – % Yes = % No

Comments:

Strengths:

CHAPTER NINE

Beyond Illness to Recovery

What Is Recovery?

Recovery for people who have a severe, persistent mental illness can mean many different things. Some people use the term *recovery* to mean that all symptoms are gone, never to return; some people use the term to mean *cure*. In this book we use *recovery* to mean something different from *cure*. Recovery for us is the process of experiencing more in life than just illness. It is the process of going from being a patient or a client to being a *person* who may continue to have symptoms from mental illness but also has more in his or her life than just being a client. Recovery is the process of finding out who you are, of choosing who you are, and deciding who you want to be, beyond your illness. You may be someone who likes to read, who makes art, who has a job, who has friends, who is part of a bowling league. Recovery is the process of having as full a life as possible, despite problems related to your illness. Your illness may make some things more difficult, but your illness makes nothing impossible. Recovery is having your own goals about what you want your life

to be like, and then working toward accomplishing those
goals.

The Recovery Process

When you first became ill, the illness probably took over
everything in your life. Everyone around you may have gotten
to the point of thinking of you as the illness, and you might
have too. You and your family and your friends may have
forgotten the rest of who you are. The people around you may
think of you as merely "a mental patient," "a schizophrenic," or
"a manic–depressive." It may be hard to remember that you are
a student, a brother, a sister, a person who enjoys art or music.
Recovery is the process of taking back yourself, your personhood, and becoming more of who you want to be. The following points provide an overview of the recovery experience.

1. Recovery from a major mental illness is an ongoing process
   of working to achieve more of one's own life goals, despite
   illness. It is the process of discovering more to life than just
   illness. In this sense, recovery is a continuing process that
   is available to everyone, a process that focuses on hopes
   and goals and accomplishments, and is possible even if
   symptoms and problems from the illness remain.

   Not everyone uses the word "recovery" in the same way.
   Some people think of recovery as something that can be
   accomplished. For people with this view of recovery, there
   may one day be a sense of "arrival" and "accomplishment:"
   of "sustaining recovery" instead of "working toward recovery." Whether you believe recovery is a continuing
   process or a goal that can be attained and must be sustained, it is important to understand that recovery does not
   mean cure. The authors of this book use the term recovery
   to mean something quite different than cure. For us, recovery is the process people engage in to make life more
   like what they want it to be. For people struggling with a

serious illness, recovery is the process of having as full a life as possible, despite the problems caused by illness.

2. Recovery can occur even if you continue to have symptoms.
3. Recovery starts in different ways for different people. For one person it may start by taking a walk every day. For another person it might start by making a friend. For another it may begin by getting a volunteer job or by going back to church.
4. Recovery has ups and downs. The journey may go very well for a while, and then go through periods of more difficulty. It is important not to get too frustrated or discouraged if you go through a difficult period.
5. Recovery can go through periods when it may appear as though nothing is happening, like dormant periods in plant growth. People recover in different ways at different speeds. It is not unusual for some people to appear "dormant" for periods of time, when they may be taking time to get ready or prepare themselves for the next change.
6. Recovery from the stigma of having a mental illness may be more difficult than recovery from the illness itself. If you begin to think of yourself as nothing but your illness, then it can be hard to think of yourself in any other way. If other people think of you only in terms of your illness, they may expect you to be a certain way and might not recognize or support your recovery.

Recovery Is an Ongoing Process

Most people continue to work to make their life better, while also maintaining what they have already achieved. For people with a major mental illness, recovery is the process of not allowing their identity, their personhood, to be defined by their illness. It can be hard work to make life what we most want it to be. Once we achieve a goal, it can also be a challenge to hold onto what we have achieved. This can be even more difficult for people who also have to cope with the problems caused by a major mental illness.

People who are recovering from mental illness have identified a number of things that seem most helpful in the process of recovery. What things do you believe are most important for your recovery?

☐ 1. A determination to get better
☐ 2. An understanding of my illness
☐ 3. Taking responsibility for myself
☐ 4. Managing my illness
☐ 5. Having friends and family who accept and support me
☐ 6. An optimistic attitude
☐ 7. Spiritual beliefs that helped me find meaning in my life

Think about the boxes you have checked. How can you strengthen those things you have chosen as most important to your own recovery? How can you use these to begin or further your own recovery process?

The Goal of Mental Health Treatment

The overall goals of mental health treatment are for you to have a better life and to hold onto what you want in life, once you reach your goals. However, getting better means something different for each individual. Most people have their own ideas about what a better life would be like. No one else can really decide for you what would make your life better. Some things are common to most of us. Most of us want to be safe, feel happy, live in an environment that we like, have productive things to do, and have people around whom we like and who like us.

Every person has different ideas about what these things mean. Every person will have his or her own idea about what it would take to be safe or what a nice place to live in would look like. Each person has specific things that are important to him or her. For one person it may be getting a car; for another person it may be going back to school.

What do you want to make your life better?

_____

_____

_____

This can actually be a complicated question. It is a bit easier to answer if you start by thinking about goals.

Think about Your Life Goals

The process of recovery is helped when you start thinking about your personal life goals. Choosing your own short-term and long-term goals are important steps in the process of recovery.

It may actually be difficult to think about your goals. It might be hard to allow yourself to want anything, especially if you have been disappointed over and over. Even if you have goals, it might be hard to go from big general goals like "I want my life to be better" to more specific goals that you can actually work on.

The more specific and concrete your goals are, the more likely you are to actually reach them. Goals can be separated into short-term ones and long-term ones. Short-term goals are things you can work toward over the next few months. Long-term goals are things that may take years. Dreams are also important. Goals are things that may be difficult but that are also possible. Dreams are things that may not be possible, but that we still think about and hope for. Getting a part-time job may be a short-term goal—something that may be difficult but is possible to accomplish over the next couple of months. Finishing school may be a long-term goal; it may take years of work. Becoming an astronaut may be a dream. It is unlikely that any adult could become an astronaut if they had a significant gap in school or work or had a serious illness. Even if it is unrealistic, it is good to have dreams. Dreams help to keep hope alive, and there is always the hope that a dream can come true.

What goals are most important to you?
☐ 1. I want to get a better place to live.
☐ 2. I want to have a job.
☐ 3. I want to own a car.
☐ 4. I want to have more friends.
☐ 5. I want to go back to school.
☐ 6. I want to _____

Now let's get more specific and break down goals into short- and long-term goals:

My short-term goals: Things I would like to accomplish in the next 3 months. Be as specific as possible. For example, if you want a job, think about what kind of job you might want. If you want to return to school, think about what classes you might want to take and where you might want to go.

Your short-term goals: What do you want to accomplish in 3 months? _____

My long-term goals: Things I would like to work toward, even if it takes years to accomplish. Do not be afraid to list long-term goals that might appear unrealistic or impossible. Long-term goals are an important part of creating your recovery action plan.

Your long-term goals: What would you like to accomplish in 3 years? _____

What changes would make your life better? _____

What are you willing to work on to move toward your goals?

_____

And let's not forget your dreams . . .

Dreams: Things I have always wanted. _____

_____

Put Together Your Own Recovery Team

Who are the people in your life that support your recovery? Recovery can be much easier if you put together your own recovery team. Most people find it a lot harder to pursue the process of recovery all alone. Help and support can make your recovery journey much easier. Think about who is supportive of your recovery. Your recovery team will usually include your prescriber, your therapist, as well as other people who are important for your recovery. Your recovery team may include members of your family, a good friend, a minister, or even an employer. It may include someone who knows you very well or someone who is supportive who does not know you all that well. Different members of your recovery team may help you in very different ways.

Someone on your recovery team might join you in your meeting with your prescriber. However, your whole recovery team might not all meet together in a room, and in some cases, may not even know each other. They are still part of the team that supports you in your recovery. Some members of your recovery team may help you think about your personal goals or help you come up with your recovery plan. Some members of your team may have more limited roles. An employer or a minister might not meet with other members of your recovery team, but he or she may provide important support for achieving your goals and may also play an important role for members of your team. Members of your recovery team do not necessarily meet together in one place; they are simply all the people who support you in your recovery.

Think about the people on your recovery team. Write down a list of all of the people who support your recovery. It is easy to overlook important people who may be part of your team. Think about who is on your team. Then think again and consider whom you may have forgotten to list as members of your team. Who in your life do you want to include on your team?

My Recovery Team

_____   _____

_____   _____

_____   _____

_____   _____

_____   _____

Put Together a Specific Plan to Pursue Your Goals

It is one thing to want something; it is very different to come up with a specific plan to actually achieve your goal. It is easy to want something to change; it is much harder to make the change really happen. Like all of the other steps in recovery, putting together a plan sounds easy but can be harder than it seems. Goals can be so big that they seem to be overwhelming. It may be difficult to know where or how to start. It is important that each piece of a plan be small enough that you believe that you can do it. Part of your recovery plan may include learning specific information and skills that you need to be able to achieve your goals. Some members of your recovery team may be very helpful in putting together your personal recovery plan. Consider discussing your goals and plans with members of your recovery team.

There are usually a number of steps involved between wanting a change and making that change real:

1. _Decide what you really want to change._ Personal choice is very important. If you allow yourself to be pushed into agreeing to a change because of pressure from someone else, then real change is less likely to happen. If you make a choice based on "should" and "ought to," then success is more doubtful. What

are some things YOU really want to change about your life?

_____

2. *Decide which changes are most important to make now.* Sometimes it is a good idea to choose changes that are most important, or that are easiest, or that you have the most help and support for. No one can change everything all at once. What do you want to change first? _____

3. *Put together a concrete plan to make the change you have chosen.* Be sure that each part of the change is something that you can really do. Break big changes that might be over-whelming into small pieces. For example, if you want to go back to school, how would you begin? We provide a sample of what a plan to go back to school might look like. Check the steps that would be important for you and fill in the blanks.

☐ A. Decide what school you want to go to: _____
☐ B. Get a list of the classes that are offered.
    a. How will you get this list? _____
    b. Who could help you get this list? _____

☐ C. Decide which class looks interesting: _____
    a. Do you want to take it for credit?
    b. Do you want to just sit in the first time around?

☐ D. Sign up for the class.
    a. How/where do you sign up? _____
    b. How much does it cost? _____
    c. How will you pay for the class? _____
    d. How many books are required for the class?

       _____

    e. How much will the books cost? _____
    d. Who can help you figure this out? _____

☐ E. What do you need to do to succeed at the class?

_____

a. Would a coach or tutor help? _____

b. Do you need help with making a study calendar?
_____

c. Who can help you if the class gets difficult?
_____

☐ G. Think about what problems might occur and plan ahead.
a. Will it be difficult getting to class every time?
_____

b. How will you make sure you can get to class?
_____

c. Will it be hard getting to class on time? _____
d. How can you make sure you can get to class on time?
_____

e. What other things might be hard about being successful at school? _____
f. How can you overcome these problems? _____

☐ H. How are you going to motivate yourself to keep working toward your goal?
a. Every time I make a step I will mark it on a calendar so I can see my progress
b. I will journal what has gone well every day
c. I will involve other people in my support group to give me encouragement
d. I will give myself a reward when I accomplish my goal
e. other

4. *Make a series of small changes over time.* Avoid setting yourself up for failure by working on too many changes at once. Recognize when you get off track and get yourself back on course again.

5. *Decide who on your recovery team can help you put together your recovery plan.* It may be very difficult to put together an entire plan by yourself. When you work on a plan alone, it

can be easy to overlook difficulties, make individual steps too big, or get stuck in how to break big steps into smaller, more manageable pieces. Use people on your recovery team to make sure that you have a solid, achievable recovery plan. Once you have some ideas written down, discuss them with some of the members of your recovery team. Get their ideas and consider their input. The choices and goals will still be your own, but input can sometimes be quite valuable.

6. *Keep working toward your goals.* Do not get discouraged if your plan, or part of your plan, does not work the first, second, or even third time. If you put together a plan that does not work, talk with people on your recovery team. Figure out what did not work and what you could do differently the next time. Change is very difficult. The important thing is to keep learning, to decide what you will do differently the next time, and to keep working toward your goals.

What Is the Connection between Managing Mental Illness and Achieving Goals?

There is more to life than having a mental illness. You can manage your illness and have a better life.

> "I have a mental illness, but my mental illness does not have me."

Managing your illness to achieve your life goals does not mean that you must be symptom free. Many people continue to experience symptoms while working toward personal life goals. However, managing your mental illness usually makes it easier to be a person with many

> "I am a person who has a mental illness. I am not a mental patient."

different roles and personal life goals, instead of being just a "mental health client." Managing your illness means getting your symptoms under control to the point that they don't keep you from reaching your personal life goals. If your symptoms are severe, distressing, or hard to deal with, they will probably be more likely to interfere with your efforts to reach your goals. Talk with your prescriber and therapist about any symptoms that might be getting in the way of reaching your goals. Work with your team to manage your illness so that you can move forward with your recovery goals.

What symptoms might be getting in the way of achieving your personal life goals?

☐ 1. I have trouble ignoring hallucinations.

☐ 2. I have trouble thinking clearly.

☐ 3. I have trouble ignoring delusional thoughts and ideas.

☐ 4. I have trouble keeping my mind on anything for very long.

☐ 5. I have trouble remembering things.

☐ 6. I have trouble ignoring paranoid thoughts.

☐ 7. I have trouble feeling happy.

☐ 8. I have trouble getting motivated.

☐ 9. I have trouble enjoying anything.

☐ 10. I have trouble keeping my moods under control.

☐ 11. I have trouble getting enough sleep at night.

☐ 12. I have trouble showering, brushing my teeth, and keeping myself clean.

☐ 13. I have trouble remembering and following instructions.

☐ 14. I have trouble understanding what people say.

☐ 15. I have trouble getting up and getting going.

☐ 16. I have trouble sticking to a task until it is done.

☐ 17. I have trouble explaining things so that people understand me.

☐ 18. I have trouble being around people without feeling anxious and afraid.

☐ 19. I have trouble thinking positively about anything.

☐ 20. I have trouble thinking thing things through.

☐ 21. I have trouble _____

☐ 22. None of the above. I do not have any symptoms that get in the way of reaching my life goals.

Managing Your Illness

Managing your illness is an important part of achieving your personal life goals. There are a number of ways to manage your illness. Medication, symptom management skills, and recovery lifestyle habits are some of the main tools you can use to help make your recovery successful. The most important job of your medication is to help you manage your illness so that you can put energy into achieving your personal life goals.

Medication Is a Tool

Taking medication and managing your illness are important throughout your recovery journey. Taking medication correctly is not the goal. Medication is a tool. Medicine can help you reach your goals of role recovery, functional recovery, and a better life. (We'll explain the difference between role and functional recovery in the next section.) If your symptoms are severe, distressing, and out of control, they are likely to make it much harder to do everyday things. Uncontrolled mental illness can get in the way of taking care of yourself, having fun, making friends, reading, planning for the future, working, being successful in school, and having a better life. Managing your illness helps put *you* in control. Work with your prescriber and therapist to find a medication that works well for you. Many people find it helpful to learn about their illness and how to manage their persistent symptoms so that the illness does not interfere with achieving their life goals. You may find it helpful to learn about your medication, recognize and monitor your symptoms, manage medication side effects, use symptom management skills, learn and practice recovery lifestyle habits, and be an active participant in medication-related decision making. These are all important steps that

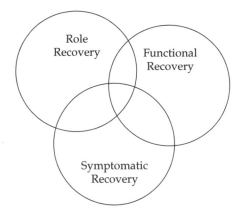

Figure 9.1. Different types of recovery
can affect each other, but one can also
occur without the other.

you can choose to take to help yourself achieve your recovery
goals.

What Is Role Recovery?

Role recovery involves...

A. Working toward achieving your personal life goals.
B. Having roles in life other than those of *patient, client, consumer,* or *person with mental illness.*
C. Having a sense of identity beyond your mental illness.
D. Working toward personhood instead of having your whole life focus on patienthood.

The following checklist can help you identify the roles you've already achieved as well as those you'd like to achieve some day.

What Roles Have You Already Achieved? "I am a…"	What Roles Do You Want to Achieve Some Day? "I want to be a…"
☐ 1. Grandmother/ grandfather	☐ 1. Grandmother/ grandfather
☐ 2. Mother/father	☐ 2. Mother/father
☐ 3. Wife/husband	☐ 3. Wife/husband
☐ 4. Daughter/son	☐ 4. Daughter/son
☐ 5. Sister/brother	☐ 5. Sister/brother
☐ 6. Girlfriend/boyfriend	☐ 6. Girlfriend/boyfriend
☐ 7. Friend	☐ 7. Friend
☐ 8. Church/synagogue/ mosque member	☐ 8. Church/synagogue/ mosque member
☐ 9. Student	☐ 9. Student
☐ 10. Worker/employee	☐ 10. Worker/employee
☐ 11. Volunteer	☐ 11. Volunteer
☐ 12. Artist	☐ 12. Artist
☐ 13. Athlete	☐ 13. Athlete
☐ 14. Writer/author/poet	☐ 14. Writer/author/poet
☐ 15. Musician	☐ 15. Musician
☐ 16. Singer/choir member	☐ 16. Singer/choir member
☐ 17. Gardener	☐ 17. Gardener
☐ 18. Advocate	☐ 18. Advocate
☐ 19. Card player	☐ 19. Card player
☐ 20. Sports fan	☐ 20. Sports fan

What Roles Have You Already Achieved? "I am a..."	What Roles Do You Want to Achieve Some Day? "I want to be a..."
☐ 21. Bowler	☐ 21. Bowler
☐ 22. Person who has a mental illness	☐ 22.
☐ 23.	☐ 23.
☐ 24.	☐ 24.
☐ 25.	☐ 25.

a. How can managing your mental illness help you get and keep the roles you want in life? _____

b. What knowledge, skills, and supports do you need to help you get and keep the roles you want in life? _____
_____

What Is Functional Recovery?

Functional recovery involves...

A. Being able do things for yourself.
B. Being able to take care of yourself and your needs.
C. Being able to do everyday things such as taking a shower, paying bills, washing clothes, grocery shopping, cooking, driving a car.
D. Being able to read, understand, learn, follow instructions, and think clearly.
E. Being able to talk to, and get along with, people.
F. Being able to "make it" in the world.

The following checklist can help you identify the functional skills you already have and those you want to improve or learn.

What Functional Skills Do You Already Have? "I am able to..."	What Functional Skills Do You Want to Improve or Learn? "I want to be able to..."
☐ 1. Ride the bus	☐ 1. Ride the bus
☐ 2. Drive a car	☐ 2. Drive a car
☐ 3. Pay bills	☐ 3. Pay bills
☐ 4. Wash clothes	☐ 4. Wash clothes
☐ 5. Manage money without running short	☐ 5. Manage money without running short
☐ 6. Live on my own	☐ 6. Live on my own
☐ 7. Find, get, keep, and change jobs	☐ 7. Find, get, keep, and change jobs
☐ 8. Read and understand information	☐ 8. Read and understand information
☐ 9. Carry on conversations	☐ 9. Carry on conversations
☐ 10. Handle anger	☐ 10. Handle anger
☐ 11. Be assertive with people	☐ 11. Be assertive with people
☐ 12. Solve problems well	☐ 12. Solve problems well
☐ 13. Keep myself neat and clean	☐ 13. Keep myself neat and clean
☐ 14. Study and pass tests in school	☐ 14. Study and pass tests in school
☐ 15. Use positive self-talk	☐ 15. Use positive self-talk
☐ 16. Eat healthy foods and manage my weight	☐ 16. Eat healthy foods and manage my weight
☐ 17. Do aerobic exercise	☐ 17. Do aerobic exercise
☐ 18.	☐ 18.

What Functional Skills Do You Already Have? "I am able to ..."	What Functional Skills Do You Want to Improve or Learn? "I want to be able to ..."
☐ 19.	☐ 19.
☐ 20.	☐ 20.

a. How can managing your mental illness help you get and keep functional skills? _____
b. How can improving your functional skills help you achieve your personal life goals? _____

What Is Symptomatic Recovery?

Symptomatic recovery involves ...

A. Managing your symptoms so that they do not keep you from reaching your life goals.
B. Learning and practicing recovery lifestyle habits.
C. Getting treatment for substance abuse problems.
D. Preventing relapse.

The following checklist can help you identify the symptom management skills you already have as well as those you want to learn or practice more often.

What Symptom Management Skills Do You Already Have? "I am managing my illness by ..."	What Symptom Management Skills Will You Learn or Practice More Often? "I will manage my illness by ..."
☐ 1. Taking medication	☐ 1. Taking medication
☐ 2. Practicing relaxation skills	☐ 2. Practicing relaxation skills
☐ 3. Doing exercise	☐ 3. Doing exercise

What Symptom Management Skills Do You Already Have? "I am managing my illness by…"	What Symptom Management Skills Will You Learn or Practice More Often? "I will manage my illness by…"
☐ 4. Sleeping 7–9 hours at night	☐ 4. Sleeping 7–9 hours at night
☐ 5. Eating healthy foods	☐ 5. Eating healthy foods
☐ 6. Choosing low-sugar food/drinks	☐ 6. Choosing low-sugar food/drinks
☐ 7. Choosing decaffeinated drinks	☐ 7. Choosing decaffeinated drinks
☐ 8. Staying away from street drugs	☐ 8. Staying away from street drugs
☐ 9. Staying away from alcohol	☐ 9. Staying away from alcohol
☐ 10. Staying out of bed during the day	☐ 10. Staying out of bed during the day
☐ 11. Staying busy during the day	☐ 11. Staying busy during the day
☐ 12. Getting support from family/friends	☐ 12. Getting support from family/friends
☐ 13.	☐ 13.
☐ 14.	☐ 14.
☐ 15.	☐ 15.
☐ 16.	☐ 16.
☐ 17.	☐ 17.
☐ 18.	☐ 18.
☐ 19.	☐ 19.

a. What symptoms are getting in the way of achieving your personal life goals? _____

b. How can managing your illness help you achieve your personal life goals? _____

CHAPTER TEN

Recovery Lifestyle Habits: Recovery Is a Way of Life

Sometimes we talk about medication so much that we overlook the other things you can do each day to recover from mental illness. Taking medication every day is an

| Medication alone is not enough. |

important part of a recovery lifestyle. In fact, as you will see, for most people taking medication is at the top of the list of recovery lifestyle habits. However, although medication may be necessary, medication alone is not enough. Your everyday habits—the things you do, the choices and decisions you make—help determine how successful you are at managing your illness and reaching your goals. Your daily lifestyle habits can help you recover, improve your health and wellness, and reduce your risk of relapse. The opposite is also true: Your daily lifestyle habits can make it harder for

> Your everyday habits—the things you do each day, the choices and decisions you make—help determine how successful you are at managing your illness and reaching your goals.

you to recover, make your illness worse, and increase your chances of relapse.

• *Choice and practice.* The more recovery lifestyle habits you choose and practice, the better. Recovery lifestyle habits can help get your symptoms under control, help you feel better, and lower your risk of relapse. Learn, choose, practice, and gradually make recovery lifestyle habits part of your everyday life over time. New habits are a matter of thoughtful choice and mindful daily practice. Really deciding to practice a new habit is more likely to lead to change than if you just

> New habits require deliberate choice and mindful daily practice.

commit yourself to "trying." Saying "I'll try to do better" can be a way of not committing yourself to really making the change. *Try* is a word that people use when they are not truly ready to make a change. If your goal is to try, failure may be built in. "I tried" is a way to avoid change while giving the impression that you made some attempt to change. Instead, make choices, set realistic goals, practice, and make a series of small changes over time. If you change your mind, make a new choice and set a new goal.

• *Don't make too many changes at the same time.* Avoid setting yourself up for failure by working on too many changes at once. There are 13 recovery lifestyle habits described in this chapter. It is usually not a good idea to change a lot of habits all at the same time. For most people, changing one or two habits at a time works best. You will probably be more interested in practicing some of the habits than others. You will be given the opportunity to choose a sentence that best describes how interested you are in practicing each recovery lifestyle habit. There are no right or wrong answers. Start with what you are most interested in, with what is most important to you. Recognize when you get off track and renew your commitment to practicing the good habits you have chosen. Practice recovery lifestyle habits every day to improve your overall health and wellness, get your symptoms under better control, reduce your risk of relapse, and achieve recovery.

Medications

Medications are an important part of recovery for most people with serious mental illness. Medications do not "cure" mental illness. What medication can do is to help you decrease the impact of symptoms and make it easier for you to manage your own life. The issue is how you can use this tool—how you can use medication—as effectively as possible. Taking a medication is never a goal of treatment. The goal of treatment is to make it possible for you to achieve your own goals. Medications alone are never enough, but they *can* help.

Because there is no known cure for mental illness, the goal is to get your symptoms under control. When medication works well, it gets rid of some of your symptoms and makes other symptoms easier to deal with. Medication may not take away all your symptoms. However, medicine can control your symptoms so they do not cause as much trouble. Medication can also decrease your risk of relapse. Learn about how your medications work and what happens to make symptoms return if you stop taking your medication.

For medication to help you the most, you must make sure that you are on the right medication, at the right dose, and then you must take it every day. Getting on the right medication at the right dose requires that you are able to talk with your prescriber and your therapist about what you want the medication to do, what your goals are, how well the medication is working, and what problems or side effects the medication might be causing. Medication is an important part of recovery lifestyle habits. You, your prescriber, your therapist, and other members of your support team must be clear about your plan and about the role of medication as a part of this plan.

Three ways of thinking can help you get the most from your medication (adapted from Pat Deegan, National Empowerment Center, http://www.power2u.org/articles/selfhelp/reclaim.html):

Think differently about your medication.
a. There are no magic bullets.
b. Medications are only a tool.
c. Using medications is not a moral issue.
d. Learn to use medications in the prescribed way.
e. Learn as much as possible about your medications; the more you know about them, the better you will be able to use them.
f. Medications are never enough; medications need to be combined with other coping strategies.

Think differently about yourself.
a. Learn to trust yourself.
b. Remember, it is *your* recovery.
c. Focus on your own goals.
d. Recognize that your questions are important.

Think differently about prescribers.
a. Your prescriber has information that you can use for your own recovery.
b. Prescribers are not experts on everything.
c. Most prescribers are very busy, and might miss something important or not have enough time to give you all the information you may want and need.
d. Sometimes prescribers are wrong.

Two actions can help you get the most from your medication (adapted from Pat Deegan, National Empowerment Center, http://www.power2u.org/articles/selfhelp/reclaim.html):

Prepare to meet with your prescriber.
a. Work with your therapist to set an agenda for the meeting (e.g., "I_____").
b. Work with your therapist to organize your thoughts and concerns.

c. Be specific.

d. Write down your questions.

e. Role-play; practice with your therapist or with a friend what you want to say to your prescriber.

Take charge of the meeting with your prescriber.

a. Bring a pad and pen to the meeting.

b. Think about tape-recording the meeting so that you can remember what was said.

c. Say your agenda at the beginning of the meeting.

d. Consider bringing a friend or advocate to the meeting.

Remember that having both positive and negative thoughts about medication is not unusual. Most of us would prefer not to take medication. Even those of us who accept that we need medication would like not to have to take it. There are concerns about risk and side effects. There is the sense that when we are taking medication we are somehow dependent on it, or dependent on the person who prescribes it. Every pill we take may remind us of the illness that we are treating. It is easier to just forget the medication and the illness and hope that it will all work out and let us get better. Unfortunately, if we have a serious illness, avoiding it and forgetting medication just makes it worse. We can know this but still not like it.

People are much more likely to take medication if they believe it will help them. They probably will not take it if they believe it will not help. Beliefs are important. We all make decisions based on what we believe to be true. Consider these three important questions:

a. What is your belief about your illness?

_____

b. What is your belief about how to best treat this illness?

_____

c. Do you believe that medication will help?

_____

Recovery Lifestyle Habits

In the remainder of this chapter we explore 13 recovery life-style habits that can help you manage your illness and create the kind of life you want to live.

1. Take Your Medications Every Day

It is important to make sure that your medication works as well as possible to help you decrease your symptoms, stay in control of your own be-havior, and allow you to follow your plan. Most medication will work much better if it is taken every day. Unfortunately, it can be hard to take medication every day. It can be hard to remember to take it. It might be hard to talk yourself into taking it if it is causing uncomfortable side effects. At times, it may seem that people are pressuring or forcing you to take the medication, and it may seem natural to "fight back" by skipping doses. At other times, each dose of medication you take may remind you of the problems in your life. There may be a natural hope that if you just avoid the medication, maybe everything else will go back to the way it used to be. It can almost seem like medication is part of the problem rather than part of the solution.

> Take medication every day even when symptoms go away.

Unfortunately, your illness and your problems are very un-likely to go away or get better if you miss doses of medication. Assuming that you are on the right medication, your life is likely to be better if you take your medication consistently. Things are likely to get much worse if you skip many doses. Taking the medication every day might be hard, but it is an important part of being able to achieve your goals. When medication works well, it gets rid of some of your symp-toms and makes other symptoms easier to deal with. Medica-tion may not take away all your symptoms, but medicine can control your symptoms enough so they do not cause as much trouble.

Medication can also decrease your risk of relapse. Learn about how your medications work and what happens to make symptoms return if you stop taking the medications. Learning and living by the saying, *"Take medication the right way, every day, even when symptoms go away"* can be quite a challenge for many people. Unfortunately, without effective and regular use of medication, it is likely to be much more difficult for you to follow your recovery plan. For some people, a long-acting shot (injectable medication) may be easier than taking a pill every day. Even if you are on a long-acting shot, taking your medication regularly is still important. With an injectable medication, taking your medication regularly means getting your injection on the day it is due, every time that day comes around.

Give some thought to your medication-taking habits by answering the following questions.

A. How many times have you forgotten, missed, or skipped some of your medicine in the past week? _____

B. When was the last time you changed the dose of some of your medication, without discussing it with your prescriber?_____

C. When was the last time you stopped taking some of your medicine?_____

D. Are you willing to take your medication every day? What would be good reasons to take your medication regularly?_____

E. What keeps you from wanting to take your medication regularly?_____

Check the box that applies to you:

☐ a. I am not planning to take my medication every day.
☐ b. I am thinking about taking my medication every day.
☐ c. I am planning to start taking my medication every day very soon.
☐ d. I am ready to start taking my medication every day.
☐ e. I am already working on taking my medication every day.

☐ f. I already take my medication every day, and I am going to keep practicing this habit.

What reminders or aids would help you take your medication every day? Check the boxes that apply to you:

☐ a. I will use a weekly pillbox.

☐ b. I will ask someone to remind me or help me with my medication.

☐ c. I will talk with my prescriber about the advantages and disadvantages of taking a long-acting shot once or twice a month instead of taking pills every day.

☐ d. I will keep my medicine where I will see it when it is time to take it...
  ☐ On my dresser
  ☐ Next to my alarm clock
  ☐ At my place on the dinner table
  ☐ Next to my toothbrush
  ☐ On my pillow on my bed
  ☐ Next to my glasses
  ☐ On top of my radio or TV
  ☐ Beside my favorite chair
  ☐ Inside my shoe
  ☐ Other _____

☐ e. I will take my medicine when I do something else that I do every day...
  ☐ When I brush my teeth
  ☐ When I put my shoes on in the morning
  ☐ When I take my shoes off at night
  ☐ When I eat breakfast, lunch, or dinner
  ☐ When I feed my cat/dog
  ☐ When I _____

☐ f. I will put a reminder note where I will see it; I will be careful not to leave my medication out where children might get it.

☐ g. I will ask someone to remind me to take my medication.

☐ h. I will talk with my prescriber or therapist about the problems I am having with my medication; it is not that I forget, it is that I decide not to take it.

☐ i. None of the above; I like taking my medication when I think I need it and am not planning on changing this right now.

2. Get Regular Exercise

Exercise is another important recovery lifestyle habit. Regular exercise can help you deal with stress, improve your mood, cope with medication side effects such as weight gain and sedation, sleep better, and improve your health and wellness. Exercise that you can do for a period of time (e.g., 20–30 minutes or more) and that raises your pulse is called aerobic exercise. Lifting weights may be helpful in keeping you strong, but aerobic exercise is more important for helping you stay healthy and deal with stress. Aerobic exercise includes walking, running, biking, swimming, and even dancing. You might choose to begin walking 15 minutes a day, 3 days a week. Then gradually work up to 20–30 minutes a day, 3–5 days a week. How do you know if you are putting enough into your exercise to get the benefits? Find your target heart rate on the table below.

While you are exercising, press two fingers to the side of your throat or on your wrist. Count the number of times your heart beats in 10 seconds. Compare your 10-second heart rate to your target heart rate. You are getting the benefits of exercise when you reach your target heart rate. When you start exercising it is usually a good idea to choose a beginner target heart rate, based on your age.

Most people can do light exercise 15–30 minutes per day without risking injury or

---

Exercise Can Help You...
Deal with stress
Improve your mood
Cope with medication side effects
Sleep better
Improve your health and wellness

Table 10.1

Target Heart Rate		
10 Second Count		
YOUR AGE	Beginner Heart Rate	Intermediate Heart Rate	Advanced Heart Rate
20–24	20	23	28
25–29	20	23	28
30–34	19	22	27
34–39	19	22	26
40–44	18	21	26
45–49	18	20	25
50–54	17	20	24
55–59	17	19	23
60–64	16	19	23
65–69	16	18	22
70+	15	18	21

health complications. However, if you are overweight or have a heart condition or any other health problem, talk to your doctor before you start exercising. In almost all cases, regular exercise will help the medical condition. Even if you are in good health, if you have *any* question, doubt, or concern about whether exercise is safe for you, talk with your prescriber or family doctor before adding exercise to your recovery lifestyle. If you have a health problem that limits your exercise choices, talk to a health care professional. A recreational therapist, occupational therapist, personal trainer, or physical rehabilitation specialist may be able to help you come up with some exercises that are helpful and safe, based on your health.

Give some thought to your exercise needs, preferences, and any limitations by thinking about the following questions and checking the boxes that apply to you.

A. Do you have any health problems that make it necessary for you to talk to a doctor before you start regularly exercising?
   ☐ a. I am overweight.
   ☐ b. I have back problems.
   ☐ c. I have problems with my knees (or other joints).
   ☐ d. I have high blood pressure.
   ☐ e. I have diabetes (if you check this box, see Appendix 1).
   ☐ f. I have problems with my lungs or with breathing.
   ☐ g. I have a heart condition.
   ☐ h. I have questions, doubts, or concerns about whether exercise is safe for me.
   ☐ j. I have _____ (other health problem).
   ☐ k. I do not have any health problems, questions, doubts, or concerns.
   ☐ l. I do not have any health problems, but I will talk to my doctor just to be on the safe side.

B. Are you willing to exercise regularly? We all know we should exercise regularly, but many of us do not, even though we know we would feel better if we did. Is regular exercise something you are ready to do now?
   ☐ a. I am not planning to do regular exercise.
   ☐ b. I am thinking about doing regular exercise.
   ☐ c. I am planning to start doing regular exercise soon.
   ☐ d. I am ready to start doing regular exercise.
   ☐ e. I am already working on doing more regular exercise.
   ☐ f. I already exercise regularly, and I am going to stick with my good habit.

C. What choices will you make to get into the habit of exercising regularly?

☐ a. I will walk.　　　　　☐ g. I will hula-hoop.

☐ b. I will rollerblade.　　☐ h. I will do jumping jacks.

☐ c. I will skateboard.　　☐ i. I will bicycle.

☐ d. I will jump rope.　　 ☐ j. I will swim.

☐ e. I will jog.　　　　　 ☐ k. I will dance.

☐ f. I will march in place.　☐ l. I will ＿＿＿＿＿＿＿＿.

☐ m. None of the above; I am not planning to do regular exercise.

D. When will you exercise?

a. Which days? (circle) Sun Mon Tue Wed Thu Fri Sat

b. What time?　＿＿＿＿＿＿＿＿＿＿＿＿＿＿＿＿＿＿＿

c. When will you start? ＿＿＿＿＿＿＿＿＿＿＿＿＿＿＿＿

E. What is your target heart rate? ＿＿＿＿＿＿＿＿＿＿＿＿

3. Eat Healthy Meals

Eating healthy food is another important part of recovery and wellness. Choosing healthy food instead of junk food can help your brain work better, help keep your mood stable, and keep up your energy level. It is easy to grab a hamburger and an order of fries instead of a bowl of soup and a salad. A hamburger, with its high fat contact, might taste better, is easier to eat "on the run,"

> Eat brain food instead of junk food.

and may even be less expensive. A bag of potato chips may be more appealing than a piece of fruit. The people who sell us fast food understand how to get us to eat what they want to sell, instead of what is good for us. Unfortunately, high-fat, high-sugar food will usually cause us to feel less energetic or "sharp." Choose food wisely. Pick brain food instead of junk food.

Eating regular meals, especially breakfast, is also important, rather than just grabbing a candy bar or other snack. Breakfast does not need to be expensive or hard to make. Many cereals are inexpensive, easy to fix, and good for you. A sandwich can be made with a lot less fat than a hamburger, and even if you are not much of a cook, it is easy to warm up a frozen dinner in a microwave, healthy, and much less expensive than eating out at a fast food place.

Think about how you feel when you eat healthy food. Consider changing your eating habits for 3 weeks. This is probably the shortest possible time to experience much of a difference. Do you feel any differently? Do you feel any more alert, or can you concentrate better, or do you just feel a bit more energetic? Do your friends or other people on your support team notice a difference? Do your activities change? Do you do more things or different things when you are eating healthy food? This is easier said than done. Many of us are not in the habit of eating well. Eating food that is healthy, inexpensive, easy to fix, and that tastes good requires that we think about what we are doing instead of just grabbing what is easiest.

Skipping meals or replacing meals with snacks that have little nutritional value can make it hard to control your mood, energy level, and thinking. Are you in the habit of eating healthy meals? Consider the following questions fill in the blanks, and check the boxes that apply to you.

A. What meals do you usually eat?
   ☐ Breakfast
   ☐ Lunch
   ☐ Dinner
   ☐ Other

B. What do you usually eat?
   Breakfast: _____
   Lunch: _____
   Dinner: _____

C. How willing are you to eat healthier meals?
   ☐ a. I am not interested in changing what I eat.
   ☐ b. I am thinking about eating healthier meals.
   ☐ c. I am planning to start eating healthier meals soon.
   ☐ d. I am ready to start eating healthier meals.
   ☐ e. I am already working on eating healthy meals.
   ☐ f. I already eat healthy meals, and I am going to keep practicing this good habit.

D. What healthy foods will you choose?
   Breakfast: _____
   Lunch: _____
   Dinner: _____
   None of the above; I'm not planning to change my eating habits right now.

4. Limit Caffeine and Sugar

You may not realize how much caffeine and sugar you take in during the day. A 2-liter bottle of cola has a huge load of both. The sugar can lead to weight gain as well as mood instability. Too much caffeine can keep your medication from working and make your symptoms worse. The more caffeine and sugar you take in, the harder it is to control your illness. Unfortunately, caffeine can be addictive. If you regularly use a lot of caffeine, you probably do not realize you are "hooked." You might be thinking, "I drink coffee and soda all day, and it doesn't bother me." You cannot really know what effect caffeine and sugar may be having on you untill you go without them for a while. Consider the following questions, fill in the blanks, and check the boxes that apply to you.

A. How much of soda, coffee and tea do you usually drink a day?
   a. I usually drink _____ of soda a day.
   b. I usually drink _____ of coffee a day.
   c. I usually drink _____ of tea a day.

B. How often do you usually eat sweets? _____
C. What are your favorite sweets?
- ☐ a. Candy
- ☐ b. Cookies
- ☐ c. Pie
- ☐ d. Cake
- ☐ e. Sweet rolls
- ☐ f. Donuts
- ☐ f. Ice cream
- ☐ f. _____

Choosing caffeine-free soda, coffee, and tea can help decrease anxiety and reduce the severity of other symptoms. Cutting back on sugar can help you feel better while also cutting calories and helping you lose weight. Your brain may go through withdrawal if you suddenly stop all caffeine or suddenly cut down on sugar. If you have been using a lot of caffeine and stop it suddenly, you may have a few days of headaches, crankiness, and low energy. Some people prefer to just stop caffeine all at once. Some people prefer to cut down on caffeine intake over a period of time, taking less every day until they are off it completely after a few weeks. Once you are off all caffeine and have cut down on your sugar, pay attention to how you feel. Some people switch to water. Other people like the flavor of soda so they switch to caffeine-free and sugar-free soda. There are many different sugar-free and caffeine-free drinks that you can choose.

Again, it is hard to really know what caffeine and sugar may be doing unless you stop or at least limit these substances for 3 weeks or so, and then step back and evaluate how you feel. Can you tell a difference? Can people on your support team tell a difference? Is your sleep different? Are your symptoms less distressing or easier to manage? Do you feel less anxious? Do you feel any less moody? Have you been able to lose any weight? Are you gaining less weight?

Some people do better with no caffeine. Other people find that they feel better and concentrate better if they take some caffeine. The important word here is *some*. The problem is that most people take much more caffeine than is helpful, because the amount tends to go up over time due to tolerance and addiction. This extra caffeine can cause you to feel more anxious, interfere with sleep, and make other symptoms worse. Once you have stopped all caffeine for at least 3 weeks so you know how it feels to be caffeine free, think about whether or not your symptoms are less distressing, or less difficult to manage. This approach is usually especially helpful for people who are on higher doses of medication, or multiple medications, but still have problems with distressing symptoms. Consider these questions and check the boxes that apply to you.

A. Are you willing to cut down on caffeine or sugar to see if this helps?
   a. I'm not interested in cutting down on either caffeine or sugar at this time.
   b. I am thinking about cutting down on ☐ caffeine, ☐ sugar, or ☐ caffeine and sugar.
   c. I am planning to start cutting down on ☐ caffeine, ☐ sugar, or ☐ caffeine and sugar soon.
   d. I am ready to start cutting down on ☐ caffeine, ☐ sugar, or ☐ caffeine and sugar.
   e. I am already working on cutting down on ☐ caffeine, ☐ sugar, or ☐ caffeine and sugar.
   f. I already cut down on ☐ caffeine, ☐ sugar, or ☐ caffeine and sugar, and I am going to keep practicing this good habit.

B. What healthier choices will you make?
   ☐ a. I will drink water instead of soda, tea, or coffee.
   ☐ b. I will drink sugar-free and caffeine-free soda, tea, or coffee.

☐ c. I will replace sweets with healthy snacks and treats.

☐ d. I will _____

☐ e. None of the above; I am not planning to change the amount of sugar or caffeine that I eat/drink at this time.

5. Get Enough Sleep

Regular sleep habits are an important part of recovery. Different people need different amounts of sleep, but most people will do better if they sleep between 7 and 9 hours a night. You can force yourself to sleep less, but allowing yourself to get enough sleep each night may help you control your symptoms, keep your mood stable, give you more energy during the day, and help your brain work better. If you have trouble sleeping at night, this may be a recovery lifestyle habit that you might choose to change.

* *Sleeping pills.* Some people find it hard to get to sleep or stay asleep. The common response if someone cannot sleep is to take a sleeping pill. Actually, there are a lot of things you can do to improve the quality of your sleep besides just taking a sleeping pill. Talk with your treatment team if you practice good sleep habits but you still have trouble sleeping.

* *Boredom.* Some people who complain of not being able to sleep actually have no problem with sleep but have a major problem with boredom. Some people who have little to do may want to pass time by trying to sleep 10 or 12 hours a day, or even more. If you try to sleep more than your body needs as a way of passing time, you will not be able to do it. This is not a sleep problem but a boredom problem.

* *Sleep disorders.* Some people can't sleep at night because they have a specific disorder that can cause them to wake up many times during the night. The most common sleep disorders are sleep apnea and restless leg syndrome. Both of these conditions cause people to wake up feeling very tired, even if they

spend a lot of time in bed trying to sleep. People with sleep apnea actually stop breathing while they are asleep, and their body wakes them up when they need more oxygen. This can happen 50 times a night or even more. People with sleep apnea almost always snore very loudly. Snoring does not mean that you have sleep apnea, but if you do snore, sleep apnea is more likely. People with restless leg syndrome will move and jerk and kick so much that they keep waking themselves up many times during the night. You can ask your health care physician, nurse, or psychiatrist for more information about these two sleep disorders.

• *Anxiety.* Many people do not have any specific sleep disorder, but they get so anxious that they cannot get to sleep. They may worry so much about getting to sleep that it gets in the way of falling asleep. Especially if someone has had trouble getting to sleep in the recent past, he or she may be so afraid that he or she will not sleep tonight that the fear of not sleeping will interfere with sleep. The more afraid you are that you will not be able to sleep, the more likely that this fear will keep you awake. When anxiety interferes with your sleep, paying attention to good sleep habits can help. Some useful relaxation skills will be discussed later in this chapter.

• *Sleep diary.* If you are having trouble with your sleep, keeping a "sleep diary" can be very useful. A sleep diary is a calendar where, every day, you write down what time you got to bed, what time you woke up, and a few other things connected to sleep. This can include whether or not you exercised, used alcohol, took a nap, had some unusual stress during the day, etc. This kind of record keeping can give you information about the pattern of your sleep. For example, do you have problems sleeping every day, or just weekends, or just after you get your paycheck? It is often hard to figure out these patterns without keeping a sleep diary.

• *Early warning sign of relapse.* A major change in your sleep pattern can be an early warning sign of relapse. People who are getting manic, depressed, or more psychotic often have a change in sleep pattern before things get very bad. Sleep problems often happen before there are other signs or symptoms of relapse. Talk with your treatment team. You might need a medication change or you may need to encourage yourself to sleep more instead of staying up so late at night. Anything that disrupts your sleep can increase your risk of relapse.

• *Changing habits.* Choosing new sleep habits could help you sleep better and feel better. Keep in mind that changing your sleep habits takes persistence and practice. You will not sleep better right away. That is true of changing any habit. Make healthy a choice and practice over and over again until you have a new habit that works well for you.

> Getting 7–9 hours of sleep at night can help your recovery.

Getting 7 9 hours of sleep at night may help you feel better, keep your symptoms under better control, and reduce your risk of relapse. Consider the following questions and check the boxes that apply to you.

A. What sleep habits do you have?
  ☐ a. I often get less than 7 hours of sleep at night.
  ☐ b. I frequently stay up late at night or get up early.
  ☐ c. I usually have a lot of trouble falling asleep at night.
  ☐ d. I often wake up in the middle of the night and can't get back to sleep.
  ☐ e. I usually sleep more than 9 hours at night.
  ☐ f. I _____.
  ☐ g. I usually get 7–9 hours of sleep.

B. How interested are you in changing your sleep habits?
  ☐ a. I am thinking about changing my sleep habits.
  ☐ b. I am planning to start changing my sleep habits soon.
  ☐ c. I am ready to start changing my sleep habits.
  ☐ d. I am already changing my sleep habits.

      ☐ e. I do not sleep 7–9 hours each night, but I am not ready to make any changes in my sleep habits right now.

      ☐ f. I already sleep 7–9 hours each night, and I am going to stick with my good sleep habits.

C. What good sleep habits will you practice?

      ☐ a. I will go to bed at about the same time each night. What time? _____

      ☐ b. I will wake up at about the same time each morning. What time? _____

      ☐ c. I will stay awake and out of bed during the day.

      ☐ d. I will exercise each morning. What time? _____

      ☐ e. I will shower in the morning instead of at night. What time? _____

      ☐ f. I will practice a relaxation skill at bedtime to help me get to sleep. What time? _____

      ☐ g. I will drink a cup of warm milk to help me get to sleep. What time? _____

      ☐ h. I will avoid alcohol (which some people thinks helps sleep but actually interferes with it).

      ☐ i. I will decrease the amount of liquid I drink before bed, because I keep waking up to go to the bathroom.

      ☐ j. I will decrease the amount I smoke (heavy smokers actually wake up during the night because they go through nicotine withdrawal).

      ☐ k. I will _____.

      ☐ l. None of the above. I'm not planning to change my sleep habits right now.

6. Practice Relaxation Skills

Most of us have a list of things that we do when we are upset. Each person's list is a bit different, but some things are common. For example, if you are upset, does it help if you take a walk, or is it better for you if you stay in your room? Does it help if you listen to music, read, watch TV, talk to a friend, take some deep breaths, or e-mail a support group? Do you find that it helps if you work on a jigsaw puzzle, knit, or draw? Praying helps some people, while other people cannot even imagine how praying might help. Keeping busy is often helpful as long as the activity is not too demanding. The one sure point is that what helps varies from one person to another.

It might be a good idea to make a list of the activities that help you cope with stress and symptoms. This list can be an important part of your personal recovery lifestyle habits.

What activities help you cope with distress and symptoms? Check the box(es) that applies to you.

☐ a. I take a walk to cope with distress and symptoms.
☐ b. I pray to cope with distress and symptoms.
☐ c. I call a friend to cope with distress and symptoms.
☐ d. I listen to music to cope with distress and symptoms.
☐ e. I read a book or magazine to cope with distress and symptoms.
☐ f. I watch TV to cope with distress and symptoms.
☐ g. I clean the house to cope with distress and symptoms.
☐ h. I exercise to cope with distress and symptoms.
☐ i. I e-mail a support group to cope with distress and symptoms.
☐ j. I practice relaxation skills to cope with distress and symptoms.
☐ j. I _____ to cope with distress and symptoms.

Doing What Helps

Choosing things that work well and getting yourself to do those things may be a challenge. Some people naturally and easily do activities that help them calm down and cope better. Other people may know what they need to do, but find it more difficult to talk themselves into doing those things. Still other people seem to get stuck in a habit of doing things that are not really very helpful. What about you?

☐ a. When I am upset, I naturally do things that help me calm down.
☐ b. When I am upset, I need to force myself to do things that help me feel better.
☐ c. When I am upset, I have a habit of doing things that are not really very helpful.

The activities that are already on your list are probably things that you do naturally, often without practice. You do not have to practice to take a walk or talk to a friend. There may also be some new skills you could learn and practice that would help you.

Relaxation Skills

Many people find that practicing relaxation skills help them deal with stress, calm down, and cope with distressing symptoms. There are six main kinds of relaxation skills, as listed in Table 10.2. You may find it helpful to learn and practice one or more relaxation skill to manage your persistent symptoms and cope with stress. A lot of people confuse relaxation skills with resting behaviors and leisure activities. Resting behaviors do not require new skills or practice. Relaxation skills must be learned and practiced. Many people find these learned skills helpful, regardless of whether or not they have a mental illness.

Table 10.2 Resting Behaviors and Relaxation Skills

Resting Behaviors	Relaxation Skills
Listening to music	Deep breathing
Watching TV	Muscle tensing
Sitting outside	Meditation
Taking a bath	Guided relaxation
Going for a walk	Tai chi
Reading	Yoga
Taking a nap	

Different people will find each type of relaxation more or less helpful. For example, you may find meditation very helpful but find that tai chi is not as helpful for you.

Choosing to Learn

Of course, because these are skills that must be learned, to find out if any of them will help you, you need to spend some time and energy to learn how to do them. Learning one of these skills might be a positive way to spend time and energy for some people. To learn these skills, you must also find a person, group, book, audio, or video tape that will teach the skills to you. Not all of the relaxation skills will be taught in every community. For people who are interested in more holistic and healthy ways of staying focused, managing distress, and being in control of themselves, these relaxation skills can be very useful.

What, How Much, How Often, and When?

The choice of which relaxation skills to practice is up to you. Choose the relaxation skills that are available to you and that you enjoy. For relaxation skills to help, it is important to practice often enough and long enough. It is a good idea to practice relaxation skills 20 minutes each day, and again as needed, to cope with persistent symptoms and distress. Practicing relaxation skills can help you cope with stress and manage some of the persistent symptoms that stick with you in spite of taking your medication the right way every day.

> Practice relaxation skills 20 minutes every day, and again as needed, to cope with persistent symptoms and stress.

There are, of course, other relaxation skills that are not on this list. There are also many different kinds of meditation and many different kinds of yoga. This list contains examples of relaxation skills that require learning new skills and regular practice. A growing number of people are learning to use meditation, yoga, tai chi, and other such skills to be more in control of themselves and their thoughts and feelings. Do not just try these skills a few times and then give up. Choose one or more that you like, practice every day, and stick with it until you have a new recovery lifestyle habit. Consider the following questions and check the boxes that apply to you.

A. Do you believe that it would be helpful for you to learn to be more relaxed? _____

B. Do you think that learning to be more relaxed would help you cope with your symptoms better? _____

C. How interested are you in learning relaxation skills?
   ☐ a. I am not interesting in learning relaxation skills at this time.
   ☐ b. I am interested in learning about relaxation skills.
   ☐ c. I am willing to find out what relaxation skills I can learn from a person, group, book, audio, or video tape.
   ☐ d. I am planning to start practicing relaxation skills soon.
   ☐ e. I am ready to start practicing relaxation skills.
   ☐ f. I am already working on practicing relaxation skills more often.
   ☐ g. I already practice relaxation skills every day, and I am going to continue my good habit.

D. Which relaxation skill will you learn and practice?
   ☐ a. I will learn and practice deep breathing.
   ☐ b. I will learn and practice muscle tensing.
   ☐ c. I will learn and practice meditation.
   ☐ d. I will learn and practice guided relaxation.
   ☐ e. I will learn and practice tai chi.
   ☐ f. I will learn and practice yoga.

☐ g. I am uncertain; I will find out what skills I can learn from a person, group, book, or video/audio tape that I can pay, buy, rent, or borrow from the library.

☐ h. None of the above. I'm not planning to learn and practice any relaxation skills at this time.

For many people, getting started on a new habit is more likely to happen if they choose a specific day and time to begin.

E. When (what day) will you start learning and practicing relaxation skills?

☐ a. I will begin learning and practicing relaxation on _____day.

☐ b. I already practice relaxation skills.

☐ c. I am not interested right now.

F. What time of the day will you (or do you) practice relaxation skills?

☐ a. I will practice relaxation skills at _____A.M. P.M.

☐ b. I already practice relaxation skills at _____A.M. P.M.

☐ c. I am not interested right now.

7. Stop Smoking

Tobacco is very addictive, very expensive, and causes major health problems. Tobacco is more addictive than heroin. It is harder to quit smoking than it is to quit any other drug. In part, this is because of the drug itself. Over time, nicotine does things to the brain that make you crave it, and this craving can go on for a very long time after you stop. In part, this is because smoking and reminders about smoking are all around us, so that you are always reminded or "cued." It is much harder to stay away from any drug if you go back into the place where you used that drug. Because most smokers use nicotine in every part of their life, it is almost impossible to avoid these "cues." If you are used to smoking when you first wake up in the morning, or if you are used to smoking at the end of every meal, then every time you wake up and every meal will be a cue that will renew your desire to smoke.

At the same time that it is very hard to quite smoking, quitting smoking is one of the more important things that you can do to be healthier. Smoking damages your heart and lungs, leaves you short of breath, and causes cancer. Smoking when you are younger can cause emphysema as you get older. Smoking is also very expensive. If you smoke one pack of cigarettes a day at $3.50 per pack, you are spending $105 per month on cigarettes, or $1,260 per year on cigarettes. You can go on a nice vacation in the Bahamas for a week next winter, including airfare, hotel, food, and everything else for less than $1,260. If you are a bit careful, you can even take a friend on vacation for less than the cost of smoking one pack of cigarettes a day for a year.

People with schizophrenia are much more likely to smoke than the general population. There may be something in the brain of people with schizophrenia that makes cigarettes particularly addictive. This added factor makes it hard to quit but not impossible. We know that it is much easier to quit if you are quitting at the same time as friends or other people around you are quitting. It is much harder to quit if people around you continue to smoke. We know that the stop-smoking groups help, or at least help most people. We know that the nicotine patches and other medications can help some. However, these medications work much better if they are combined with a stop-smoking group or other behavioral supports.

Stopping smoking is both very important and very hard. It does not have to be an all-or-none deal. Even if you are not ready to quit, you may be willing to cut down. Going from a pack of cigarettes a day to half a pack is still a big enough change to help you feel better, cause less risk to your health, and save you a lot of money. Put stopping or cutting down smoking on your list as part of your journey toward recovery.

Decide if this is something you are ready to do now or something that you need to put off until some other time.

How willing are you to stop smoking?
- ☐ a. I am thinking about stopping smoking.
- ☐ b. I am planning to stop smoking soon.
- ☐ c. I am ready to stop smoking.
- ☐ d. I am already working on stopping smoking.
- ☐ e. I do smoke, but I am not ready to make any changes in my smoking habits right now.
- ☐ f. I do not smoke.

8. Reach Out for Recovery Support

It can be tough to recover from mental illness. It may be even harder to recover all by yourself, without any support. *Recovery support* is the encouragement, assistance, and caring you get from people to help you stay focused on recovery.

Many things can get in the way of reaching out for recovery support. Because of your mental illness, you may have become isolated. Relationships with your family may have been strained or broken. You may have lost contact with friends. Perhaps the only support you have is from members of your treatment team. Or perhaps you have family or friends who care, but you do not reach out for their support. You may want help learning or practicing ways of reaching out to friends and family who will support your recovery. You might also want

| People who support your recovery... |
| Care about you |
| Understand your mental illness |
| Encourage recovery lifestyle habits |
| Help you stay focused on recovery |
| Encourage you to achieve your life goals |

help learning or practicing ways of giving support, to have a more balanced give-and-take relationship with the people about whom you care. Giving recovery support to other people who have mental illness can also help with your own recovery. However, you may want to learn to set limits on giving. You might want to get into the habit of reaching out for more support instead of putting all your energy into giving support to other people. Getting into the habit of reaching out for and giving recovery support can help you stay focused on recovery.

A. To whom do you reach out for recovery support? _____

_____

B. What gets in the way of reaching out for recovery support?
   ☐ a. I do not get along with anyone in my family.
   ☐ b. I do not see my family very often.
   ☐ c. I do not have any friends.
   ☐ d. I have friends or family who care, but I don't reach out for support.
   ☐ e. My family/friends do not understand my illness well enough to give me recovery support.
   ☐ f. I do not know of any peer support groups or drop-in centers.
   ☐ g. I do not know how to make friends.
   ☐ h. I give support to other people, but I do not reach out for support for myself.
   ☐ i. There are places to go for recovery support, but I do not go because _____.
   ☐ j. Other _____.
   ☐ k. Nothing gets in my way. I reach out for and give recovery support.

C. How willing are you to reach out for recovery support?
   ☐ a. I am not interested in reaching out for recovery support.
   ☐ b. I am thinking about reaching out for recovery support.
   ☐ c. I am planning to start reaching out for recovery support soon.
   ☐ d. I am ready to start reaching out for recovery support.

☐ e. I am already reaching out for recovery support more often.

☐ f. I already reach out for recovery support, and I am going to continue my good habit.

D. Where will you reach out for recovery support?

☐ a. I will reach out at home with my family.

☐ b. I will reach out at peer-support group meetings.

☐ c. I will reach out at a drop-in center.

☐ d. I will reach out at a social center.

☐ e. I will reach out at a place of worship (church, synagogue, or mosque).

☐ f. I will reach out at an advocacy group meeting (e.g., Alliance for the Mentally Ill, consumer support).

☐ g. I will reach out at a clubhouse.

☐ h. I will reach out at the mental health center.

☐ i. I will reach out at a friend's house.

☐ j. I will reach out at _____.

☐ k. None of the above. I'm not planning to reach out for support.

9. Avoid Street Drugs and Alcohol

Many people with major mental illness use or abuse street drugs and alcohol. Although some people abuse prescribed medications, our main focus here is on the types of drugs that are bought and sold "on the street," such as speed, pot, crack, and methamphetamine. We also use the term "street drugs" to be clear that we are not suggesting that you avoid all drugs. Prescription medications are sometimes called drugs. We are not suggesting that you avoid prescribed medications, just street drugs.

A. Reasons for Street Drug/Alcohol Use

There are a lot of different reasons that people with mental illness end up using street drugs. If you use drugs or alcohol, it is important to get a sense of how the substance affects your life. What do street drugs do that you like? How do drugs and alcohol get in the way of things you would like to be doing? We are not talking about abuse or whether it seems like you have a problem with street drugs or alcohol. Think about whether you use street drugs or if you drink alcohol on more than a very occasional basis. If you do—and most people with serious mental illness do—then think about the reasons. What do the drugs or alcohol do that you enjoy or that seem useful to you? In the following list, check all of the positive things connected to your drug/alcohol use.

B. How Do Street Drugs/Alcohol Help You?

- ☐ a. Street drugs/alcohol help me feel better.
- ☐ b. Street drugs/alcohol help me function better.
- ☐ c. Street drugs/alcohol help me do things that would be harder to do without them.
- ☐ d. Street drugs/alcohol help me have a good time with friends.
- ☐ e. Street drugs/alcohol help me fit in with friends.
- ☐ f. Street drugs/alcohol help me sleep.
- ☐ g. Street drugs/alcohol help me _____
- ☐ h. None of the above. Street drugs/alcohol don't help me.

C. Problems Caused by Street Drugs/Alcohol

Okay, now that you have listed how street drugs and alcohol help, think of some of the problems caused by these same substances. What problems can you think of connected to drugs and alcohol?

D. What Problems Do You Believe are Connected to Drug and Alcohol Use?

- ☐ a. Drugs/alcohol could make me more paranoid.
- ☐ b. Drugs/alcohol might make me more depressed.
- ☐ c. Drugs/alcohol could make my symptoms worse.

☐ d. Drugs/alcohol may make me angrier/more irritable/more likely to get into fights.

☐ e. Drugs/alcohol could make me more impulsive; I do things I would not do if I were not high, stoned, or drunk.

☐ f. Drugs/alcohol might make it harder for me to do things that I want to do.

☐ g. Drugs/alcohol could make it harder to concentrate or think clearly.

☐ h. Drugs/alcohol might get me arrested.

☐ i. Drugs/alcohol could get me rehospitalized.

☐ j. Drugs/alcohol might get me kicked out of where I live.

☐ k. Drugs/alcohol could _____.

E. Are Other People Concerned?

Even if you believe that your alcohol or drug use is not a problem, what does your family or therapist or other support group members say about your drug use? Do you think other people are concerned about your drug and alcohol use?

☐ a. Yes, other people are concerned about my street drug/alcohol use.

☐ b. No, no one has ever seemed concerned or said anything to me about my street drug/alcohol use.

F. Potential Problems

There are lots of problems that can be caused or worsened by street drug and alcohol use or abuse—although they might not all be a problem for you. It is possible that none of them is a problem for you but is a problem for many people. Listed below are examples of problems. Mark the ones that you have noticed, agree with, or that might be a problem for you.

G. Problems with Alcohol

☐ a. Alcohol can cause medical problems or make other medical problems much worse, including problems with liver, heart, nerves, or pancreas.

☐ b. Alcohol can make it hard to sleep.

☐ c. Alcohol can make depression much worse.

☐ d. Alcohol can make psychotic symptoms worse/more out of control.

☐ e. Alcohol can increase impulsivity/anger/fights.

☐ f. Alcohol can make it harder to work or be consistent with other activities.

☐ g. Alcohol can lead to my getting arrested, either for drunk driving, fighting, or in some other way.

☐ h. Alcohol can interfere with the action of many medications, especially antidepressants.

☐ i. Alcohol can _____.

H. Problems with Marijuana

☐ a. Marijuana can make paranoia worse.

☐ b. Marijuana can interfere with motivation or the ability to follow through with activities.

☐ c. Marijuana can make people more "spacey" or disorganized.

☐ d. Marijuana can make hallucinations worse.

☐ e. Marijuana can _____.

I. Problems with Cocaine

☐ a. Cocaine can cause people to become psychotic or paranoid, or make these problems worse in someone who already experiences these symptoms.

☐ b. Cocaine can cause people to become impulsive, angry, irritable.

☐ c. Cocaine can lead to "crashes" and depression.

☐ d. Cocaine can cause sudden death.

☐ e. Cocaine can cause medical problems.

☐ f. Cocaine use can get me arrested.

☐ g. Cocaine is expensive, and it keeps me from having money I need for other things.

☐ h. Cocaine can _____.

J. Problems with Meth (Methamphetamine)

☐ a. Meth can cause people to become psychotic or paranoid, or make these problems worse in someone who already experiences these symptoms.

☐ b. Meth can cause people to become impulsive, angry, irritable.

☐ c. Meth can lead to "crashes" and depression.

☐ d. Meth can cause sudden death.

☐ e. Meth can cause medical problems.

☐ f. Meth use can get me arrested.

☐ g. Meth is expensive, and it keeps me from having money I need for other things.

☐ h. Meth can _____.

Street Drugs, Alcohol, and Recovery

Although there are legal and addiction problems, they are not the most important reasons to quit drinking or drugging. Substance abuse makes most people more unstable, impulsive, and focused more on the drug than on their life goals. Drug and alcohol use is very likely to make your symptoms worse. Often people using drugs or alcohol find that they need a higher dose of psychiatric medications. Even with a higher dose, the medications are probably not going to work as well. Street drugs and alcohol keep you from recovering, keep your medication from working, make your symptoms worse, greatly increase your chances of relapse, and get in the way of your reaching your goals. In fact, street drugs and alcohol are the second most common cause of relapse.

You may have been told that street drugs and alcohol "don't mix" with medication. For the most part, there is little medical danger in taking most street

> Street drugs and alcohol are likely to make your medication less effective and make your illness worse.

drugs with most prescribed medication (however, there are some important dangerous interactions, so ask your prescriber about specifics). The real problem is that street drugs and alcohol are likely to make your underlying mental illness much worse and make it harder to reach your personal life goals. Even regular use of psychiatric medication is usually not enough to overcome the increase in symptoms and behavioral problems caused by street drugs.

Keep Taking Your Medication

What this means is that you should not use drugs or alcohol, but if you do use, you should keep taking your prescribed medication anyway. Talk to your prescriber about the substances you use. The medication that is prescribed for you may help a bit in preventing some of the out-of-control problems that the street drugs and alcohol could cause. It is not a good idea to stop taking medication on Friday in order to drink or drug over the weekend. You should *not* stop taking your antipsychotic, antidepressant, mood stabilizer, or side effect medications simply because you choose to drink alcohol or use street drugs.

You may be one of many people who would benefit from treatment that focuses on both your substance use and your mental illness. "Dual diagnosis treatment" helps you overcome your problems with street drugs and alcohol at the same time you get help with your psychiatric illness. It is best to get both mental health and substance abuse treatment together in the same program, if possible. However, it is better to be referred for separate substance abuse treatment than to get no substance abuse treatment at all. Staying clean and sober are very important parts of recovery. However, it may take some people a great deal of treatment and perseverance to achieve and sustain clean and sober lifestyle habits. It is important to start a clean and sober lifestyle today. It is also important to not get so frustrated that you give up if you relapse. Consider the following questions, fill in the blanks, and check the boxes that apply to you.

A. When was the last time you drank alcohol? _____
B. When was the time before that? _____
C. How much do you usually drink? _____

D. What street drugs have you used in the past 6 months?
   ☐ a. Marijuana—last use? _____
   ☐ b. Crack—last use? _____
   ☐ c. Speed—last use? _____
   ☐ d. Cocaine—last use? _____
   ☐ e. Meth—last use? _____
   ☐ f. Other drugs _____ Last use? _____
   ☐ g. None of the above. I don't use any street drugs.

E. How ready are you to quit drinking alcohol and using street drugs?
   ☐ a. I'm not planning to quit drinking alcohol or using street drugs.
   ☐ b. I am thinking about quitting ☐ alcohol, ☐ street drugs, or ☐ both alcohol and street drugs.
   ☐ c. I am planning to quit ☐ alcohol, ☐ street drugs, or ☐ both alcohol and street drugs.
   ☐ d. I am ready to quit ☐ alcohol, ☐ street drugs, or ☐ both alcohol and street drugs.
   ☐ e. I am already working on quitting ☐ alcohol, ☐ street drugs, or ☐ both alcohol and street drugs.
   ☐ f. I already avoid ☐ alcohol, ☐ street drugs, or ☐ both alcohol and street drugs, and I am going to continue my good habit.

10. Stay Busy

Most people need activities, hobbies, or responsibilities that can help them fill their day, calm down if they are upset, experience meaning in life, get things done, and work toward goals.

Staying awake, out of bed, and busy during the day can help you manage your illness and reach your goals. For most people, sitting around all day, watching TV, "hanging out" and being inactive and unproductive tend to diminish recovery and keep them from reaching their personal life goals. Consider the possibility of finding things to do each day that get you up and keep you going. You might start the day by making a list of things you could do that very day to work toward your life goals. You could write down a "to-do list" every day, mark off each item on the list after you get it done, then pick something else on the list and do it. Another option is to put together a structured daily schedule that lists what you will do at each time of the day. Many people find it helpful to balance their day with lots of different activities. Think about some of the different things you could do. Staying busy can enrich your life and help your recovery. Of course, some people are plenty busy enough already, but there are many other people who are bored because they are not busy enough. Consider the following questions and check the boxes that apply to you.

A. How interested are you in having more to do and staying busier?
   - ☐ a. I am not interested in being any busier than I am now.
   - ☐ b. I am thinking about staying busy.
   - ☐ c. I am planning to start staying busy soon.
   - ☐ d. I am ready to start staying busy.
   - ☐ e. I am already staying busy more often.
   - ☐ f. I already stay busy, and I am going to stick with my good habit.

B. What will you do to stay busy?
   - ☐ a. I will find things to do every day that get me up and keep me going.

☐ b. I will start each day by making a list of things I will do to work on my life goals.

☐ c. I will balance each day with lots of different kinds of activities. (Write one to three ideas for each activity you might be interested in:)

Having fun: _____

Being helpful: _____

Doing something challenging: _____

Practicing relaxation skills: _____

Being productive: _____

Doing exercise: _____

Eating healthy meals: _____

Getting chores done: _____

Doing something rewarding: _____

Resting: _____

Doing something for someone else: _____

Learning something new: _____

Taking medication: (when?) _____

Doing something interesting: _____

Enjoying a hobby: _____

Doing something thoughtful: _____

Being responsible: _____

Doing something enjoyable: _____

Spending time with friends and family: _____

Accomplishing something important: _____

Reading: _____

Sleeping: (what time?) _____

Other: _____

☐ d. I will put together a structured daily schedule, listing what I will do at each time of the day.
☐ e. I will _____
☐ f. None of the above. I'm as busy as I want to be.

11. Actively Manage Persistent Symptoms

In spite of taking your medication the right way every day, you may still have some persistent symptoms. Even when you are feeling your best, you may still have a few symptoms that are better but that do not completely go away. When symptoms persist in spite of medication, recognize your persistent symptoms, monitor them using symptom checklists or mood monitors, and practice symptom management skills. To successfully manage symptoms, it helps if you realize that symptoms are just that: symptoms of your mental illness. The 1990s was often called the decade of the brain. During those years scientific research helped us understand that mental illnesses are biological brain disorders. The symptoms are caused by a chemical imbalance in your brain. You can learn to remind yourself that your symptoms simply come from your brain disorder. When symptoms are bothering you, you can tell yourself, "My brain is just playing tricks on me." This is an important habit that makes it possible for you to use "intellectual override"—to use logical thinking to overcome and ignore your symptoms. You don't have to get emotionally hooked by your persistent symptoms. You can overcome persistent symptoms such as delusions, anxious thoughts, hallucinations, depressive thoughts, paranoia, and automatic negative thoughts if you make a habit of not to believing them. This is the basic idea behind symptom management skills.

Concentrating on the lyrics of a song is one way to manage persistent auditory hallucinations. Another way to manage symptoms that works with many different troublesome persistent symptoms is to apply five steps to symptom management. (Adapted from McMullin RE and Casey B. Talk. Sense to Yourself. Lakewood, CO: Counseling Research Institute; 1975.)

Five Steps to Symptom Management

1. Stop!
2. Relax
3. Replace
4. Keep Brain Busy
5. Repeat

---

1. <u>Stop!</u> Interrupt your persistent symptoms by saying *stop* to yourself several times. You can do this silently in your head when people are around or aloud when you are alone. Choose not to let symptoms control your thoughts and feelings. Be forceful about stopping your symptoms.

2. <u>Relax.</u> Use deep breathing to calm yourself. Persistent symptoms can't stress you out if you don't let them. Stay calm and in control of your thoughts and feelings. You can stay relaxed and manage your illness by controlling how you cope with, and respond to, persistent, troublesome, pesky, or disabling symptoms. To practice deep breathing:

a. Take a slow, deep, belly breath in through your nose.
b. Hold the breath while you silently and slowly count to 3.
c. Slowly blow the air out through your mouth while thinking *relax.*
d. Repeat two or more times.

3. <u>Replace.</u> Use whatever replacement thoughts work best for you. Some examples: "My brain is just playing tricks on me";

"I don't believe these symptoms, they are just my illness acting up"; "I'm in control of my thoughts and feelings"; "Automatic negative thoughts are just a part of my illness"; "I am stronger than my symptoms." Choose and use your "symptom busters" as automatic replacement thoughts. Staying in control of your thoughts will help you control your feelings.

   4.   Keep Your Brain Busy. Do something that keeps your brain busy. An idle brain invites the return of symptoms such as automatic negative thoughts, paranoid thinking, delusional thoughts, depressive thoughts, and anxious thoughts. Being in control of what your brain is doing will help you keep your symptoms under control. Puzzles, meditation, reading, writing, and math are just a few examples of ways you can choose to train your brain to focus on something productive instead of running amuck with persistent symptoms.

   5.   Repeat. The very nature of persistent symptoms is that they are *persistent.* You will probably find out that you must repeat the five steps to symptom management over and over again to gain control of your persistent symptoms. Be tougher and more persistent than your symptoms. Don't "try" these steps once, then give in to symptoms. Practice and get better and better at controlling your symptoms over time. You can control your persistent symptoms with patience and practice.

   Now consider the following questions and check the boxes that apply to you.

   A.   What persistent symptoms have been bothering you recently?
        ☐ a. Delusions (false ideas or beliefs that your brain convinces you are real)
        ☐ b. Anxious thoughts (thinking *what if,* disaster, doomsday thoughts; "awfulizing")
        ☐ c. Hallucinations (hearing voices or seeing things)

☐ d. Depressive thoughts (thinking *if only, why, never, always, impossible, nothing will change, why try*; feeling guilty, unyielding, hopeless, helpless)

☐ e. Paranoia (unrealistic suspicious thoughts with unnecessary fear)

☐ f. Automatic negative thoughts (thinking *should/ shouldn't, must/must not, can't, ought to, have to, got to, not fair, don't deserve*)

☐ g. Other: _____

☐ h. There aren't any persistent symptoms that bother me.

B. How interested are you in learning better ways to manage your persistent symptoms?

☐ a. I am not interested in changing how I manage my persistent symptoms at this time.

☐ b. I am thinking about how I could manage my persistent symptoms differently.

☐ c. I am planning to start managing my persistent symptoms soon.

☐ d. I am ready to start managing my persistent symptoms.

☐ e. I am already managing my persistent symptoms more often.

☐ f. I already manage my persistent symptoms, and I am going to stick with my good habit.

C. How will you manage your bothersome persistent symptoms?

☐ a. I will listen to the words of songs on the radio or stereo.

☐ b. I will argue with the symptoms.

☐ c. I will ignore the symptoms.

☐ d. I will talk to someone.

☐ e. I will practice a relaxation skill.

☐ f. I will do the five steps to symptom management.

☐ g. I will _____

  ☐ h. I don't plan to manage any of my persistent symptoms.

  ☐ i. I don't have any persistent symptoms.

D. What "symptom busters" will you use to replace your troublesome persistent symptoms?

  ☐ a. I will tell myself, "My brain is just playing tricks on me."

  ☐ b. I will tell myself, "I don't believe these symptoms, they are just my illness acting up."

  ☐ c. I will tell myself, "I'm in control of my thoughts and feelings."

  ☐ d. I will tell myself, "Automatic negative thoughts are just a part of my illness."

  ☐ e. I will tell myself, "I am stronger than my symptoms."

  ☐ f. I will tell myself, "Just because I think it doesn't make it true."

  ☐ g. I will tell myself, "Thinking this way just makes me feel bad."

  ☐ h. I will tell myself, "_____."

  ☐ i. I do not plan to use any symptom busters.

12. Be an Active Partner in Your Own Recovery

Recipient was once used to identify the role of people who have a mental illness. It was a label that didn't last very long. It suggested a passive role in receiving psychiatric services. Being an active partner in the recovery process is one of the most important

> Understand and fulfill your role as an active member of your treatment team

ingredients of a successful recovery lifestyle. Work with your treatment team as a central member of that team. Work together in a partnership relationship. Together you can work on more than just medication and symptomatic recovery. You and your treatment team can work together to accomplish a wide range of treatment goals, rehabilitation goals, personal life goals, and more. Understand and fulfill your role as a dependable, contributing member of your treatment team. Now consider the following questions and check the boxes that apply to you.

A. How interested are you in being an active partner in your recovery?
- ☐ a. I am not interested in being an active partner in my recovery.
- ☐ b. I am thinking about being an active partner in my recovery.
- ☐ c. I am planning to start being an active partner in my recovery soon.
- ☐ d. I am ready to start being an active partner in my recovery.
- ☐ e. I am already working on being an active partner in my recovery.
- ☐ f. I already am an active partner in my recovery, and I am going to stick with my good habit.

B. How will you be an active partner in your recovery?
- ☐ a. I will make a point of asking questions.
- ☐ b. I will consistently voice my opinions, concerns, preferences, and choices.
- ☐ c. I will be open and honest, even when I think my therapist and prescriber won't approve or agree with me.
- ☐ d. I will listen and consider the suggestions of my therapist and prescriber.
- ☐ e. I will be flexible and negotiate instead of being stubborn or resistant.
- ☐ f. I will be assertive instead of passive or aggressive.
- ☐ g. I will consider the opinions of others.
- ☐ h. I will _____
- ☐ i. I don't plan to be an active partner in my recovery.

13. Consider Complementary Approaches to Treatment

Psychiatric medication is often necessary but not sufficient to control all of the symptoms caused by mental illness. There may be a time when you consider checking out other ways of treating your illness. Herbs, vitamins, light therapy, allergy testing, elimination diets, prayer,

> If you want to add complementary approaches to your recovery lifestyle habits, talk with your prescriber.

meditation, and acupuncture are all examples of complementary approaches to recovery. You might find some of these approaches to be quite helpful when used along with your psychiatric medication. However, remember that these are complementary, not alternative, ways to achieve recovery.

There is more research support for some complementary approaches than for others. Light therapy—using very bright lights to overcome winter depression—has very good research support. Acupuncture, especially for pain, seems to be effective. Vitamins are now so well accepted that it is unclear if their use is still complementary or has become mainstream. More is known about some herbs than others. And just because something is "natural" or "herbal" or complementary does not mean that it has no risk or no side effects.

Complementary means balancing, matching, pairing, or harmonizing. Combined with psychiatric medication, one or more complementary approaches to recovery may help your feel better, help you get distressing symptoms under control, and reduce your risk of relapse. However, it is critical that you avoid the mistake of replacing psychiatric medication with complementary approaches. If you want to add complementary approaches to your recovery lifestyle habits, talk with your treatment team. Make sure your choice of approach will complement, rather than interfere with, your prescribed medication. It's best not to change or add treatment without talking to your treatment team. If you have information about a specific complementary treatment you want to start using, share the information with your therapist and prescriber. Talk with your treatment team about how it might help your recovery along with your prescribed medication. Daily symptom monitoring can help you figure out if the complementary approach helps you. Now consider the following questions and check the boxes that apply to you.

A. How interested are you in seeing if different complementary approaches might help you manage at least some of your symptoms?
- ☐ a. I am not interested in adding any complementary approach.
- ☐ b. I am thinking about adding a complementary approach.
- ☐ c. I am planning to start adding a complementary approach soon.
- ☐ d. I am ready to start adding a complementary approach.
- ☐ e. I am already adding a complementary approach more often.
- ☐ f. I am already adding a complementary approach on a regular basis.

B. What complementary approaches to recovery are you using or thinking about using?
- ☐ a. Herbs
- ☐ b. Vitamins
- ☐ c. Light therapy
- ☐ d. Allergy testing
- ☐ e. Allergy elimination diet
- ☐ f. Prayer/meditation
- ☐ g. Acupuncture
- ☐ h. Other: _____
- ☐ i. I don't plan to add any complementary approaches.

There's more to recovery than just taking medication. Choose and practice recovery lifestyle habits every day to improve your overall health and wellness. With each new habit you add to your recovery lifestyle, you may increase your chances of getting your symptoms under better control and reduce your risk of relapse so that your illness will be less of an obstacle to reaching your personal life goals.

CHAPTER ELEVEN

Relapse Management

Relapse management **means** reducing the risk of relapse when possible, seeing the danger signs before a re lapse gets out of control, and learning effective ways to deal with the problems if a relapse does occur. Learning ways to decrease the problems caused by relapse is an important part of recovery.

What Is Relapse?

Relapse means getting sick again. A relapse is an increase in symptoms severe enough that it causes major problems in your life. For some people with a mental illness, symptoms are fairly constant; their symptoms stay pretty much the same over time. For other people, symptoms seem to have a lot of ups and downs; they get somewhat worse, then better, over time. Relapse is more than just the usual ups and downs of symptoms. A relapse is a major increase in how distressing your symptoms are, or behavior changes that threaten to get in the way of what you want in life. Any big change in symptoms, function, and distress level can lead to major life disruptions. When symptoms start getting in the way of your personal life goals—when the illness takes control—you are experiencing a relapse.

Learning from Your Own Experiences

What have you learned about your periods of relapse? The five worksheets in this chapter are a way of helping you organize your experiences and learn more about your relapses. Knowing more about your relapse experiences can help you (1) decrease the risk of another relapse, (2) act quickly so that you can stop a relapse early before it gets out of control, and (3) minimize the problems caused by a relapse, if one were to happen. It would be great if you never have another really bad time, if you never have to go through another relapse. It may not be possible to avoid all relapses, but there are actions and approaches that can help. Thinking about relapse ahead of time can help you stay more in control of your life, even if you go through a bad time.

The Cost of Relapse

Every relapse costs you something. The most obvious costs are the real-world losses that relapse can cause. During a relapse, you could lose an apartment, a job, or even friends. Your behavior could lead to your being hospitalized or even arrested. Especially if your behavior has been frightening or destructive, it may take other people in your life some time to get over their own fear that it could happen again. You could do real damage to yourself or others during a bad relapse. Finally, it may take you a period of time before you trust yourself that another relapse would not happen.

Worksheet 1: What Problems Have Past Relapses Caused for You?

Personal Costs of Relapse

It is hard to think about old problems. It would be nice to keep them in the past and not have to keep thinking about them over and over again. However, thinking about past problems can help you avoid the same problems in the future. By thinking about past relapses, you may be able to avoid having another one. You may be able to figure out ways to keep the consequences from being so bad, even if you do have another relapse. You can also realize how big a problem relapse has been for you in the past, which could help you decide how important it is to work on avoiding relapse in the future.

Think about what you have lost during past periods of relapse. What are some of the problems you have had during times of relapse? Check the boxes that apply to you.

☐ 1. I lost a place to live that I like.
☐ 2. I ended up homeless.
☐ 3. I had more problems in my relationships with my family.
☐ 4. I had more problems in relationships with my friends.
☐ 5. I lost a job that I liked.
☐ 6. I ended up dropping out of (or getting behind in) school.
☐ 7. I ended up in the hospital.
☐ 8. I ended up in jail.
☐ 9. I lost control of my own money.
☐ 10. I ended up broke.
☐ 11. People trusted me less or worried about me more.
☐ 12. Other: _____

Which problems would be the most difficult for you to handle if they happened to you now? _____.

Which problems are most important for you to avoid in the future? _____.

Psychological Costs of Relapse

A relapse can also have psychological costs. Relapse can interrupt your recovery journey. People often count the weeks, months, or years since their last hospitalization, last arrest, or last period of homelessness. Some people count how long they have held a job or maintained an important relationship. Relapse can result in your having to "start over" in these areas—which can be frustrating and demoralizing. A painful relapse can leave lingering concerns that it could happen again at any time, causing feelings of hopelessness and discouragement. Many people find that the disorganization and confusion that are part of relapse to be extremely upsetting. If you have gone through a bad relapse, you may have become fearful that it could happen again. This fear could get in the way of your hope and willingness to continue working toward your recovery goals.

Think about the psychological cost of your past periods of relapse and check the box(es) that applies to you.

☐ 1. I had less self-confidence.
☐ 2. I went through a period when I gave up on trying to make things better for myself.
☐ 3. I believed that relapse would keep happening no matter what I did.
☐ 4. I started thinking that I could never accomplish my recovery goals.
☐ 5. I told myself that everything I did would go wrong.
☐ 6. I believed that I was not as smart, or strong, or attractive as other people.
☐ 7. I lost some of my motivation, commitment, or belief in recovery.
☐ 8. Other: _____

Which psychological cost would be the most difficult if it happened to you now? _____.

Which psychological cost would be the most important for you to avoid in the future? _____.

Other Costs of Relapse

There is also concern that relapsing may be bad for your brain. The more times you relapse, the harder it may be on you and your brain. It seems that "the more often you get sick, the sicker you get." Your illness may get worse—it might get harder to control. Research in this area is just beginning, but it is possible that untreated symptoms and serious relapse might cause your underlying illness to get worse. Relapse can make things worse, not just during the relapse but for a long time afterward.

The long-term impact of relapse is very different for different people. The severity of major mental illness can change over time. Symptoms and life disruptions can get worse or better. There are data from long-term follow-up studies indicating that many people who have a difficult and less stable course to their illness when they are younger can go on to have a much stabler life and a good recovery as they get older. People can learn to better manage their life and their illness and to successfully work toward their goals. The idea of recovery is that people can learn to overcome problems that seemed overwhelming in the past. Relapse can set back this process. Learning to manage relapse is an important part of your recovery. It is important to be aware of the five areas in which relapse can negatively affect recovery:

1. *More persistent symptoms.* With repeated relapses, you could develop symptoms that stay with you in spite of taking medication and practicing recovery lifestyle habits. Some of your symptoms might not go away completely. If you have been dealing with mental illness for years, you might have some persistent symptoms. Persistent symptoms are the ones that do not go away—even when you take your medication. There is a risk that after repeated relapses, fewer symptoms might go into remission. Even after the relapse is over, your persistent symptoms may be more intense, more frequent, or last longer than they did in the past.

2. *Medication does not work as well.* After repeated relapses, your brain may become less responsive to medication, and you might notice that the medication does not do as good a job. You

also could be more likely to have breakthrough symptoms when you are under stress. Relapses may cause your brain to resist medication. Sometimes people say that medication "runs out of gas" and quits working. It might be more accurate to say that your brain may have become treatment resistant. Relapse may cause your brain to resist the positive effects of the medication.

3. *Need more medication.* You might need to take higher doses of medication to control your symptoms after repeated relapses. When you got sick for the first time, a low dose of medicine probably did a good job of controlling your symptoms. After repeated relapses, it might take a higher dose of medication or more than one medication to control your symptoms.

4. *Takes longer to recover.* It takes some people longer to bounce back following many relapses. Early in your illness it might only take a few days to start feeling better again after a relapse. After many relapses it might take weeks or months. Repeated relapse can take a toll on your brain, on your sense of confidence, and on your friends and family.

5. *More severe impairments.* Repeated relapses might also make it harder and harder to do everyday things. It might make it more difficult for you to be successful at work, school, independent living, and relationships. Relapse could make it harder to function, make every day life more difficult, and might make it more difficult to achieve your personal life goals.

Think about the other costs of your past periods of relapse and check the box(es) that applies to you.

☐ 1. *I have more persistent symptoms.* Some of my symptoms keep happening even when I take my medication. Some of them do not go away anymore, even when I take medication.

☐ 2. *My medication does not work as well.* I get breakthrough symptoms when I am going through a lot of stress. My persistent symptoms are stronger, more intense, or happen more often than they used to.

☐ 3. *I need more medication.* I need more medicine than I used to; I need a higher dose, or several medications, to control my symptoms. Less medicine does not seem to do as good a job of controlling my symptoms.

☐ 4. *It takes longer for me to recover.* It seems to take me longer to bounce back from relapse. The medication does not seem to work as quickly as it did before. I recover a lot more slowly than I did in the past.

☐ 5. *I have more severe impairments.* My symptoms make it harder for me to do things now than in the past. My symptoms are making it more difficult to work, go to school, have friends, or live on my own.

☐ 6. *None of the above.* None of these problems seems to fit my situation.

Worksheet 2: What Are Your Signs of Relapse?

It can be helpful to recognize that you may be starting to relapse. The earlier you can recognize the problem, the more you can do about it, and the more you can avoid problems caused by it. This worksheet is about the three stages of relapse. Some people may not experience all three stages of relapse, and the stages may not always happen in this order. However, learning the stages and thinking about your personal signs of relapse may help you manage relapses in the future.

Stage 1: Early Warning Signs Appear

Early warning signs are usually the first changes that tell you that a relapse may be starting. Early warning signs are changes that start before any change in symptoms. It is very useful for you to identify what early warning signs–changes in your thoughts or feelings or behavior–are your first signs of possible relapse. If you recognize some early warning signs and know that you are at risk for things getting worse, you can do things to head off problems before they get bad. Although different people have very different early warning signs, a particular person is likely to have the same early warning signs each time a relapse happens. For example, if you always have trouble sleeping before a relapse, then sleep problems become an early warning sign for you. If you tend to stop spending time with friends or family before you relapse, then this becomes an early warning sign for you. Now consider the following questions and check the boxes that apply to you.

How do your thoughts or feelings change before you experience a relapse?

- ☐ 1. I start having trouble concentrating.
- ☐ 2. I become more forgetful.
- ☐ 3. I have less energy and feel run down.
- ☐ 4. I get into an irritable mood; I feel impatient.
- ☐ 5. I cannot think as clearly as usual.
- ☐ 6. I feel nervous, worried, or anxious.
- ☐ 7. Other: _____

How does your behavior change before you experience a relapse?

- ☐ 1. My sleep habits change.
- ☐ 2. I spend more time in bed.
- ☐ 3. I quit doing activities (e.g., going to work, volunteer job, class).
- ☐ 4. I stop doing things around the house.
- ☐ 5. I become cranky or argumentative.
- ☐ 6. I become more withdrawn.
- ☐ 7. Other: _____

Stage 2: Persistent Symptoms Get Worse

As relapse continues, your usual symptoms—your persistent symptoms—may become more of a problem.

Frequency

Your persistent symptoms may happen more often than usual. For example, Josh says that voices usually bother him in the evening, but when he relapses, they start bothering him more often throughout the day.

What persistent symptoms do you have that happen more often than usual when you relapse? _____

Intensity

Your persistent symptoms might get stronger, harder to ignore, more distressing, or harder to manage. For example, Saul explains that he always has problems with "dark moods," but when he relapses, the sense of doom becomes much stronger and harder to shake off.

What persistent symptoms do you have that get stronger, harder to ignore, or harder to manage when you relapse?

_____

Duration

Your persistent symptoms might last longer than usual when you are relapsing. Your symptoms may last hours or days instead of going away quickly. For example, Maria reported that when she relapses, her periods of paranoid thinking last for hours at a time.

What persistent symptoms do you have that last longer than usual when you relapse? _____

Stage 3: Remitted Symptoms Return

In the third stage of relapse, your old symptoms may come back again. Remitted symptoms are the symptoms that are usually controlled by medication and recovery lifestyle habits. If the relapse gets bad enough, your remitted symptoms may return. For example, you may start hearing voices again, even if you have not heard them for some time.

What remitted symptoms return when you relapse?_____

_____

Sometimes people do not even remember how they behaved during a relapse. When friends, family members, or a therapist tells you about your behavior during a relapse, do you believe them, or do you think that they are making it up or exaggerating? _____

What kind of information would help you decide whether your family, friends, or therapist were being accurate and that your brain was too messed up for you to remember, or that your brain was reporting accurately and it was other people who were confused or wrong? For example, in the film *A Beautiful Mind* John Nash, a brilliant mathematician with schizophrenia, figured out that a girl who befriended him must have been a delusion, because she never aged.

Worksheet 3: What Caused Your Relapse in the Past?

It may not always be clear why a relapse happens. Different people in your support system, including yourself, might have different ideas about what caused a relapse. Often, relapse is not caused by one thing. Rather, there are usually several things that happen all around the same time.

Common Causes of Relapse

There are a number of common causes of relapse. Learning what makes relapse more likely for you can help you learn to reduce your risk of relapse. These common causes can also be used as a "Relapse Checklist" to figure out what might have caused a relapse and help you know what might help stop a relapse once it has started.

Read through each common causes of relapse. Mark the ones that may have caused you to relapse in the past.

1. Too Much Stress Can Cause a Relapse

Stress is a common cause of relapse. This can be good stress, such as a new job or a new friend, or a bad stress, such as losing an apartment or illness of a family member. Some people are very sensitive to some kinds of stress but not to others. For example, one person may have a hard time if they have to be around too many people, while another person may be fine around others, as long as they are not expected to answer a lot of questions. Having a small relapse after doing something new—a new job or going back to school—does not mean that you should not do new things in the future. It does mean that you need to plan how to handle this stress so that it does not get in the way of your recovery. Learning and practicing stress management skills, making one change at a time, and making changes in small steps can help reduce the risk of stress causing a relapse.

Are you sensitive to stress? If so, what kind? _____

In the past, my relapse may have been connected to good stress—doing new things, going after my life goals (check the box[es] that apply to you):

- ☐ 1. Starting a new job.
- ☐ 2. Finding a new place to live.
- ☐ 3. Making a new friend.
- ☐ 4. Feeling better, and then getting scared that it would not last.
- ☐ 5. Other: _____
- ☐ 6. None of the above. I do not think my relapses have been connected to good stress.

In the past, my relapse may have been connected to bad stress—things that upset my life:

☐ 1. I lost a friend.
☐ 2. I got a different therapist.
☐ 3. I had to move.
☐ 4. I ran out of money.
☐ 5. I did not have enough to do during the day.
☐ 6. Someone close to me became ill or died.
☐ 7. Other: _____
☐ 8. None of the above. I do not think my relapses have been connected to bad stress.

How will you manage stress? Check the box(es) that applies to you.

☐ a. I will practice relaxation skills (e.g., deep breathing, muscle tensing, meditation, guided relaxation, tai chi, yoga) at least 20 minutes each day and as needed to deal with stress and/or symptoms.
☐ b. I will talk with my therapist about the problems I am having.
☐ c. I will talk about the stress with my family or friends.
☐ d. I will make sure that I keep doing things that keep me healthy, such as spending time with friends or doing activities I enjoy.
☐ e. I will work on solving problems so I do not get over-whelmed.
☐ f. I will make just one change at a time.
☐ g. I will make important changes more slowly.
☐ h. I will _____.

2. Not Taking Care of Yourself Can Cause a Relapse

Many decisions that people make about how they live their life can make a relapse more likely. These are things that you have a choice over. Not all of these things are equally likely to cause relapse. However, not taking good care of yourself can sometimes make it harder to keep your illness under control.

Think back to the last time you relapsed. Think about the things you were doing, or not doing, to take care of yourself. Which of these things might have increased your risk of relapse in the past?

☐ a. I was drinking a lot of caffeine (soda, coffee, tea).

☐ b. I was eating/drink a lot of sugar (soda, hot cocoa, coffee, tea, cookies, candy, pie, cake, ice cream, etc.).

☐ c. I was not doing any exercise besides just my everyday activities.

☐ d. I was not practicing relaxation skills for 20 minutes each day (deep breathing, muscle tensing, meditation, guided relaxation, tai chi, or yoga).

☐ e. I was not eating healthy meals.

☐ f. I was not getting 7–9 hours of sleep each night.

☐ g. I stopped talking with friends or other support people in my life.

☐ h. I stopped activities that helped me feel good about myself.

☐ i. I _____.

☐ j. None of the above. I do not think how I took care of myself had any connection with my past relapse.

What will you do to take better care of yourself? Check the box(es) that apply to you.

☐ a. I will limit or stop drinking caffeine (soda, coffee, tea).

☐ b. I will limit sugar (soda, hot cocoa, coffee, tea, cookies, candy, pie, cake, ice cream, etc.).

☐ c. I will exercise daily.

☐ d. I will practice relaxation skills for 20 minutes each day (deep breathing, muscle tensing, meditation, guided relaxation, tai chi, or yoga).

☐ e. I will eat healthy meals.

☐ f. I will get 7–9 hours of sleep each night.

□ h. I will force myself not to withdraw from family or friends if I go through a difficult period.

□ i. I will make myself to do something active every day.

□ j. I _____.

□ k. None of the above. I do not think how I took care of myself had any connection with my past relapse.

3. Medication Changes Can Cause a Relapse

Many relapses are connected to some kind of medication change. The person may stop taking medication or stop taking it as consistently. Sometimes a relapse is connected to a decision between client and prescriber to try a new medication or to stop an old one. Consider the following possibilities and check the boxes that apply to you.

"My Relapse May Have Been Connected to My Stopping My Medication." If you have ever stopped taking your medication, you are not alone. Most people who have an illness that requires that they take medication over a long period of time wonder if they really need it, what would happen if they stopped it, or wonder if the side effects are worth it. Stopping medication is the #1 cause of relapse for people with major mental illness. It is not the only reason for relapse, but it is pretty common.

Realizing that a relapse may be connected to your decision to stop taking your medication is only part of the story. What were some of the reasons that you decided to stop the medication at that time? Check the box(es) that apply to you.

□ a. I was having too many side effects.

□ b. I started using drugs or alcohol.

□ c. I thought I did not need the medication any longer.

□ d. My decision was a reaction to some other stress.

□ e. I was forced or pressured to take medication and never really agreed to it.

□ f. It was not clear to me what the medication was supposed to do.

☐ g. I did not think that the medication was doing what it was supposed to.

☐ h. Other: _____

☐ i. None of the above. I have not quit taking my medication.

If stopping medication may have been part of your past relapse, figure out what happened, make a plan, and choose solutions that can help you keep taking your medication. "Take medication the right way, every day" is a message that is important for you to learn and live by. You may not like it, you may not think it is fair, and you may want the illness and the medication and everything else to just go away. And if you think this way you will be right. It is not fair for you to have an illness, and it is not fair that you have to take a medication. Being fair has nothing to do with it. It is unfair, and now you can choose to make the best of it all, so that you can live your life the way you want to, despite having an illness that sometimes makes this difficult.

For most people who have a serious mental illness, stopping medication eventually leads to relapse. For the first few days after stopping medication, you may feel okay, maybe even better than when you were taking medication. The relapse will not happen in a day or two, because it often takes several weeks for all the medication to get out of your brain. Sometimes people can do well for weeks or even months without medication, but the risk of eventual relapse is very high. Taking medication in a way that allows it be effective will help you manage your illness, reach your life goals, and reduce your risk of relapse. This almost always means taking medication every day. Talk with your therapist and prescriber about the problems you've had with taking your medication. Make a plan that will help you stay on your medication. Talk to your therapist and prescriber about changing your medication if side effects are a problem. Now think about these questions and check the boxes that apply to you.

What happened that you stopped taking your medication?

☐ a. I decided that I did not need medication anymore because I was feeling good.
☐ b. I just did not get around to refilling the medication.
☐ c. I decided that the medicine was not helping me.
☐ d. I decided I did not need to take medication; I do not have an illness, and there is nothing wrong with me.
☐ e. I had problems with the medicine and decided to quit taking it until my next appointment with my prescriber.
☐ f. I took the advice of someone who told me it would be a good idea to stop taking medication.
☐ g. I could not stand the side effects of the medication.
☐ h. I could not afford to pay for the medication.
☐ i. I thought I would do okay without the medication.
☐ j. I got tired of taking medication.
☐ k. I did not make it to my appointments and I ran out of refills.
☐ l. I have a medical illness and thought that my psychiatric medication would make it worse.
☐ m. I was embarrassed to take medication in front of my friends.
☐ n. I got tired of my therapist or family pressuring me to take medication all of the time.
☐ o. Other: _____
☐ p. None of the above. I have never stopped taking any of my medication.

What will you do to keep taking your medication?

☐ a. I will remind myself that the reason I am feeling better is because the medication is working.
☐ b. I will talk to my prescriber or therapist and explain the reasons that I want to stop taking my medication.
☐ c. I will refill my medication on time so I do not run out.
☐ d. I will remind myself to take it, even if I think I might not need it.

☐ e. I will ask my therapist or prescriber if I could take a long-acting injection instead of pills.

☐ f. I will tell myself that I know I'll get sick again if I stop taking medication.

☐ g. I will reach out for recovery support by talking to some-one who will encourage me to keep taking my medication.

☐ h. I will talk with my prescriber and therapist about how taking medication might help me.

☐ i. I will _____.

☐ j. None of the above.

"My Relapse May Have Been Connected to Missing Doses of Medication." Medication is more effective if it is taken regularly, every day. It is hard for anyone to take medication every day without missing on occasion. It is more difficult if your life is different every day, and nothing is particularly structured or regular. It is also difficult if you are not completely sure if you always want to take your medication. It is sometimes hard to figure out if a missed dose of medication is just due to forgetting it, or if you halfway did not want to take it anyway, or perhaps a bit of both. And you might have thought it would not be a big deal if you missed or skipped some doses. Unfortunately skipping, missing, or forgetting doses makes it more likely that your symptoms would get worse and that you would have a relapse. Now think about these questions and check the boxes that apply to you.

What happened that you skipped, missed, or forgot to take your medication?

☐ a. I meant to take it, but sometimes I just forgot.

☐ b. Sometimes I fell asleep before taking my nighttime dose.

☐ c. I cut down on the number of pills I took because I decided that I was on too much medication.

☐ d. I waited several days to get my medication refilled after I ran out.

☐ e. I decided to take it just when I thought I needed it—when I felt stressed out or when I'd had a bad day.

☐ f. I kept forgetting to take my medicine with me when I left home for the day.

☐ g. The medicine was too expensive, so I decided to make the bottle of medicine last longer by taking fewer pills.

☐ h. I was not sure if the medication was really helping. I hated the idea of taking it, so sometimes I did and sometimes I did not take it.

☐ i. Other: _____

☐ j. None of the above. I almost never skip, miss or forget to take my medication.

What will you do to make missing, skipping, or forgetting doses of medicine less likely?

☐ a. I will use a pillbox so that I can easily see if I have taken my medication for the day.

☐ b. I will talk to my prescriber or therapist and explain why I want to cut down on my medication.

☐ c. I will ask someone I trust to help me stick with taking my medication.

☐ d. I will remind myself that I need to take my medication every day; the medication cannot help me if I only take it on the days that I think I needed it.

☐ e. I will ask my therapist or prescriber if I could take a long-acting injection instead of pills.

☐ f. I will talk with my therapist and prescriber about the problems I'm having with missing, skipping, and forgetting doses.

☐ g. I will get my medication filled on time so I do not run out.

☐ h. I will talk to my prescriber or therapist about getting my medication from a pharmacy that will mail it to me each month.

☐ i. I will take my medication an hour earlier so I do not fall asleep before taking it.

☐ j. I will tie a reminder on my doorknob so I do not leave home without my medicine.

☐ k. I will _____

☐ l. None of the above.

"In the Past, My Relapse May Have Been Connected to a Medication Change." A change in medication can make things better, which is usually the main reason people decide to make such a change. Although a medication change can make things better, it can also make things worse. If a new medication does not work as well as the old medication, it could make your symptoms worse. There is no way of knowing ahead of time whether or not a certain medication will work well for you. Now think about the following question and check the box(es) that apply to you.

What will you do to reduce your risk of relapse the next time your medication is changed?

☐ a. I will keep a record of my symptoms each day and call my therapist or prescriber if my symptoms get worse.

☐ b. I will involve friends, family, or other people on my support team to help me handle the stress of a medication change and to monitor my symptoms to make sure things are not getting worse.

☐ c. I will develop a plan to reduce stress during the period around my medication change.

☐ d. I will ask my prescriber if I can stay on the usual dose of my old medication for several weeks so that my new medication has time to get up to a high enough level to control my symptoms.

☐ e. I will make a list of my early warning signs and watch for them; I will call my therapist or prescriber right away if my early warning signs appear.

☐ f. I will ask my prescriber what side effects to expect.

☐ g. I will ask my prescriber what to do if I get side effects.

☐ h. I will talk with my prescriber about what to do if I start having breakthrough symptoms during the change.

☐ i. I will talk to my pharmacist or prescriber before I take an over-the-counter medication to find out if it will interfere with the medications I am already taking.

☐ j. I will _____.

☐ k. None of the above.

"In the Past, My Relapse May Have Been Connected to Taking a Low Dose of Medicine." There are many possible reasons that a person might be on a small dose of medication. Perhaps your prescriber started you on a low dose of medication. Maybe your dose of medicine was decreased because of side effects. Your prescriber might have talked to you about taking more medication, but you decided you did not want to increase the dose. Maybe you and your prescriber decided it was important to use the lowest possible dose. There are natural ups and downs in symptoms over time. If you were not taking enough medication to handle an increase in symptoms, this could be one of the reasons your illness got out of control.

Maybe you have been doing well for a long time on a low dose of medication and then relapsed because of some outside stress. Whatever the reason, if you relapsed while you were taking a small dose of medication, taking a higher dose might be useful. You might want to consider taking a higher dose of medication and seeing how you feel. You might want to see if your symptoms are better, if you function better, and if you feel better on a bit more medication. If your life has been going pretty well except for the relapse, and if you feel better on a low dose of medication than on a higher dose, then it may work for you to know when you need to temporarily increase your dose without necessarily staying on the higher dose. Now think about the following question and check the box(es) that applies to you.

What will you do to reduce your risk of relapse if you are taking a low dose of medication?

☐ a. I will ask my prescriber what the usual dose is so I know where I am on the dosage range.
☐ b. I will talk with my prescriber about the advantages and disadvantages of increasing the dose, and of decreasing the dose, so I understand my choices.
☐ c. I will keep a record of my symptoms each day, and I'll call my therapist or prescriber if my symptoms get worse.
☐ d. I will consider my prescriber's advice about taking a higher dose if my symptoms get worse.
☐ e. I will make a list of my early warning signs, watch for them, and call my therapist, prescriber, or member of my support team right away if any appear.
☐ f. I will ask my prescriber if it would be possible for me to have some extra medication to take when I need it to control my symptoms.
☐ g. I will talk with my treatment team about whether increasing my dose might help if I go through another period when my symptoms get worse.
☐ h. I will _____.
☐ i. None of the above.

4. Using Street Drugs or Alcohol May Cause a Relapse

Some people have been told that street drugs and alcohol do not mix with medication. They think that street drugs or alcohol could cause a bad reaction with medication, so they skip their medication whenever they drink or got high. They do not realize that with most medications used to treat mental illness, it is usually a better idea to keep taking the medications even on days they drink or get high. Other people believe that if they do not use "too much" or do it "too often," their drug usage will not make their illness worse. Many people do not realize that street drugs and alcohol can keep medication from working and make their illness worse. Substance abuse is one of the most common causes of relapse. Even if you know the risk of relapse, it can be hard to resist the urges and temptations to drink and drug. You are not alone. More than half the people who have serious mental illness use street drugs or drink alcohol. Now think about the following question and check the box(es) that applies to you.

What will you do to stay off street drugs and alcohol?

☐ a. I will make a list of the ways in which street drugs and alcohol interfere with my achieving my life goals.

☐ b. I will go to self-help, mutual support, AA (Alcoholics Anonymous), NA (Narcotics Anonymous), double trouble, peer support, or dual recovery meetings.

☐ c. I will talk with my therapist about getting involved in a treatment program.

☐ e. I will move to a "clean and sober" residence.

☐ e. I will actively practice how to say "no."

☐ f. I will remind myself of what my goals are and how using can get in the way of reaching those goals.

☐ g. I will stay away from places, people, and things that might tempt me to use.

☐ h. I will spend time in places, with people, doing things that actively support my sobriety.

☐ i. I will _____.

☐ j. None of the above.

5. Other Medical Problems May Cause Relapse

Sometimes when people get physically ill, their psychiatric illness worsens. A cold, the flu, and a chronic medical problem that gets worse are examples of medical problems that can increase the risk of psychiatric relapse. The sooner you get treatment for medical problems, the better your chances of staying stable and reducing your chances of relapse. Now consider the following question and check the box(es) that applies to you.

What will you do to manage your physical health and medical problems?

- ☐ a. I will get medical treatment right away if I get physically ill.
- ☐ b. I will go to regular, scheduled appointments with my medical doctors and nurses, even if I do not think I need to go.
- ☐ c. I will talk with my doctors and nurses about what I can do to manage my physical illness and improve my health.
- ☐ d. I will take the medications prescribed for my physical health, the right way, every day.
- ☐ e. I will talk with my medical doctors and nurses before I stop taking, or cut back on, medications used to treat my physical health.
- ☐ f. I will choose and practice at least one healthy habit that will help me manage my physical illness, recover my health, or improve my health.
- ☐ g. I will _____
- ☐ h. None of the above.

6. An Illness Cycle May Cause a Relapse

For some people, one of the ways to find the cause of a relapse is to take a look at their relapse patterns. If you think about it, you may be able to find predictable periods of relapse. Although more common in bipolar disorder and depression, some people with schizophrenia may also experience a predictable cycle of ups and downs. One person may relapse every spring, another might experience an increase in symptoms every December, still another might have flair-ups every other month. Recognizing a symptom cycle can help you see the increased symptoms coming, use extra illness management skills, and work toward breaking the cycle.

Do you think your past relapse has been connected to a symptom cycle? _____

If so, what is the cycle you experience? _____

Worksheet 4: Making a Relapse Action Plan

Making a relapse action plan is a lot like having a plan for what to do if there is a fire. It is good to have a plan to keep people safe, call for help, prevent the fire from spreading, and put out the fire if possible. Having a plan is likely to lead to a much better outcome than if you try to figure out what to do after the fire starts. We hope we never have to use the plan, but we know that we will deal with an emergency better if we are prepared ahead of time. In the same way, we come up with a relapse action plan. These kinds of plans about how to recognize, avoid, and cope better with crisis or relapse can be called by different names, Relapse Management Plan, Relapse Action Plan, Wellness Recovery Action Plan (WRAP)™, Crisis Intervention Plan, or Emergency Plan. Whatever you call the plan, the goal is to keep a relapse from interfering with your recovery. However, even with the best plan, relapse can still happen. Planning what to do if you have a relapse can help you cope with it much better.

Staying Safe

Sometimes when people relapse, there is a greater chance that someone will get hurt. Think about the relapses you have experienced in the past. Was there a possibility that you or someone else might have been injured? What might have helped keep you and everyone else safe? Think about what could be done during a future relapse to decrease the chances that anyone would be hurt, injured, threatened, or put in danger. Use the information included in the next few pages to write down what you would need to do to stay safe if you ever had another relapse, and the names of the people who will help you stay safe. If there is no risk that you or anyone else would be hurt, injured, threatened, or put in danger, skip this part of the relapse action plan.

If you relapse, what needs to be done to help make sure that you will be safe and that other people will be safe too? Use Table 11.1 to help figure out what things need to be done to decrease the chances that anyone will be hurt, injured, threatened, or put in danger. Which of these things are important for your safety? Not all of the ideas on this table will apply to you.

Table 11.1. Harm Prevention Plan

What will help me stay safe if I relapse?		Who can help me do this?
☐ a.	Lock up or remove guns from the house.	
☐ b.	Lock up or remove knives, razor blades, and other sharp objects from the house.	
☐ c.	Make sure I do not have bottles of pills or other things that I could use to hurt myself.	
☐ d.	Make sure I am not left alone.	
☐ e.	Make sure I have some place to go.	
☐ f.	Make sure I do not drive my car until I feel better.	
☐ g.		
☐ h.		

Add other safety issues to this table, as needed, to cover your own personal safety needs.

Planning steps involved in your harm prevention plan:

1. List the people you will ask to help you with your safety plan.
2. Discuss your safety plan with the people you have chosen.
3. Ask each person if he or she is willing to do the things you have listed.
4. Ask each person if he or she has other safety suggestions that could be added to your list.

Planning Ahead

There are probably things you can do that help you feel better, and other things that are less likely to be helpful for you. One person calms down by taking a walk, while another person becomes more anxious when taking walks. Table 11.2 is a list of some ideas of things that might help you get back in control if you are in the beginning of a relapse or a crisis. The problem is that when you are going through a difficult period, it might be hard to remember what helps and what does not. At times it seems like *nothing* helps. When you are calm and not having difficulty, think about (1) what you like and (2) what is helpful. These may not always be the same thing. For example, I might not like to exercise if I am upset, but I might also know that if I force myself to do some exercise, I will feel better and be more in control. This list is just to give you some examples. Your own list is likely to be much longer, and uniquely yours. If you cannot think of anything, keep working on it. Almost everyone has things that they regularly use to help themselves calm down and feel better.

There may also be some things that friends and family would be willing to do to give you help and support. When you make a list of activities, also include who can be helpful and supportive to you in doing these things.

Table 11.2. What and Who Will Help

If I relapse, these things are likely to help me. This list includes things I can do for myself plus things that friends and family might be willing to do for me or with me.		
What will be done?		**Who will do it?**
☐ a.	Talk to people by phone.	
☐ b.	Have people come visit me.	
☐ c.	Go to church, temple, synagogue, mosque	
☐ d.	Go grocery shopping.	
☐ e.	Remind me to take my medication.	
☐ f.	Encourage me to get up in the morning.	
☐ g.	Take a walk.	
☐ h.	Stay with me for a few days.	
☐ i.	Invite me over for a visit.	
☐ j.	Go to a support group meeting.	
☐ k.	Go out to eat.	
☐ l.	Practice relaxation skills.	
☐ m.	Do art work.	
☐ n.	Work on a jigsaw puzzle.	
☐ o.	Listen to music.	
☐ p.	Read.	
☐ q.	Go to appointments with me.	
☐ r.	Help me solve sleep problems.	
☐ s.	Make a list of things to do each day.	

☐ t.	Do some exercise.	
☐ u.	Visit someone.	
☐ v.	Stay busy by _____	
☐ w.		
☐ x.		

Planning steps involved in setting up things that are likely to help you if you relapse:

1. Write your name beside the things you are willing to do for yourself.
2. Write down who you will ask to do the other things on your list.
3. Discuss your plan with the people you have chosen.
4. Explain what you would like them to do if you relapse.
5. Find out if they are willing to do the things you listed.
6. Get their ideas about other helpful and supportive things they could do.

It is also important to have a list of things to avoid—things that are not very helpful—when we are going through a difficult time (Table 11.3). There will be well-meaning friends and professionals who may want to help by making suggestions. The list of things to avoid can help these people not make suggestions that would likely make things worse for you.

Once you have your lists, you need to decide with whom to share them. You may want to share your lists with a friend or family member. Your therapist and prescriber will probably be important participants in the discussion. There may also be a crisis service that you could involve. If you give your support team more information, they may be able to do a better job in helping you when you are in crisis. These lists provide advance

Table 11.3. Things to Avoid When Upset

Things to avoid when I am upset	Who can help me with this?
☐ a. Reading	
☐ b. Doing art work	
☐ c. Taking a walk	
☐ d. Listening to music	
☐ e. Doing a jigsaw puzzle	
☐ f. E-mailing friends	
☐ g. Talking to friends over the phone	
☐ h. Being told what to do	
☐ i. Being alone	
☐ j.	
☐ k.	

directions that can help your support team do a better job of helping you.

Calling for Assistance

Sometimes it helps to reach out to your support team during a relapse—to those friends, family members, neighbors, and others whom you trust and who could help you during a difficult period. Every person has his or her own support team. It could include a minister, the people at a drop-in center, your boss, a coworker. Making a list of names and phone numbers may make it easier for you to get help when you need it. Having a list of names and telephone numbers may also be a good idea if you need someone else to make phone calls for you during a relapse. In Table 11.4 you can list the name and contact information of each person who might be called and asked to help you deal with the relapse.

Getting Help from Mental Health Professionals and Places

Mental health professionals are also an important part of your support team. These can include your therapist or your psychiatrist, whom you already know well, or people at your drop-in center or emergency services, even if you do not know them personally. In Table 11.5 make a list of the hospital, emergency room, crisis stabilization unit, doctor, and other places and people whom you trust and prefer. Include the name, address, and phone number of each. If there are certain places or people with which you prefer *not* to have contact

Table 11.4. Contact Information of Relapse-Support People

If I relapse, these are trusted family, friends, peer specialists, and other members of my support team to call for assistance:		
Name	**Relationship**	**Phone Number(s)**
24-hour crisis line: _____		

Table 11.5. Contact Information of Mental Health Places
and Professionals

If I relapse, these are the mental health professionals and places I prefer:		
Name	**Phone Number**	**Address**
Hospital		
Emergency room		
Crisis stabilization unit		
Crisis intervention team		
Mental health center		
Psychiatrist		
I prefer *not* to go to: _____ The person who will help me get help, if needed: _____		

during a relapse, you may want to write that information down too. Talk with your support team members and let them know where you prefer to go for help when you need it.

Planning steps involved in calling for assistance:

1. Make a list of places you prefer to go for help.
2. Talk with the people who help you in times of relapse.
3. Discuss your plan with the people you have chosen.
4. Let them know where you do prefer to go for help when you need it.

Worksheet 5: How to Use Medication to Help When You Are Beginning to Relapse

Some people know that taking some extra medication or using a medication that they take only when necessary can be very helpful. Medication can help some people sleep better, avoid getting as frightened, think more clearly, and stay in better control. Other people have not found medication as helpful. Most people have some medication that helps, at least a little, and other medication that does not help or might actually make the situation worse.

Talk with your therapist and your prescriber about which medications might be helpful if you were beginning to relapse. Involve your support team. Find out what the people who know you well—your family and friends—think about using extra medications during the warning signs of a relapse, which medications they would choose for you, and if these are the same medications that your therapist and prescriber think would help. See if you can all agree on a plan about which medications to use, when to use them, and with what target symptoms or goals in mind. Also agree on which medications *not* to use and why. Write down this information in Table 11.6.

Table 11.6. Extra Medication to Take During a Relapse

Plan on which medications you will use if you have a relapse and note what you are hoping each medication will do.	
Medications that help when I am beginning to relapse	Target symptom or goal for this medication
Medications that I think do *not* help	Problems caused by this medication in the past

Two important questions to consider include:

- Do you already have some of the medications that you can take, or do you need to call your prescriber to get some?
- What can you, your therapist, and prescriber do to plan ahead, to make sure that you can quickly and easily get medication that you may need?

Always remember that there are lots of things that you can do to cope with the beginning of a relapse in addition to taking medication. Medication is always part of a larger plan. Medication is an important tool, but medication alone is rarely enough. Develop your own crisis plan and work with your treatment team to figure out how medication fits into that plan.

Diabetes

Diabetes is a growing concern for everyone in the United States, but it is a particular risk for people with major mental illness. Some 20.8 million people in the United States, or 8% of the population, have diabetes. The most common kind of diabetes is Type II. Historically, this type was often called adult-onset diabetes and primarily affected older people. Unfortunately, people are now developing Type II diabetes earlier; indeed, it is not uncommon for people to develop it in their 30s or 40s. People who are obese, people of color, and people with major mental illness are all much more likely to develop Type II diabetes. Diabetes is a leading cause of blindness, leg amputation, and kidney failure. It is associated with a painful condition, peripheral neuropathy, in which nerve damage can cause people to feel pain, burning, or itching. Finally, diabetes is associated with stroke and heart disease. In short, diabetes is a very common disease that causes a tremendous amount of pain, disability, and death. It is at epidemic levels in the United States, especially among people with major mental illness.

Type I Diabetes

There are two main kinds of diabetes. Type I, or what used to be called juvenile diabetes, is a genetic disorder that almost always runs in families. It usually starts in childhood or early teen years and is caused by the body not making enough insulin. The insulin that is made works normally, but there is not enough of it.

Type II Diabetes

Type II diabetes is much more common than Type I, and it is the kind that is most likely to affect people with mental illness, especially as they grow older. In Type II diabetes the cells in a person's body become resistant to insulin. Insulin is a hormone that transports glucose (sugar) in the blood into a cell where the cell can use it to produce energy. If there is not enough insulin, or if the cell is resistant to insulin, then the glucose level builds up in the blood, causing damage, and is not available inside the cell where it is needed.

At the beginning of this process the body can overcome this insulin resistance by just producing more and more insulin. During this early phase, the blood sugar or serum glucose level may be normal, but it takes more and more insulin to keep it normal. After a period of time, which may be years or even decades, the insulin resistance gets worse and more insulin is required. At the same time, the cells that produce insulin start to die because of the stress of trying to produce increasing amounts of insulin. When the insulin-producing cells cannot produce enough insulin to keep up with the increasing demand, blood sugar goes up and diabetes develops. Although this process can take years to develop, the final stage can be very fast. A person may have few symptoms of diabetes and not even know he or she is developing it, before the blood sugar suddenly gets so high as to be medically very dangerous.

Thirteen percent of people with schizophrenia have Type II or adult-onset diabetes. There are many reasons why people with major mental illness have an increased chance of getting diabetes. It appears that just having schizophrenia may increase a person's risk of developing diabetes.

This increased risk associated with having schizophrenia is well documented, and the biggest single risk factor is obesity. Increased weight increases the risk of developing diabetes, especially as people grow older. Shockingly, 65% of adults in the United States are considered to be overweight, and 20% are obese. People with major mental illness are even more likely to be overweight than the general population. There are many reasons why people with major mental illness tend to be overweight. Many people with major mental illness do not exercise very much and do not take care to eat in healthy ways. Many "fast foods," either from fast food restaurants or from the grocery store, are high-fat, high-caloric, high-sugar foods that can easily lead to weight gain. Clients may be taking medication that makes them thirsty, and drinking nondiet soda can add a lot of calories. Furthermore, some of the commonly prescribed medications may increase a person's appetite and lead to significant weight gain.

Some medications may be more likely to increase the risk of diabetes. Although the biggest risk factor is the weight gain that is associated with different medications, some medications may be associated with the development of diabetes apart from weight gain. Many medications for major mental illness can cause weight gain, but the second-generation (atypical) antipsychotics have been of particular concern. The FDA (Federal Drug Administration) does not distinguish between the different medications in their risk for developing diabetes. The consensus conference of the American Diabetes Association, the American Psychiatric Association, and several other organizations has suggested that there are important differences among these medications regarding both weight gain and risk for diabetes (Table A.1).

How Do You Know if You Have Diabetes?

Early symptoms of diabetes include unusual thirst, frequent urination, weight loss, and weakness. These symptoms are easy

Table A.1. Risk of Weight Gain and Diabetes in
Antipsychotic Medication

Medication	Weight Gain	Risk for Diabetes
Clozapine (Clozaril)	+++	+
Olanzapine (Zyprexa)	+++	+
Risperidone (Risperdal)	++	??
Quetiapine (Seroquel)	++	??
Aripiprazole (Abilify)	+/−	−
Ziprasidone (Geodon)	+/−	−

Note. Information from *Diabetes Care*, 2004, *27*(2), 596–601.

to miss, and a blood test to measure the amount of sugar in
your blood is needed to confirm the diagnosis. Blood sugar
normally goes up after a meal. A fasting blood sugar level (no
intake of food for 8 hours) below 100 is optimal. A fasting blood
sugar between 100 and 125 is a signal that the person is
prediabetic—that is, at risk of developing diabetes. A fasting
blood sugar above 126 on two different occasions is diagnostic
of diabetes. It is hard for some people to come in and get a blood
test before they have eaten. A random blood sugar test, although, while not diagnostic, can suggest who is likely to have
diabetes. The most sensitive way to diagnose diabetes is with an
oral glucose tolerance test. Early in the development of diabetes, a fasting blood sugar level can be normal, but the body can
still have problems reacting to a sudden load of sugar. The test
is to give the person a known amount of glucose and then
measure the blood glucose level 2 hours later. It is also possible
to test for the risk of developing diabetes, even before there is
any change in the blood glucose level. An increase in the level
of triglycerides in the blood after a 12-hour fast does not mean
that the person has diabetes, but it does suggest that the person
has an increased risk for developing diabetes in the future.

Metabolic Syndrome

Metabolic syndrome is a set of risk factors that increases the chance that the person will develop diabetes and cardiovascular disease. People with metabolic syndrome are at increased risk of coronary heart disease and other diseases related to plaque buildup in artery walls (e.g., stroke, peripheral vascular disease) and Type II diabetes. Metabolic syndrome has become increasingly common in the United States; it is estimated that over 50 million Americans have it.

The biggest risk factor for metabolic syndrome appears to be abdominal obesity and the associated insulin resistance. Insulin resistance is a generalized metabolic disorder in which the body does not use insulin efficiently. This is why metabolic syndrome is also called insulin-resistance syndrome. Abdominal fat is metabolically different from fat in other parts of the body. Most fat is designed for long-term storage of energy. Fat in a person's thighs or arms is not very metabolically active. However, abdominal fat is designed to be used more rapidly and easily when the body needs it. This abdominal fat increases levels of free fatty acids in the blood, which decreases the sensitivity of cells to insulin and leads to insulin resistance. In turn, insulin resistance increases cholesterol and triglyceride levels in the blood, which increases the likelihood that the person will develop diabetes.

Other factors associated with the syndrome include physical inactivity, aging, hormonal imbalance, and genetic predisposition. Metabolic syndrome is identified by three or more of these factors:

- Abdominal obesity (excessive fat tissue in and around the abdomen)
  Waist circumference >40 inches in men
  Waste circumference >35 inches in women

- Low HDL cholesterol or high triglycerides (measured by a blood test taken when the person has fasted for 12 hours). HDL cholesterol is "good cholesterol"; LDL is "bad cholesterol." Low HDL is part of metabolic syndrome.

HDL cholesterol < 40 mg/dl in men
HDL cholesterol < 50 mg/dl in women
Elevated triglycerides > 150 mg/dl

• Elevated blood pressure
  > 130/85 mm Hg

• Fasting blood glucose
  > 110 mg/dl

Note. Information from *Circulation*, 2002, *106*, 3143–3421. mg/dl = milligrams per deciliter (1/10 of a liter); mm Hg = millimeters.

Monitoring for Diabetes and Metabolic Syndrome

The current suggestion is that anyone taking any antipsychotic medication, or anyone with schizophrenia should have regular screenings. This screening includes asking about family history, obtaining both weight and waist circumference at regular intervals, and getting regular blood pressure measurements and fasting blood tests. Not every clinic will be able to do all parts of this monitoring, and not every client will accept, or need, all parts of this monitoring. Still, we know that many people have early diabetes and do not know it.

The consensus recommendations on diabetes monitoring, from the American Psychiatric Association, American Diabetes Association, American Association of Clinical Endocrinologists, and the National Association for the study of Obesity are shown in Table A.2.

Managing Weight, Diabetes, and Metabolic Syndrome

As with many other problems, an ounce of prevention is worth a pound of cure. It is important to prevent weight-related health problems whenever possible. Most people in the United States, not just people with mental illness, would benefit from

Table A.2. Consensus Recommendations on Diabetes Monitoring

	Baseline	4 weeks	8 weeks	12 weeks	3 months	12 months	5 years
Personal/family history	X					X	
Weight (body mass index)	X	X	X	X	X	X	X
Waist circumference	X					X	
Blood pressure	X			X		X	
Fasting glucose	X			X		X	
Fasting lipid profile	X						X

Note. Information from *Diabetes Care*, 2004, 27(2), 596–601.

making wiser food choices, getting more exercise, and losing weight. For people who are not overweight, preventing weight gain can help reduce the risk of health complications. Working ahead of time to prevent weight gain and other metabolic problems is particularly important for people who are taking medications that can worsen these problems.

If a client is taking a medication that can cause increased appetite, talking about this possible side effect ahead of time and recommending strategies to manage this side effect can help avoid significant weight gain. For people who are already overweight, losing weight through healthy eating habits and physical activity can help reduce the risk of health complications.

If monitoring detects that a client has diabetes, metabolic syndrome, elevated lipids, high blood pressure, or obesity, then it is important for the treatment team either to provide the services needed to help manage the problem or to link that individual to another provider for the necessary services. Unfortunately, such services, although both effective and important, are too often not available. Many treatment teams find it a daunting challenge just to monitor for medical problems, and treating medical problems may not be feasible. Helping clients to link with health care providers can be challenging as well.

Concern about weight gain and diabetes should be one of the considerations in making medication decisions. When possible, medications less likely to cause metabolic problems should be considered, especially for clients who are at particular risk for diabetes, either because of family history, obesity, or other current risk factors. A medication change should be considered if a client gains significant weight in the first few weeks after starting a medication that is commonly associated with significant weight gain. Although behavioral strategies are effective in helping many people control weight gain, they do not work for everyone. Not every client is willing or able to participate in behavioral strategies to control weight, and professional support for such strategies are not always available.

Medications by Brand Names

Brand Name	Generic Name	Primary Use
Abilify	aripiprazole	psychosis
Adderall	amphetamine + dextroamphetamine	ADHD
Adderall XR	amphetamine + dextroamphetamine extended	ADHD
Akineton	biperiden	motor side effects
Ambien	zolpidem	sleep
Ambien CR	zolpidem controlled release	sleep
Anafranil	clomipramine	OCD
Antabuse	disulfiram	substance abuse
Aricept	donepezil	dementia
Artane	trihexphenidyl	motor side effects
Asendin	amoxapine	depression
Ativan	lorazepam	anxiety
Benadryl	diphenhydramine	motor side effects
Buprenex	buprenorphine	substance abuse
BuSpar	buspirone	anxiety

Brand Name	Generic Name	Primary Use
Campral	acamprosate	substance abuse
Catapres	clonidine	drug withdrawal
Celexa	citalopram	depression
Clozaril	clozapine	psychosis
Concerta	methylphenidate sustained release	ADHD
Congentin	benztropine	motor side effects
Cylert	pemoline	ADHD
Cymbalta	duloxetine	depression
Cytomel	liothyronine	thyroid replacement
Dalmane	flurazepam	sleep
Depakene	valproate	mood stability
Depakote	divalproex	mood stability
Depakote ER	divalproex extended release	mood stability
Desyrel	trazodone	sleep
Dexadine, Adderall	dextroamphetamine	ADHD
Dolophine	methadone	substance abuse
Effexor	venlafaxine	depression
Effexor XR	venlafaxine extended release	depression
Elavil	amitriptyline	depression
Ensam (daily patch)	selegiline patch	depression
Eskalith	lithium	mood stability
Eskalith CR	lithium controlled release	mood stability
Exelon	rivastigmine	dementia
FaxaClo	clozapine quick dissolve wafer	psychosis
Focalin	dexmethylphenidate	ADHD
Gabitril	tiagabine	anxiety
Geodon	ziprasidone	psychosis
Halcion	triazolam	sleep

Brand Name	Generic Name	Primary Use
Haldol	haloperidol	psychosis
Haldol Deconoate	haloperidol deconoate	psychosis
Inderal	propranolol	motor side effects
Klonopin	clonazepam	anxiety
Lamictal	lamotrigine	bipolar depression
Lexapro	escitalopram	depression
Librium	chlordiazepoxide	anxiety
Lithobid	lithium	mood stability
Loxitane	loxapine	psychosis
Ludiomil	maprotiline	depression
Lunesta	eszopiclone	sleep
Luvox	fluvoxamine	depression
Lyrica	pregabaline	nerve pain
Marplan	isocarboxazid	depression
Mellaril	thioridazine	psychosis
Meridia	sibutramine	substance abuse
Minipress	prazosin	PTSD
Moban	molindone	psychosis
Namenda	memantadine	dementia
Nardil	phenelzine	depression
Navane	thiothixene	psychosis
Neurontin	gabapentin	anxiety
Norpramin	desipramine	depression
Pamelor	nortripyline	depression
Parnate	tranylcypromine	depression
Paxil	paroxetine	depression
Paxil CR	paroxetine controlled release	depression
Prolixin	fluphenazine	psychosis
Prolixin Deconoate	fluphenazine deconoate	psychosis
Provigil	modafanil	fatigue
Prozac	fluoxetine	depression
Remeron	mirtazapine	depression

Brand Name	Generic Name	Primary Use
Remeron SR	mirtazapine sustained release	depression
Reminyl	galantamine	dementia
Requip	ropinirole	sleep
Restoril	tempazepam	sleep
ReVia	naltrexone	substance abuse
Risperdal	risperidone	psychosis
Risperdal Consta	risperidone 2-week injection	psychosis
Risperdal M tabs	risperidone quick-dissolve tablets	psychosis
Ritalin	methylphenidate	ADHD
Ritalin SR	methylphenidate sustained release	ADHD
Rozerem	ramelteon	sleep
Serax	oxazepam	anxiety
Serentil	mesoridazine	psychosis
Seroquel	quetiapine	psychosis
Serzone	nefazodone	depression
Sinequan	doxepine	depression
Sonata	zaleplon	sleep
Stelazine	trifluperazine	psychosis
Strattera	atomoxetine	ADHD
Suboxone	buphrenorphine + naloxone	substance abuse
Surmontil	trimipramine	depression
Symbyax	fluoxetine + olanzapine	bipolar depression
Symmetrel	amantadine	motor side effects
Synthroid	levothyroxine	thyroid replacement
Tegretol	carbamaxepine	mood stability
Tenex	guanfacine	PTSD
Thorazine	chlorpromazine	psychosis
Tofranil	imipramine	depression
Topamax	topirimate	substance abuse
Tranxene	clorazepine	anxiety
Trilafon	perphenazine	psychosis
Trileptal	oxcarbazepine	mood stability

Brand Name	Generic Name	Primary Use
Valium	diazepam	anxiety
Vistaril	hydroxyzine	sleep
Vivactil	protriptyline	depression
Wellbutrin	bupropion	depression
Wellbutrin SR	bupropion sustained release	depression
Wellbutrin XL	bupropion extended release	depression
Xanax	alprazolam	anxiety
Xanax XR	alprazolam extended release	anxiety
Xyrem	sodium oxybate	sleep
Zoloft	sertraline	depression
Zydis	olanzapine quick-dissolve tablets	psychosis
Zyprexa	olanzapine	psychosis

Medications by Generic Names

Generic Name	Brand Name	Primary Use
acamprosate	Campral	substance abuse
alprazolam	Xanax	anxiety
alprazolam extended release	Xanax XR	anxiety
amantadine	symmetrel	motor side effects
amitriptyline	Elavil	depression
amoxapine	Asendin	depression
amphetamine + dextroamphetamine	Adderall	ADHD
amphetamine + dextroamphetamine extended	Adderall XR	ADHD
aripiprazole	Abilify	psychosis
atomoxetine	Strattera	ADHD
benztropine	Congentin	motor side effects
biperiden	Akineton	motor side effects
buprenorphine	Buprenex	substance abuse

Generic Name	Brand Name	Primary Use
bupropion	Wellbutrin	depression
bupropion extended release	Wellbutrin XL	depression
bupropion sustained release	Wellbutrin SR	depression
buspirone	BuSpar	anxiety
carbamaxepine	Tegretol	mood stability
chlordiazepoxide	Librium	anxiety
chlorpromazine	Thorazine	psychosis
citalopram	Celexa	depression
clomipramine	Anafranil	OCD
clonazepam	Klonopin	anxiety
clonidine	Catapres	drug withdrawal
clorazepine	Tranxene	anxiety
clozapine	Clozaril	psychosis
clozapine quick-dissolve wafer	FaxaClo	psychosis
desipramine	Norpramin	depression
dexmethylphenidate	Focalin	ADHD
dextroamphetamine	Dexadine, Adderall	ADHD
diazepam	Valium	anxiety
diphenhydramine	Benadryl	motor side effects
disulfiram	Antabuse	substance abuse
divalproex	Depakote	mood stability
divalproex extended release	Depakote ER	mood stability
donepezil	Aricept	dementia
doxepine	Sinequan	depression
duloxetine	Cymbalta	depression
escitalopram	Lexapro	depression
eszopiclone	Lunesta	sleep
fluoxetine	Prozac	depression

Generic Name	Brand Name	Primary Use
fluoxetine + olanzapine	Symbyax	bipolar depression
fluphenazine	Prolixin	psychosis
fluphenazine deconoate	Prolixin Deconoate	psychosis
flurazepam	Dalmane	sleep
fluvoxamine	Luvox	depression
gabapentin	Neurontin	anxiety
galantamine	Reminyl	dementia
guanfacine	Tenex	PTSD
haloperidol	Haldol	psychosis
haloperidol deconoate	Haldol Deconoate	psychosis
hydorxyzine	Vistaril	sleep
imipramine	Tofranil	depression
isocarboxazid	Marplan	depression
lamotrigine	Lamictal	bipolar depression
levothyroxine	synthroid	thyroid replacement
liothyronine	Cytomel	thyroid replacement
lithium	Eskalith	mood stability
lithium	Lithobid	mood stability
lithium controlled release	Eskalith CR	mood stability
lorazepam	Ativan	anxiety
loxapine	Loxitane	psychosis
maprotiline	Ludiomil	depression
memantadine	Namenda	dementia
mesoridazine	Serentil	psychosis
methadone	Dolophine	substance abuse
methylphenidate	Ritalin	ADHD
methylphenidate sustained release	Concerta	ADHD
methylphenidate sustained release	Ritalin SR	ADHD
mirtazapine	Remeron	depression

Generic Name	Brand Name	Primary Use
mirtazapine sustained release	Remeron SR	depression
modafanil	Provigil	fatigue
molindone	Moban	psychosis
naltrexone	ReVia	substance abuse
nefaxodone	Serzone	depression
nortripyline	Pamelor	depression
olanzapine	Zyprexa	psychosis
olanzapine quick-dissolve tablets	Zydis	psychosis
oxazepam	Serax	anxiety
oxcarbazepine	Trileptal	mood stability
paroxetine	Paxil	depression
paroxetine controlled release	Paxil CR	depression
pemoline	Cylert	ADHD
perphenazine	Trilafon	psychosis
phenelzine	Nardil	depression
prazosin	Minipress	PTSD
pregabaline	Lyrica	nerve pain
propranolol	Inderal	motor side effects
protriptyline	Vivactil	depression
quetiapine	Seroquel	psychosis
ramelteon	Rozerem	sleep
risperidone	Risperdal	psychosis
risperidone 2-week injection	Risperdal Consta	psychosis
risperidone quick-dissolve tablets	Risperdal M tabs	psychosis
rivastigmine	Exelon	dementia
ropinirole	Requip	sleep
selegiline patch	Ensam (daily patch)	depression
sertraline	Zoloft	depression

Generic Name	Brand Name	Primary Use
sibutramine	Meridia	substance abuse
sodium oxybate	Xyrem	sleep
Suboxone	buphrenorphine + naloxone	substance abuse
tempazepam	Restoril	sleep
thioridazine	Mellaril	psychosis
thiothixene	Navane	psychosis
tiagabine	Gabitril	anxiety
topirimate	Topamax	substance abuse
tranylcypromine	Parnate	depression
trazodone	Desyrel	sleep
triazolam	Halcion	sleep
trifluperazine	Stelazine	psychosis
trihexphenidyl	Artane	motor side effects
trimipramine	Surmontil	depression
valproate	Depakene	mood stability
venlafaxine	Effexor	depression
venlafaxine extended release	Effexor XR	depression
zaleplon	Sonata	sleep
ziprasidone	Geodon	psychosis
zolpidem	Ambien	sleep
zolpidem CR	Ambien Controlled Release	sleep

Medication History Charts

Antidepressant Medication History

Type	✓ each that has been taken	Brand Name	Generic Name	Dosage Range (mg)	Start & Stop Dates	Highest Dose Taken	Side Effects Experienced	Reason(s) Stopped
Selective Serotonin Reuptake Inhibitors (SSRIs)		Celexa	citalopram	20–80				
		Lexapro	escitalopram	10–20				
		Paxil	paroxetine	10–50				
		Prozac	fluoxetine	20–80				
		Serzone	nefazodone	300–600				
		Zoloft	sertraline	50–200				
		Cymbalta	duloxetine	30–60				

Category	Brand	Generic	Dose				
Dual Action Medications (increase serotonin and norepinephrine)	Elavil	amitriptyline	100–300				
	Remeron	mirtazapine	15–45				
	Norpramin	desipramine	100–300				
	Pamelor	nortriptyline	50–150				
	Effexor	venlafaxine	75–375				
	Tofranil	imipramine	100–300				
	Parnate	tranylcypromine	10–60				
	Nardil	phenelzine	45–90				
	Marplan	isocarboxazid	20–60				
	Ensam	selegiline patch	6–12				
Other	Wellbutrin	bupropion	200–450				

Antipsychotic Medication History

Type	✓ each that has been taken	Brand Name	Generic Name	Dosage Range (mg)	Start & Stop Dates	Highest Dose Taken	Side Effects Experienced	Reason(s) Stopped
Atypical (second generation)		Abilify	aripiprazole	10–30				
		Clozaril	clozapine	100–900				
		Geodon	ziprasidone	80–320				
		Risperdal	risperidone	2–6				
		Risperdal Consta	risperidone injection	25–50 q 2 wks				
		Seroquel	quetiapine	300–800				
		Zyprexa	olanzapine	10–30				

Typical (first generation)								
Haldol[+]	haloperidol	2–100						
Loxitane	loxapine	50–250						
Navane	thiothixene	5–120						
Prolixin[+]	fluphenazine	2.5–20						
Stelazine	trifluoperazine	5–200						
Trilafon	perphenazine	8–64						
Prolixin Dec	fluphenazine deconoate	12.5–37.56 q 2 wks						
Haldol Dec	haloperidol deconoate	100–400 q 4 wks						

[+]Can be taken as long-acting injection.

Mood Stabilizer Medication History

Type	✓ each that has been taken	Brand Name	Generic Name	Dosage Range (mg)	Blood Level	Starts & Stop Dates	Highest Dose Taken	Side Effects Experienced	Reason(s) Stopped
		Eskalith, Lithonate, Eskalith CR, Lithobid	lithium, lithium carbonate, LiCo3	900–1500	.50–1.00 mEq/l				
		Depakote, Depekene, Depakote ER	divalproex, valproate, sodium valproate, valproic acid	1000–2500	50–120 µg/mL				
		Tegretol	carbamazepine	400–1600	4–12 mg/l				
		Trileptal	oxcarbazepine	200–600	NA				
		Lamictal	lamotrigine	100–400	NA				

Atypical	**Abilify**	aripiprazole	15–30	NA				
	Clozaril	clozapine	100–900	NA				
	Geodon	ziprasidone	80–320	NA				
	Risperdal[+]	risperidone	2–6	NA				
	Seroquel	quetiapine	300–800	NA				
	Zyprexa	olanzapine	10–30	NA				

[+]Can be taken as a long-acting injection.

Medications Used to Treat Motor Side Effects of Antipsychotic Medications

✓ each that has been taken	Brand Name	Generic Name	Dosage Range	Start & Stop Dates	Highest Dose Taken	Side Effects Experienced	Reason(s) Stopped
	Cogentin	benztropine	1–6 mg				
	Benadryl	diphenhydramine	25–100 mg				
	Symmetrel	amantadine	100–300 mg				
	Artane	trihexphenidyl, trihexy-5	5–15 mg				
	Inderal	propranolol	10–80 mg				

Bibliography

Journal Articles

Aquila R, Emanuel M. Weight Gain and Antipsychotic Medications. *J Clin Psychiatry.* 1999;60(5):336–337.

Ball MP, Coons VB, Buchanan RW. A program for treating olanzapine-related weight gain. *Psychiatr Serv.* 2001;52(7): 967–969.

Bartsch DA, Shern DL, Feinberg LE, Fuller BB, Willett AB. Screening CMHC outpatients for Physical Illness. *Hosp and Community Psychiatry.* 1990;41(7):786–790.

Consensus Development Conference on Antipsychotic Drugs and Obesity and Diabetes: Consensus Statement from the American Diabetes Association, American Psychiatric Association, American Association of Clinical Endocriniologists, and North American Association for the Study of Obesity. *Diabetes Care.* 2004;27(2):596–601.

Deegan PE. The importance of personal medicine: A qualitative study of resilience in people with psychiatric disabilities. *Scand J Public Health.* 2005;33:29–35.

Deegan PE, Drake RE. Shared decision-making and medication management in the recovery process. *Psychiatr Serv.* 2006;57(11).

Diamond RJ. Enhancing medication use in schizophrenic patients. *J Clin Psychiatry.* 1983;44(6–Sec. 2):7–14.

Diamond RJ. Antipsychotic drugs and the quality of life: The patient's point of view. *J Clin Psychiatry.* 1985;46(5–Sec. 2):29–35.

Diamond RJ. Recovery from mental illness: A psychiatrist's point of view. *Post Graduate Medicine Special Report: New Directions in Psychopharmacology and Recovery in Schizophrenia.* 2006;54–62.

Dubin WR, Weiss KJ, Zeccardi JA. Organic brain syndrome. The psychiatric imposter. *JAMA.* 1983;249:60–62.

Gutheil TG. Psychodynamics in drug prescribing. *Drug Therapy.* 1977;7(7):82–95.

Hall RCW, Popkin MK, De Vaul R, Faillace LS, Stickney, SK. Physical illness presenting as psychiatric disease. *Arch Gen Psychiat.* 1978; 35(11):1315–1320.

Johnson R, Ananth, J. Physically Ill and Mentally Ill. *Can J Psychiatry.* 1986;31:197–201.

Katerndahl DA. Non psychiatric disorders associated with depression. *J of Family Practice.* 1981;13(5):619–24.

Koran LM, Sheline Y, Imai K, Kelsey TG, Freedland KE, Mathews J, Moore M. Medical disorders among patients admitted to a public-sector psychiatric inpatient unit. *Psychiatr Serv.* 2002 Dec;53(12): 1623–1625.

Korrin MK, Sox HC, Marton KI, et al. Medical Evaluation of Psychiatric Patients: Results in a State Hospital System. *Arch of Gen Psychiatry.* 1989;46(8):733.

Littrell KH, Hilligoss NM, Kirshner CD, Petty RG, Johnson CG. The Effects of an Educational Intervention on Antipsychotic-Induced Weight Gain. *J Nurs Scholarship.* 2003;35(3):237–241.

Mechanic D. Sources of power of lower participants in complex organizations. *Administrative Science Quarterly.* 1962;7:349–364.

Menza M, Vreeland B, Minsky S, Gara M, Radler DR, Sakowitz M. Managing atypical antipsychotic-associated weight gain: 12-month data on a multimodal weight control program. *J Clin Psychiatry.* 2004;65(4):471–47.

Reeves RR, Pendarvis EJ, Kimble R. Unrecognized Medical Emergencies Admitted to Psychiatric Units. *American J of Emergency Psychiatry.* 2000;18(4):390–393.

Scheifler PL, Weiden PJ. Beyond psychopharmacology: Psychosocial strategies for getting the best results when switching antipsychotic medications. *Post Graduate Medicine Special Report: New Directions in Psychopharmacology and Recovery in Schizophrenia.* September 2006;45–53.

Slater E. Diagnosis of "hysteria." *Brit Med J.* 1965;1:1395–1399.

Sox HC Jr, Roran LM, Sox HC, Marton RI, Dugger F, Smith T, et al. A medical algorithm for detecting physical disease in psychiatric patients. *Hosp and Comm Psych.* 1989;40(12):1270–1276.

Vreeland B, Minsky S, Menza M, Rigassio Radler D, Roemheld-Hamm B, Stern R. A Program for Managing Weight Gain Associated with Atypical Antipsychotics. *Psych Serv.* 2003;54(8):1155–1157.

Weiden, PJ. Switching in the Era of Atypical Antipsychotics: An Updated Review. *Post Graduate Medicine Special Report: New Directions in Psychopharmacology and Recovery in Schizophrenia.* Sept 2006;27–44.

Weiden PJ, Miller AL. Which side effects really matter? Screening for common and distressing side effects of antipsychotic medications. *J of Psychiatr Practice.* 2001;7(1):41–47.

Weissberg MP. Emergency room medical clearance: An educational problem. *Am J Psychiatry.* 1979;136:6.

Wirshing DA, et al. Novel antipsychotics: comparison of weight gain liabilities. *J Clin Psychiatry.* 1999;60(6):358–363.

Wise MG, Taylor SE. Anxiety and Mood Disorders in Medically Ill Patients. *J of Clin Psychiatry.* 1990;51(Suppl): 27–32.

Chapters

Becker M, Diamond R. Quality of life measurement in persons with schizophrenia: Are we measuring what's important? In: Katschnig H, Freeman H, eds. *Quality of Life in Mental Disorder.* Chichester, UK: Wiley; 2005:111–126.

Curtis LC, Diamond RJ. Power and coercion in mental health practice. In: Blackwell B, ed. *Treatment Compliance and the Therapeutic Alliance.* Amsterdam: Harwood Academic; 1997:97–122.

Diamond RJ. Multidisciplinary teams. In: Vacarro JV, Clark GH, eds. *Community Psychiatry: A Practitioner's Manual.* Washington, DC: American Psychiatric Press; 1996:343–360.

Diamond RJ. Coercion and tenacious treatment in the community: Applications to the real world. In: Dennis D, Monahan J, eds. *Coercion and Aggressive Community Treatment: A New Frontier in Mental Health Law.* New York: Plenum Press; 1996:51–72. Reprinted in Drake RE et al., eds. *Readings in Dual Diagnosis.* Columbia, MD: International Association of Psychosocial Rehabilitation Services; 1998:431–449.

Diamond RJ, Stein LI, Schneider-Braus K. The psychiatrist's role in mental health center administration. In: Breakey W, ed. *Modern Community Psychiatry.* New York, Oxford University Press; 1996: 87–102.

Mechanic D. Sources of power of lower participants in complex organizations. In: Porter DE, Applewhite PB, ed. *Studies in Organizational Behavior and Management.* Scranton, PA: International Textbook; 1964.

Books

Crowley K. *The Power of Procovery in Healing Mental Illness: Just Start Anywhere.* San Francisco, CA: Kennedy Carlisle Publishing; 2000.

Diamond RJ. *Instant Psychopharmacology: A Guide for the Nonmedical Mental Health Professional.* 2nd ed. New York: Norton; 2002.

Floersch J. *Meds, Money and Manners: Case Management of Severe Mental Illness.* New York: Columbia University Press; 2002.

Hall RCW, ed. *Psychiatric Presentations of Medical Illness.* New York: SP Medical and Scientific Books; 1980.

Havens, L. *Making Contact: Uses of Language in Psychotherapy.* Cambridge, MA: Harvard University Press; 1986.

Jefferson JW, Marshall JR. *Neuropsychiatric Features of Medical Disorders.* New York: Plenum Medical Book Company; 1981.

Meyer JM, Nasrallah HA. *Medical Illness and Schizophrenia.* Washington, DC: American Psychiatric Press; 2003.

Miller WR, Rollnick S. *Motivational Interviewing: Preparing People to Change.* 2nd ed. New York: Guilford Press; 2002.

Mueser KT, Noordsy DL, Drake RE, Fox L. *Integrated Treatment for Dual Disorders: A guide to Effective Practice.* New York: Guilford Press; 2003.

Rapp CA, Goscha RJ. *The Strengths Model: Case Management with People with Psychiatric Disabilities.* 2nd ed. New York: Oxford University Press; 2006.

Shea SC. *Psychiatric Interviewing: The Art of Understanding.* 2nd ed. Philadelphia: Saunders; 1998.

Sidler JZ. *Descriptions Prescriptions: Values, Mental Disorders and the DSMs.* Baltimore: Johns Hopkins Press; 2002.

Soreff SM, McNeil GN. *Handbook of Psychiatric Differential Diagnosis.* Littleton, MA: PSG Publishing; 1987.

Tasman A, Riba MB, Silk KR. *The Doctor–Patient Relationship in Pharmacotherapy.* New York: Guilford Press; 2000.

Taylor RL. *Mind or Body: Distinguishing Psychological from Organic Disorder.* New York: Springer; 1990.

Psychoeducational Resources

Ascher-Swavum H, Krause A. *Psychoeducation Groups for Patients with Schizophrenia.* New York: Aspen Publishers; 1991.

AstraZeneca Pharmaceuticals. *Caring Outreach Partnership Education* (COPE). Wilmington, DE: AstraZeneca Pharmaceuticals; 2005.

AstraZeneca Pharmaceuticals. *Success Stories.* Wilmington, DE: AstraZeneca Pharmaceuticals; 2005.

Baker L, Landwehr K. *Pebbles in the Pond: Achieving Resilience in Mental Health.* Gig Harbor, WA: Directions in Education, Training & Consultation; 1996 (revised 2006).

Bellack AS, Mueser KT, Gingerich S, Agresta J. *Social Skills Training for Schizophrenia: A Step-by-Step Guide.* 2nd ed. New York: Guilford Press; 2004.

Bisbee CC. *Educating Patients and Families about Mental Illness.* Hawthorne, NY: Wellness Reproductions; 1991 (revised 1995).

Bristol-Myers Squibb. *Mental Health and Wellness Resource Center.* NY, NY: Bristol-Myers Squibb; 2004.

Cathcart T. *The Recovery Workbook Series.* Nashville, TN: Foundations Associates; 2004.

Copeland ME. *Wellness Recovery Action Plan*™ (WRAP). West Dummerston, VT: Mental Health and Recovery; 1997.

Copeland ME. *Living without Depression and Manic Depression.* Oakland, CA: New Harbinger; 1994.

Copeland ME. *Winning against Relapse.* Oakland, CA: New Harbinger; 1999.

Eli Lilly and Company. *Living with Bipolar Disorder.* Indianapolis, IN: Eli Lilly and Company; 2004.

Foxx RM and Bittle RG. *Thinking It Through: Teaching a Problem-Solving Strategy for Community Living.* Champaign, IL: Research Press; 1989.

Janssen Pharmaceutical, *Connections and Care: Constant Connections.* Titusville, NJ: Janssen Pharmaceutical; 2005.

Johnston B. *Enhancing Recovery from Psychosis.* Port Adelaide, Australia: Department of Human Resources; 1998.

Liberman RP. *Social and Independent Living Skills: Medication Management.* Los Angeles: UCLA Dept of Psychiatry; 1986.

McMullin RE and Casey B. *Talk Sense to Yourself.* Lakewood, CO: Counseling Research Institute; 1975.

Moller M, Freeman M. *Recovering from Psychosis: A Wellness Approach.* Nine Mile Falls, WA: Psychiatric Resource Network; 1998 (revised 2002).

Mueser K and Gingerich S. *Illness Management and Recovery.* Rockville, MD: Substance Abuse and Mental Health Services Administration; 2005.

Ryan S, Littrell K, Kirshner C, and Peabody C. *Solutions for Wellness.* Indianapolis, IN: Eli Lilly and Company; 1999 (revised 2005).

Substance Abuse and Mental Health Services Administration. *Developing a Recovery and Wellness Lifestyle.* Rockville, MD: SAMHSA; 2002.

Scheifler PL. *Relapse Management: A Computerized Workbook.* Sylacauga, AL: Partnership for Recovery; 2003.

Scheifler PL. Recovery Lifestyle Habits. Sylacauga, AL: Partnership for Recovery; 1995.

Scheifler PL. Effective Educational Strategies: Skills and Techniques for Teaching People Who Are Recovering from Severe Persistent Mental Illness. Sylacauga, AL: Partnership for Recovery; 1995.

Scheifler PL. Effective Educational Strategies: Tailored Psychoeducation for People Who Have Severe Persistent Mental Illness. Sylacauga, AL: Essential Learning; 2004.

Scheifler PL, Bisbee CC. Symptom Tracker. Sylacauga, AL: Partnership for Recovery; 2006.

Vreeland E. *Solutions for Wellness Update.* Indianapolis, IN: Eli Lilly and Company; 2005.

Weiden PJ, Garrett DG, Kopelowicz AJ, Mendelowitz AJ, Moller M, Ross R, et al. *Treatment Resources for Understanding Schizophrenia Therapy* (TRUST). NY, NY: Pfizer; 2001.

Weiden PJ, Scheifler PL, Diamond RJ, Ross R. *Breakthroughs in Antipsychotic Medications.* New York: Norton; 1999.

Weiden PJ, Scheifler PL, McCrary KJ, Gilmur D, Griffin EW, and Mueser KTl. *Team Solutions.* Indianapolis, IN: Eli Lilly and Company; 1997 (revised 2005).

Williams E. *Interventions for Schizophrenia.* Oxfordshire, UK: Speechmark; 2004.

Index

Note: Figures and tables are indicated by *f* and *t*, respectively, following page numbers.